Dressing the Elite

Dressing the Elite

Clothes in Early Modern England

Susan Vincent

Oxford • New York

First published in 2003 by
Berg
Editorial offices:
1st Floor, Angel Court, 81 St Clements Street, Oxford OX4 1AW, UK
838 Broadway, Third Floor, New York NY 10003–4812, USA

Berg is an imprint of Oxford International Publishers Ltd.

Library of Congress Cataloging-in-Publication Data
A catalogue record for this book is available from the Library of Congress.

British Library Cataloguing-in-Publication Data
A catalogue record for this book is available from the British Library.

ISBN 1 85973 746 3 (Cloth)
1 85973 751 X (Paper)

Typeset by JS Typesetting Ltd, Wellingborough, Northants.
Printed in the United Kingdom by Biddles Ltd, Guildford and King's Lynn.

www.bergpublishers.com

For my parents, John and Barbara

Sure this robe of mine does change my disposition.

William Shakespeare, *The Winter's Tale*, IV, 4, 134.

Contents

Illustrations

Acknowledgements

Many people have, of course, contributed in varying and valuable ways towards this book. I especially wish to thank, however, my doctoral supervisor, Dr Mark Jenner. Throughout the course of the research that ultimately led to this, he was unstintingly generous with his time and academic expertise, full of excellent suggestions and unfailing encouragement. The acquisition of images to illustrate the text has also led me into contact with many helpful individuals, and institutions. I wish particularly to note the Borthwick Institute for giving permission to reproduce a document in their custody. I would also like to make special mention of the Earl of Mexborough, and the Duke of Bedford and the Trustees of the Bedford Estates: my sincere thanks for their generosity. Although undoubtedly benefiting from the suggestions and advice of colleagues, any errors that remain in this work are my own. The publication of this book has been assisted by a grant from the Scouloudi Foundation in association with the Institute of Historical Research.

Conventions and Abbreviations

Spellings in most quotations are original. However, the i/j u/v y/th usage has been modernized for clarity. Similarly, certain contractions have been silently expanded. The following abbreviations have been used:

APC   *Acts of the Privy Council*
BIHR   Borthwick Institute of Historical Research
BL   British Library
Bod. Lib.   Bodleian Library
CA   College of Arms
CJ   *Journals of the House of Commons*
CSPD   *Calendar of State Papers Domestic*
Diary   *The Diary of Samuel Pepys*, ed. by Robert Latham and
            William Matthews, 11 vols (London, 1970–1983)
HMC   Historical Manuscripts Commission
LJ   *Journals of the House of Lords*
PRO   Public Record Office
SP16   Public Record Office, State Papers Domestic, Charles I
SR   *Statues of the Realm*

Introduction: 'When I am in Good Habitt'

History and Dress

In his diary entry for 8 October 1666, Samuel Pepys recorded the beginnings of a new look. England was at war with France and London reeling from the aftermath of the Great Fire, and so the King intended to create a fashion for clothes that was both anti-French and anti-extravagance. 'It will be a vest', wrote Pepys, but 'I know not well how'. By the following week, however, Pepys had discovered more:

> This day the King begins to put on his Vest, and I did see several persons of the House of Lords, and Commons too, great courtiers, who are in it – being a long Cassocke close to the body, of black Cloth and pinked with white silk under it, and a coat over it, and the legs ruffled with black riband like a pigeon's leg – and upon the whole, I wish the King may keep it, for it is a very fine and handsome garment.

The rush on tailors for the new style must have been considerable, for within days the fashion was being flaunted and sartorial gossip was rife: 'The Court is all full of Vests; only, my Lord St. Albans not pinked, but plain black – and they say the King says the pinking upon white makes them look too much like magpyes, and therefore hath bespoke one of plain velvet.' Not to be behindhand, Pepys too plunged into the fashionable stream and ordered a matching outfit. It arrived on 4 November: 'Comes my Taylors man in the morning and brings my vest home, and coat to wear with it, and belt and silver-hilted sword. So I rose and dressed myself, and I like myself mightily in it, and so doth my wife.' However, in the afternoon Pepys was to discover some less positive aspects of his new garments, for the weather was cold and he became 'mighty fearful of an ague (my vest being new and thin, and the Coate cut not to meet before upon my breast)'. In time it seems that Pepys learnt how to wear this style satisfactorily – or at least learnt how to accommodate the worrying possibility of an ague – for seven months later he was re-vamping an old outfit: 'I to my tailor's about turning my old silk suit and cloak into a suit and vest'.[1]

While clothing has been pushed to the margins of historiography, Pepys's reflections remind us that, by contrast, dress was central to the lives of historical subjects. Fernand Braudel, until very recently one of the few historians to consider the area, suggests that the clothing practices of an age are a window onto its underlying *mentalité*. The way in which people dress is an 'indication of deeper phenomena – of the energies, possibilities, demands and *joie de vivre* of a given society, economy and civilisation'.[2] We have only to return to Pepys's narrative to see this complexity beneath such apparently unremarkable events. Scrutinize his experience for a moment and we find the politics of foreign relations and national identity; the significations of status as the court jostles for position; the creation of a new aesthetic as judgements decree just where that hair line is to be placed that divides beauty from magpie absurdity; the policing of gender roles as Elizabeth Pepys looks on, but does not try on; Pepys's delight in his dressed self; and the disciplining and education of his body to find pleasure in apparently unpleasant physical sensations. Thus, far from being merely an index of utility, clothing has immense symbolic importance. It gives form to a society's ideas about the sacred and secular, about exclusion and inclusion, about age, beauty, sexuality, and status. So wide-ranging is the cultural practice of dress that any investigation needs, as Philippe Perrot has written, to 'venture into the terrain of gestures, anatomy, sexuality, hygiene, economics, signs, rituals, morality and the law'.[3]

Given clothing's complex and important position in relation to human experience, it is surprising how many of its studies are prefaced by justifications. Even as recently as 2001 one scholar's opening statement declared that, 'To engage in research on dress is to place oneself at the fringe of academic respectability.'[4] In the main, academically respectable historians would seem to have agreed. There has been no place in nine-teenth- and twentieth-century history departments for costume studies. Instead, as the profession developed its emphasis on state affairs, matters of dress became the province of antiquarian scholars on the one hand, and, on the other, art historians seeking to date and identify works of art. Even recent cultural historiography perpetuates the neglect of clothing. For example, despite its centrality to corporeality, histories of the body most often overlook the small matter of adornment. Even while acknowledging the body as 'the subject of culture, or in other words as the existential ground of culture', the cultural work of dress is strangely ignored.[5] If the body is not actually naked, the body's clothing is usually of the hermeneutically see-through variety. Indeed, studies of the Renaissance body are instead strikingly visceral, presenting a subject both discursively and physically anatomized and dismembered.[6]

The one area of historiography in which dress has featured, has been the history of consumption. This scholarship, in tracing patterns of ownership and use in the early modern economy, has offered enormous insights into the value of material culture to people from the past. Specifically, ownership of textiles and clothing has demonstrated the gradually increasing wealth and social aspirations of humbler folk, and also illuminated the hitherto hidden economy of a second-hand trade bolstered by peddling and theft.[7] However, such studies concentrate on the economic and functional importance of dress, treating garments as commodities that are variously owned and disposed of. They are an index of social standing and personal comfort, and selling or stealing them can generate cash. They are not, however, construed as items that in turn shape and 'use' their owners, or nuanced as objects in which multiple meanings reside. Furthermore, the literature of clothing consumption has a marked predilection for the poorer and middling sort of the eighteenth century, and tends not to address the importance of dress for other people or other periods.

The Meaning of Clothing and the Clothing of Meaning

In the retrieval of clothing practices of the past, few would dispute that the meanings of dress are arbitrary, relational, and culturally constructed. That is, a garment or style is only intelligible in respect to other items or styles of dress. There is, for instance, no essential and unchanging quality that signifies 'practicality'. Rather a garment is only indicative of utility in contrast to others that are not, and vice versa. Furthermore, this ascription of meaning will change over time so that the same garment ten years later may, in relation to the wider clothing system, be encumbering and impractical. The same goes for any other possible meaning such as status, allure or fashion. Residing only fleetingly in a garment these signifieds can exist only by virtue of the existence of others from which they are different. To illustrate this we can return to Pepys's experience. The particular style of vest that became fashionable in Restoration England fell from favour in 1670 when ridiculed by visiting French dignitaries. Nothing changed about the garment, except its relationship with other garments and the concept of modishness. Similarly, instead of devising the vest in 1666, Charles II might just as easily have opted for a different garment altogether: a new cut of cloak or doublet, for instance.

However, Pepys's account of wearing the vest alerts us to a way in which clothing *does* have inherent meaning. When, on the afternoon of 4 November Pepys went to Whitehall by river, he was cold and chilled because his vest was thin, and his coat was cut in such a way as to not cover his chest. There was something, in other words, essential to those garments that caused certain physical sensations. Wearing a cloak – although perhaps just as potent a signifier of status, or fashion, or gender – would not have had the same effect. For the material nature of clothing *matters*. Its weight, colour, fabric, shape, texture and even smell are significant. The physical properties of dress are inalienable, inherent qualities, and they affect the meaning that cultures then ascribe to clothes. Thus materiality puts the limits on the physical performance of dress. However, the values ascribed to that performance remain relative and revisable: they are created by the interpretative viewer. For example, wearing a laced corset will always produce the sensations of enclosure, binding and tightness. At various times and by various viewers, these sensations have been interpreted as supportive, comfortable and natural. The same sensations have been equally read as restrictive, uncomfortable and deforming. Or returning to Pepys, the cold and open sensations of the vest and coat he re-learned and reinterpreted as being appropriate and desirable.

Studies of material culture can also help enormously in our interpretation of dress, for this scholarship foregrounds what is often overlooked, particularly by historians: that is, objects are not inactive, but predispose toward particular modes of behaviour, and thought. As Chandra Mukerji has noted, they translate ideas into material form which then remain in the environment. In doing so they also provide a setting in which only certain activities and patterns of thought will be congruent, or meaningful.[8] Objects then do not just express culture, they also create it. For clothing, what might this mean? Its forms and materiality discipline the body, ornamenting its surface, affecting size, shape, gesture, temperature, posture and movement.[9] Dress, indeed, creates a certain body and then influences behaviours and thoughts, and relationships with others. For example, a woman's garment that dictates physical isolation creates certain cultural possibilities. A society in which elite women wear farthingales is likely to hold particular views about the gendering of space, proximity and intimacy. The value ascribed to such a physical arrangement is by no means predetermined: it is equally possible to read marginalization through exclusion, or empowerment through incorporation, or both. What is incontrovertible is that the vestimentary shaping of the body helps shape cultural context and individual personality, because, owing to its fundamental relationship with the self, clothing is vital to the formation of identity. Pepys wrote when he dressed himself in his vest that 'I like myself mightily in it'. His phrase opens up the possibility that he might not like himself out of it. Or to push the point a bit further, he might be another self out of it, or dressed in another garment. For 'fashion is not so much a consequence of choice but, instead, some kind of causal agent. Clothes, in a very real sense, do "make" the man and woman.'[10]

Early Modern England

This book, then, argues that clothing was an expression of early modern culture but in turn contributed to societal formation. It was fundamental to an individual's experience and creation of self, and mediated his or her relationships with others. As well as being commodities of utility and economic value, garments enjoyed a rich discursive life, participating in moral, religious and political debates. There were few, if any, areas of sixteenth- and seventeenth-century life in which concerns were not voiced about appearances. So much might be said, perhaps, for any moment in any society. However, in the period under study, *c.* 1550 – *c.* 1670, clothing had an extremely overt and often acknowledged importance. Indeed, at a time when the correspondence between the body politic and the body personal was taken with immense seriousness, matters of dress and deportment were central to social and political relations. Moreover, in a period covering the Reformation and the Civil War, times of extreme religious and political unrest, we find appearance invested with a weighty moral significance. For example, the Puritan writer Philip Stubbes (fl. 1581–1593) violently objected to all extremes of fashion: 'But this sinne of excess in Apparell, remayneth as an Example of evyll [evil] before our eyes, and as a provocative of sinne, as Experience daylye sheweth . . . for doth not the apparell styrre uppe the heart to pride? doth it not intice others to sinne? and doth not sin purchase hell the guerdon of pride?'[11] However, against such denunciations of finery, the Renaissance courts glittered with a hitherto unmatched conspicuous display. So great was elite expenditure on dress that it frequently, or so contemporaries maintained, led directly to bankruptcy and the insolvency of landed estates.

Thus, this investigation focuses on the elite of the sixteenth and seventeenth centuries and asks how their apparel structured their daily experience. This is not to say that non-elite clothing was not imbued with meaning, or that it was not equally important to its wearers. However, this importance is extremely difficult to retrieve for it has left little historical record. As a cultural production of the privileged, though, apparel had a declared centrality to the realization of power, wealth, status and gender. As such, elite dress was guaranteed a cultural visibility so marked that today we can still perceive it even from our historical distance. Clearly, though, this broad categorization of privilege and exclusion needs refining, for Tudor and Stuart society was far more complex than it suggests. Indeed, debate about social formation and questions of demographic structure and definition continue to exercise scholars of the period.[12] Such historiographical problems aside, this study takes as its subjects those participating in courtly and aristocratic circles, the gentry, wealthy urban professionals, and those at the top end of the middling sort. In terms of the population as a whole, this is a small group. According to Peter Laslett, of all the people alive in Tudor and Stuart England at most a twentieth belonged to the gentry and above.[13] To this modest number belonged a disproportionate amount of land, money, goods – and garments. It is the stories of these garments, the stories of how they participated in the lives of their wearers, that we will trace.

Finding sources for this type of study has its difficulties. Despite, or perhaps because of the way apparel featured in daily life, evidence is everywhere, and nowhere. To borrow from John Kasson, it is like looking for salt in the sea.[14] Typically, commentary about clothing is dispersed widely throughout a range of records whose main subject is almost always something other than dress. Thus sources as various as, for example, court proceedings, sermons and drama are all littered with brief mentions of apparel. Very few, however, offer sustained commentary. This multiplicity of mentions has been noted by Daniel Roche. 'So the history of clothes has its sources' he writes, 'they are abundant, though difficult to master from one single approach'.[15] Furthermore, again due to the quotidian nature of dress practices, which were participated in by all, there is generally a high level of assumed knowledge in contemporary writings on the subject. Putting on garments was something that everyone did, so there were many shared understandings that are now nearly opaque for the modern reader.

One of the few sources that does form both a discrete and continuing commentary is sumptuary law, that body of acts and proclamations specifying what any particular person could, or more precisely, could not wear. Although the first English act of apparel appeared as early as 1337, it was the sixteenth century that witnessed the most vehement and committed attempts to control how the population dressed. Repealed early in the seventeenth century, sumptuary law made an apparently uncontested exit from the statute books. However, and this is seldom noted, the next fifty years continued to see determined efforts to retrieve the control of appearances, and keep it as a matter for parliamentary prerogative.

From the declaration of state authority, we turn to less official opinions about vestimentary seemliness. One area in which we hear this voiced is the war, waged via the medium of pamphlet and treatise, on stage practices. Developing alongside the flowering of Renaissance drama, anti-theatricalism articulated anxieties about stage mimesis that contributed, ultimately, to the 1642 closure of the playhouses. Fundamental to this anxiety were concerns about dissimulation, and the dangers of counterfeiting appearances by donning forbidden raiment. In the context of all-male acting companies, this most obviously led to fervid denunciations of the cross-dressed confusion of gender.

A further debate about appearances can be found within the pages of conduct manuals, and their tangential controversy about the place and behaviour of women. There was nothing new about written guides to social behaviour. Classical commentary, biblical pronouncements and medieval definitions of courtly etiquette had all prescribed ways of acting in public. In the sixteenth and seventeenth centuries, though, this literature expanded rapidly. Developing from a small core of texts, conduct books were translated, adapted, penned and parodied. The developing notion of gentlemanly (and gentlewomanly) conduct they described was produced for an increasingly urban, educated and socially mobile population. In this context an individual's relationship to self, society, the wider world and God was emerging as more creative and contingent than in the past. New ways of acting out lives were a possibility and – as the communicating surface between the private and public – physical appearances were of the utmost importance.

Alongside these textual sources I have drawn on pictorial evidence, particularly portraits. On a purely representational level such iconographic remains clearly have an illustrative value. Aileen Ribeiro, author of a recent study of fashions as depicted in the National Portrait Gallery collection, claims that in sixteenth-century portraits 'the literal truth in dress is what we do see'.[16] Certainly in these paintings the apparel and adornment of the sitters was described more meticulously than their faces. Ribeiro points out that an artist's reputation depended in great part on his ability to capture the details of lavish costumes; while for Peter Stallybrass and Ann Jones, English Renaissance portraits were 'mnemonics to commemorate a particularly extravagant suit, a dazzling new fashion in ruffs, a costly necklace or jewel'.[17] However, portraits also bear a different sort of witness to the importance of clothing in their culture, for they record the choices of self-presentation that each subject made for the occasion.

Behind each image were decisions about dress, and the meanings that particular garments embodied.

Underpinning the whole is the evidence of personal documents. From letters, diaries, memoirs and autobiographies, account and commonplace books we gain an unparalleled glimpse of the subjective experience of clothing and its place within the writer's life. Perhaps most important, personal narratives help us to sidestep our own deep-seated prejudices about appearances and come closer to a view concordant with early modern attitudes.

Chapter 1, 'Fashioning Appearances', first of all addresses some of the difficulties that we have when faced with garment styles that have long since disappeared. For if the past is a foreign country, then it certainly dresses in alien ways. Thus the opening section, 'The Wardrobe', discusses the basic forms of sixteenth- and seventeenth-century costume for both men and women, in order to familiarize the reader with this different vestimentary order. 'Reviewing the Wardrobe', however, returns us to a reconsideration of early modern dress styles. It explores the prevailing aesthetic more fully, and considers how the forms and structure of garments determined a vocabulary of movement, and defined the 'work' of dress.

From this more generalized beginning, 'Addressing the Body', turns to actual individuals and their experience of clothing in relation to their physical well-being. Specifically, it examines the intimate, almost organic relationship between cloth and skin, and how garments sustained, protected and purified the body. Whereas uncovered flesh was vulnerable to disease and cold, garments encased the wearer in defensive layers that left only face and hands exposed. Clothing also defended the wearer from internal dangers by cleansing the body of its polluting secretions. So fundamental was clothing to bodily well-being, that it is not surprising to find dress also connected with the apprehension of physical maturation and transition. Thus garments became both a way of thinking about ageing, and the means of structuring rites of passage. 'Clothing Grief', looks in depth at one such moment: that of death. In doing so, it principally investigates the changing forms of mourning apparel and how they functioned to help early modern society manage issues of mortality and bereavement.

'Clothes Make the Man', turns from the wearer's physical well-being to focus on ways that clothing structured his or her social body. This chapter presents evidence of individuals consciously using particular styles of dressing as a means of creating a desired identity, and also as a way of judging others. These desired identities might foreground aspects of personality, gender, political allegiance, or religious belief. Moving from the latter to a consideration of the Puritan stereotype of plain and sober apparel, we find that the 'way' of wearing was just as significant as the 'what' of wearing. In other words, not only did garment choice carry meaning for sixteenth- and seventeenth-century viewers, but also the manner in which these garments were borne, displayed and manipulated. An example of this is hat honour, the social subtext governing the use and handling of male headwear. Through focusing on clothing as it shaped social personae, the chapter goes on to show that the process was a public undertaking. The sartorial project, although begun in private, generated most meaning when viewed by others. 'To See and be Seen' explores this facet of early modern dress experience, identifying arenas of visual engagement where people took the opportunity to assess one another's appearance. Costumed portraits and the wearing of livery are also considered as different means of extending the visibility of the self. These were all ways of establishing credit through public witness. By openly demonstrating an inappropriate or unseemly dressed persona, discredit was formulated in a similar fashion. Indeed, in 'Punishment and Shame' we see that in the early modern world sartorial misuse was a signifier of social dysfunction. Finally, 'A Very Good Fancy in Making Good Clothes' explains why the relationship between social and sartorial reputation was so very intimate and binding in the past. Before the mechanisms of mass production, consumers took a much more active part in the creation of their clothing, their choices determining the colour, cut, fabric and style of a new garment. Individuals thus 'made' their clothes; in turn the public response to this vestimentary project made or unmade the self.

While Chapter 3 traces the establishment of social identities through the agency of clothing, Chapter 4 turns to the regulation of this process. For so important was the matter of public appearance that, via the mechanisms of sumptuary law, both Parliament and Crown sought to exercise authority over the way people dressed. The considerations that made dress control so attractive a proposition to lawmakers were weighty, and covered economic, moral, and social issues, for not far beneath the apparel acts lay fears of financial hardship, social dysfunction, crime, and immorality. Furthermore, despite a repeated rubric that castigated the lower orders, a careful reading of the acts and proclamations reveals instead a concern to control the appearances of the upper sort in general, and young men in particular. The most startling discovery is the omission of women from the apparel orders until 1574, followed by a sudden inclusion that seems to have been closely connected to the politics and person of the monarch. The chapter closes with a discussion of the effectiveness of the sumptuary project, confronting the common apprehension that these laws were unenforceable, and therefore foolish. It concludes that the nature and parameters of sumptuary legislation did indeed impose severe limitations on its effectiveness. However, this did not make the laws of apparel a bad idea. On the contrary, they were a reasonable response to serious concerns and had, if not practical support, then widespread theoretical approval.

One of the fears prompting the sumptuary orders was that clothing might be used to misrepresent the wearer, and deceive and mislead the viewer. Despite an apparent desire for a simple transparency of self-presentation, early modern people knew 'seeming' might not be the same as 'being'. Chapter 5 explores this further. By contrasting the figures of the vagabond and the courtier it becomes clear that attitudes to disguise were profoundly political, and access to this strategy was rigorously policed. For the privileged, the manipulation of appearances was a culturally sanctioned technique for advancement, or prudent self-preservation. More ordinary folk might also employ sartorial counterfeit but they risked censure or, as some court records indicate, retribution. In the case of the marginal and socially excluded, the use of disguise was inherently suspicious and enmeshed the perpetrator in the imputed motivations of deceit and duplicity. The punishments for those who dared to appear as other than they were, were brutal and disfiguring, permanently inscribing on their bodies the 'truth' of their marginalized identity. One specific aspect of disguise played with perceptions of gender. This is a subject that has drawn vociferous comment, both from modern scholars and early modern moralists. Looking more closely at the discursive treatment of cross-dressing, however, reveals the real target of complaint to be the extremes of elite fashion. The transgression was chiefly framed in sartorial terms and not, as it might first appear, in terms of gender. By contrast, cross-dressing that occurred in real life rather than discursive space, like any other aspect of disguise, is found to be inflected by class. That is, for those who were powerful enough, wearing another's raiment – whether they be from a different status group or different sex – was an allowable strategy. For those without influence, it was dishonest and punishable. As occasion necessitated, then, false beards or borrowed breeches could be worn with impunity, but only by the privileged.

Thus this book looks at the importance of clothes in people's lives. It traces their involvement in physical processes, in bodily transitions, in the organization of individual identity, and in the policing and misrepresentation of social appearances. In all these contexts garments were used by their wearers, and in turn asserted themselves to shape movements, create feelings, and foster attitudes. Before we move on to Chapter 1 it is as well to return to Samuel Pepys, who briefly reminds us of this power and agency of dress. 'We had a very good and handsome dinner, and excellent wine', he wrote. But, 'I not being neat in clothes, which I find a great fault in me, could not be so merry as otherwise and at all times I am and can be, when I am in good habitt'.[18]

Notes

1. *The Diary of Samuel Pepys*, ed. by Robert Latham and William Matthews, 11 vols (London, 1970–1983), VII, 315, 8 October 1666; 324, 15 October 1666; 328, 17 October 1666; 353, 4 November 1666; VIII, 295, 26 June 1667. Hereafter *Diary*. For details of the introduction of the English vest, see Esmond S. De Beer, 'King Charles II's own Fashion; An Episode in Anglo-French Relations', *Journal of the Warburg and Courtauld Institutes*, 2 (1938–39), 105–15, and Diana de Marly, 'King Charles II's Own Fashion: The Theatrical Origins of the English Vest', *Journal of the Warburg and Courtauld Institutes*, 37–8 (1974–5), 378–82.
2. Fernand Braudel, *The Structures of Everyday Life: The Limits of the Possible*, trans. by Siân Reynolds (London, 1981), p. 323.
3. Philippe Perrot, *Fashioning the Bourgeoisie: A History of Clothing in the Nineteenth Century*, trans. by Richard Bienvenu (Princeton NJ, 1994), p. 3.
4. Efrat Tseëlon, 'Ontological, Epistemological and Methodological Clarifications in Fashion Research: From Critique to Empirical Suggestions', in *Through the Wardrobe: Women's Relationships with their Clothes*, ed. by Ali Guy, Eileen Green and Maura Banim (Oxford, 2001), pp. 237–54 (p. 237).
5. Thomas J. Csordas, 'Embodiment as a Paradigm for Anthropology', *Ethos*, 18 (1990), quoted in Julia Epstein and Kristina Straub, 'Introduction: The Guarded Body', in *Body Guards: The Cultural Politics of Gender Ambiguity*, ed. by Julia Epstein and Kristina Straub (London, 1991), p. 2.
6. For example, see Jonathan Sawday, *The Body Emblazoned: Dissection and the Human Body in Renaissance Culture* (London, 1995); and David Hillman and Carla Mazzio (eds), *The Body in Parts: Fantasies of Corporeality in Early Modern Europe* (London, 1997).

7. For example, Anne Buck, 'Clothing and Textiles in Bedfordshire Inventories, 1617–1620', *Costume*, 34 (2000), 25–38; the research by Beverly Lemire, especially *Fashion's Favourite: the Cotton Trade and the Consumer in Britain, 1660–1800* (Oxford, 1991), and *Dress, Culture and Commerce: The English Clothing Trade before the Factory, 1660–1800* (Basingstoke, 1997); Margaret Spufford, *The Great Reclothing of Rural England: Petty Chapmen and their Wares in the Seventeenth Century* (London, 1984); John Styles, 'Clothing the North: The Supply of Non-élite Clothing in the Eighteenth-Century North of England', *Textile History*, 25 (1994), 139–66; and Lorna Weatherill, 'Consumer Behaviour, Textiles and Dress in the Late Seventeenth and Early Eighteenth Centuries', *Textile History*, 22 (1991), 297–310.

8. Chandra Mukerji, *From Graven Images: Patterns of Modern Materialism* (New York, 1983), p. 15.

9. Jennifer Craik, *The Face of Fashion: Cultural Studies in Fashion* (London, 1994), pp. 1–16.

10. Arthur Asa Berger, *Reading Matter: Multidisciplinary Perspectives on Material Culture* (New Brunswick, 1992), p. 105.

11. Philip Stubbes, *The Anatomie of Abuses*, The English Experience, 489 (London, 1583; repr. Amsterdam, 1972), sigs [B7ᵛ], [C6ʳ].

12. On the structure of early modern society see Keith Wrightson, *English Society 1580–1680* (London, 1982). For a review of the historiography of social formation, particularly around the vexed issue of the middling sort, see the article by H.R. French, 'The Search for the "Middle Sort of People" in England, 1600–1800', *Historical Journal*, 43 (2000).

13. Peter Laslett, *The World We Have Lost Further Explored* (Cambridge, 1983), p. 27.

14. John F. Kasson, *Rudeness and Civility: Manners in Nineteenth-Century America* (New York, 1990), p. 4.

15. Daniel Roche, *The Culture of Clothing: Dress and Fashion in the Ancien Régime*, trans. by Jean Birrell (Cambridge, 1996), p. 20.

16. Aileen Ribeiro, *The Gallery of Fashion* (London, 2000), p. 11.

17. Ribeiro, *Gallery of Fashion*, p. 11; Peter Stallybrass and Ann Rosalind Jones, *Renaissance Clothing and the Materials of Memory* (Cambridge, 2000), p. 35.

18. *Diary*, II, 198–9, 19 October 1661.

–1–

Fashioning Appearances

Although this is an examination of the meanings and utilizations of clothing within elite early modern society, this first chapter will consider its styles and component garments. This may seem like a step in an altogether unreflective direction – a scrap of 'hemline history' – but before any scrutiny of meaning we need an appreciation of form. Without at least sharing the vocabulary of clothing with sixteenth- and seventeenth-century wearers, and to some degree being able to visualize its referent objects, our understanding of journal entries, laws, satire and pictorial records will be very partial indeed. What follows, therefore, is a broad-brush introduction to the costume of the period, divided between male and female dress.[1] After this apparently straightforward narrative of costume history, however, the chapter returns to look again at the styles of sixteenth- and seventeenth-century dress. This time we consider the possible implications of a garment's structure and shape, exploring how clothing helped form both individual bodies and cultural perceptions.

The Wardrobe – Men

The story of sixteenth- and seventeenth-century fashion can be told very simply. Our starting point is a sketch of a clothed male figure dating from the 1570s (Figure 1). The drawing comes from the marginalia of a York Archbishop's Register, and was presumably penned idly by some bored clerk.[2] The sketch indicates that our modern gestalt of the appearance of an Elizabethan was very close to theirs. The basic articles of male dress for most of the sixteenth and seventeenth centuries were the doublet, hose and cloak. As we can see in the clerk's drawing, doublets, worn over a shirt, were sleeved garments covering the torso. They were close fitting, but also well wadded and reinforced with boning. During the latter part of the sixteenth century this stiffening and padding developed into the 'peascod belly', a style which swelled belly-like out from the stomach and even, in more extreme forms, over and below the waist line (Figures 2

Figure 1 Marginal drawing, BIHR, Cons.AB. 33 (1570–2), fol. 13ᵛ. Reproduced from an original in the Borthwick Institute, University of York.

and 3). Although always appearing to open centre front, the buttons or lacing there could be merely decorative, with the real hook and eye fastenings to the side. Sleeves were either sewn into the garment, or made as separate items to be attached by long laces called points. Our clerk's drawing shows a doublet wing that might decoratively hide such an arrangement. Jerkins were very similar garments to doublets, only usually sleeveless, and were worn over the top for warmth. Due to their similarity of appearance, their presence in portraits is often very difficult to tell.

– 14 –

Figure 2 Sir Philip Sidney, after Unknown artist, date not known. By courtesy of the National Portrait Gallery, London.

Figure 4 shows a partially unbuttoned jerkin worn over a doublet that features a modest peascod belly.

Hose, which covered the legs, comprised two sections: upper and nether. Upper hose, synonymous with breeches, enclosed the body from the waist to somewhere between thigh and knee, depending on the style. These were various, but the 'typical' Elizabethan look – portrayed by the archdiocesan clerk – was of trunk hose. This was a short, full style that ballooned out from the waist and extended only to mid or upper thigh

Figure 3 Sir Francis Drake, Unknown artist, *c.* 1580. By courtesy of the National Portrait Gallery, London.

(Figures 1, 2, and 4). The remaining area of the visually isolated and elongated leg was covered by long stockings or by canions. The latter, possibly pictured by the clerk, were close fitting extensions to trunk hose, made often in a contrasting fabric and sewn into the gathered fullness of the onion-shaped uppers (Figure 4). An alternative style, increasingly popular from the last quarter of the sixteenth century, were Venetian breeches. Venetians were cut to be full and baggy around the hips and

Figure 4 Sir Walter Raleigh and Walter Raleigh, Unknown artist, 1602. By courtesy of the National Portrait Gallery, London.

thighs, but tapered to narrowness about the closed knee (Figures 3 and 4). With all styles of upper hose the lower portion of the leg was covered by a garment variously named as nether hose, nether stocks, or stockings. These were gartered either over, or underneath the breeches (Figure 4).

Although gowns continued to be worn, particularly for warmth or sobriety, from around the mid-sixteenth century cloaks were far more fashionable (Figures 3 and 5). While their claim to chic remained constant,

Figure 5 Young man against roses, Nicholas Hilliard, 1588. V&A Picture Library.

the preferred styles changed: sometimes hooded, sometimes with hanging sleeves, now shorter, now long. A younger son making his place on the fringes of Elizabethan court society, Philip Gawdy (1562–1617) wrote to his brother of an attempt to introduce one of these stylistic changes. 'Uppon Wednesday last a very specyall strayte commandement from the quene gyven by my L. chamberlayne, that no man shall come into presence, or attend uppon Her Matie wearing any long cloke beneath the knee, or therabouts.' Although inconvenient to fashionable aspirants,

Gawdy astutely remarked that, 'It commeth in a good hower for taylers and mercers and drapers'. For 'all men ar settled into longe clokes', and must perforce either rush to get them shortened, or pay for a new one – both options that spelled profit for the craftsmen.[3]

The item that lives in our minds as an inescapable vision of the second half of the sixteenth century is the ruff. Originating as a small frill drawn up at the neck of a shirt, by the 1570s the ruff had grown in size and complexity, and had become detachable. Shaped into a wide variety of styles, the quintessentially Elizabethan image is of the cartwheel ruff, whose closed pleats encircled the wearer and produced the 'head on a plate' look (Figures 3, 5, and 9). The alternative style of neckwear for both men and women was the band or, as we would name it, the collar. Again developing from the neck of a shirt or smock, it became a detachable item and was worn in two varieties: the falling and standing. The first of these was turned down in a way we would think of as being typically collar-like (Figure 4). The second, as its name suggests, stood out and up around the neck (Figure 6). Although known throughout the sixteenth century, in

Figure 6 Phineas Pett, Unknown artist, 1612. By courtesy of the National Portrait Gallery, London.

Figure 7 Henry Rich, 1st Earl of Holland, Daniel Mytens, 1633. By courtesy of the National Portrait Gallery, London.

James I's reign both varieties of band came to dominate, and the ruff disappeared from fashion. Unlike the falling band, the standing variety also declined in use, and after the 1620s was little seen. Cuffs, ranging from plain linen to complex lace and ruff styles, in form usually echoed the collar above (Figures 2 and 4).

These basic items of male dress in fact changed very little over the seventeenth century. Breeches became longer and baggier in the Jacobean period (Figure 6), bands gained supremacy, and the ruffs that remained were often worn not standing up but falling unstiffened across the shoulders. This tendency to less rigidity and to looser forms continued until, broadly coinciding with the accession of Charles I, dress presented a much softer and restrained look (Figure 7). Furthermore, despite the extraordinary social upheavals throughout the Civil War and Interregnum, mid-century fashionable dress stayed remarkably static. The individuals wielding power may have been different, but the way they were clad was often the same. Indeed, official portraits of the Interregnum rule frequently copied Van Dyck's paintings of the courtly regime, simply substituting new parliamentary heads for the old royalist ones.[4] Thus, despite the disruptions of political and social life, the visual appearance of the elite remained unbroken until the 1660s.

The Restoration did not only bring a monarch and court to England; it brought also their French styles of dress. The old guard returned with a new flamboyance, which, for men's clothes particularly, exaggerated the loose fullness of former styles to a remarkable degree (Figure 8). The tabs or skirts of the doublet disappeared, leaving a garment so short that it no longer met the breeches below. Instead lace and linen from the shirt beneath foamed out at the wearer's midriff. The independently fastened breeches burgeoned into the 'petticoat' style rather like modern culottes. The only two suits in this style that survive in England are a guide to the typical construction. Open at the knee, the breeches featured an almost unbelievable fullness, each leg measuring a phenomenal five feet two inches in circumference.[5] With so much room for a false move, it is perhaps no wonder that Mr Townend, Pepys's friend, made 'his mistake the other day to put both his legs through one of his knees of his breeches, and went so all day'.[6] The other feature typical of men's dress in the early 1660s were the garnishing ribbons. Derived originally from the points used to truss an outfit together, these laces had survived into the seventeenth century as decoration, leaving the functional work to buttons, and hooks and eyes. Adorning the post-Restoration modes, however, they fluttered to prominence; the ribbons trimming one surviving suit have been estimated as having a total length of 141 yards, while the other suit has a glorious 216 yards adorning it.[7] This cascading ensemble was finished off with a short circular cloak.

Despite the exuberance of Restoration fashions, they were short lived. Novel in 1658, already by 1665 this look had started to wane.[8] Then in October 1666 came the death knell. Charles II's act of sartorial patronage that introduced the vest, coat and breeches ensemble, ushered in the basic forms of a mode that is still with us today. Replacing the doublet, the

Figure 8 Charles II and Catherine of Braganza, Anonymous artist, 1662 or after. By courtesy of the National Portrait Gallery, London.

earliest forms of the vest were much more substantial garments than the reduced modern waistcoat. Long, and of a relatively narrow fit, this garment covered the breeches, making their fullness untenable and decorative exuberance redundant. Thereafter a neatly fitting breeches style was worn, plain and tapering to the knee. Over the top the coat, cut along very similar lines but sleeved, completed the outfit. Thus ousted, cloaks declined from fashion, remaining in use only as warm and serviceable outer coverings. The three-piece suit was born.

The Wardrobe – Women

The basic components of the woman's wardrobe were bodice, skirt and gown. The bodice, being that part of the dress above the waist, was worn over the shift and stiffened by whalebone, wood strips, or reeds.[9] Either back or front lacing, bodices that did fasten down the front would generally be worn with a stomacher. This was a stiffened triangular insert worn point down, and fastened to the bodice at either side by points, pins or ribbon ties. Functionally, the stomacher filled in the gap between the two front edges of the bodice and continued the corseting effect. Visually, the highly decorated insert took the eye from the top down to its long bottom point, making the torso appear even longer. As with men's doublets, bodice sleeves were either fixed or detachable. A number of styles emphasized certain features: some close fitting, others flaring at different points, and some sporting elaborate shoulder rolls. The most dramatic in form were trunk sleeves. Like men's trunk hose they puffed out from the limbs they covered, and were so large that their fullness was supported and held in shape by an internal framework of wire, whalebone, or wood (Figure 10). Their dimensions might be enlarged still further by the addition of gauze oversleeves, ballooning affairs that added yet another texture to the complicated assemblage (Figure 9).

The striking characteristic of the sixteenth-century skirt was its farthingale shape. The first form, popular for most of the second half of the century, was the conical Spanish farthingale (Figure 9). True to its name, this fashion originated in Spain around 1470, at least 70 years before its English appearance.[10] It was known there as a 'vertugadin', the anglicization of which results in its variant names (farthingale, vardingale, vardugal and so forth). In the 1590s the French, or wheel, farthingale took the fashionable lead, and most portraits from this period feature the distinctive 'hula hoop' round the wearer's hips over which the overskirt falls vertically to the ground. These portraits also show that the farthingale was worn tilted up at the back, and that a deep flounce often lay over the horizontal level of the skirt (Figure 10). The final basic component of sixteenth-century women's dress was the gown. This was a full-length garment worn over bodice and skirt, with a range of possible sleeve styles: hanging, puffed, sleeveless or full. The loose version was generously cut, and from the shoulders fell freely to the ground. The close bodied or fitted

Figure 9 Mary Cornwallis, George Gower, *c.* 1580–5. © Manchester Art Gallery.

gown was shaped to the waist, from where it was generally worn open to reveal the skirts beneath (Figures 9 and 11).

As with men's costume, over the sixteenth and seventeenth centuries remarkably little happened to alter the basic construction of women's apparel. The farthingale declined during James's reign as did the use of extended and enlarged sleeves (Figure 12), and this gradually developed into the softer Caroline silhouette characterized by a full draping skirt and

Figure 10 Portrait of a Lady of the Elizabethan Court, *c*. 1595 (oil on canvas), attributed to William Segar (fl. 1585- d. 1633). Ferens Art Gallery, Hull City Museums and Art Galleries, UK/Bridgeman Art Library.

short bodice (Figure 13). However, post-Restoration women's dress is simultaneously more and less complicated than the pictorial record might suggest. Taking portraits as source material would suggest that elite women appeared swathed in careless satin, with expanses of shift negligently showing at the low neckline and beneath the loosely fastened sleeves. However, these paintings actually record the contemporary vogue for posing *en déshabillé* – a state of 'undress' that outside the picture frame was only suitable for the privacy of the home. As well as purely informal poses in smock and loose nightgown, other arrangements of dress helped the sitter play at pastoral or Olympian roles.[11] Because of this vogue for

Figure 11 Portrait of Mary Denton, attributed to George Gower, 1573. York Museums Trust (York Art Gallery).

informal and fanciful images, portraits are problematic as evidence of late seventeenth-century fashion. Instead, 'information about it has to be sought in French fashion drawings, and contemporary engravings and illustrations'.[12] Looking at these alternative sources reveals a much simpler story, for the development of women's dress in the 1660s is consistent with earlier styles (Figure 8). In fact, apart from the lengthened bodice that, worn with a deeply pointed stomacher, lowered and narrowed the waistline, very little had altered from mid-century modes.

As with men's dress, change came at the end of the seventeenth century. The major alteration in form appeared in the 1670s with the development

Figure 12 Portrait of a Lady, 1618 (oil on canvas) by Marcus Gheeraerts (*c.* 1561–1635). Ferens Art Gallery, Hull City Museums and Art Galleries, UK/Bridgeman Art Library.

of the mantua, a one-piece gown that replaced the separate bodice and skirt. Fitting closely at the waist, it was worn open in front and generally fastened back to reveal an underskirt beneath. Although different in struct-ure, visually the alteration in women's dress is hard to perceive. Indeed, its major ramification was in the realm of production. For being unboned (and thus worn over a corset), the mantua was sewn by sempstresses. Thus

Figure 13 Henrietta Maria, Unknown artist, 1635. By courtesy of the National Portrait Gallery, London.

women inched their way into the production of outer wear, an industry until then the sole preserve of the male tailoring establishment.[13]

These, then, were the main components of the wardrobe. For men and women alike the basic units of dress did not change until the 1660s and 1670s brought about radically new structures. The doublet, hose and cloak ensemble was replaced by the prototypical three piece suit; and less obviously the mantua gown initiated dramatic changes in the tailoring profession, and in form looked forward to the sack dresses and side hoops of the next century. This simple story is one that is retold in innumerable texts on costume history. Fashions come and go, their duration is linked to the periodization of history by monarch, and their appearance is rendered accessible by simplified outline drawings. However, scrutinize this convenient tale for just a moment, and we find that undertaking a vestimentary history is by no means such a routine matter. The structure of garments and their techniques of assemblage and wear have certain implications for both the body within, and its relationship to other bodies, and to space. It is not enough to state merely that breeches were full or bodices were corseted, for this distension and constriction meant something for the wearer, and influenced not only physical behaviours, but also such intangibles as perceptions of beauty, grace and health. Bearing this in mind we must therefore return to our simple story of elite fashion and rescrutinize its changing forms. In doing so we will find that even the most basic dress history carries within it certain possibilities for understanding the society whose clothes it describes.

Reviewing the Wardrobe

From the mid-1500s, dress styles were characterized by extreme visual complexity. Both the male and female forms were progressively more and more unbalanced and 'distorted', with separate parts of the dressed anatomy given independent status. Rather than being subordinate to the effect of the total assemblage, each item of the late Elizabethan elite wardrobe had an independent and striking visual existence: garments were 'hooks for the eye upon which the gaze catches'.[14] Coupled to this was a decorative exuberance that loaded every point with embroidery, jewels, slashes, ribboning and pattern. Indeed, Christopher Breward has described three dimensional fashionable costume as 'a canvas or panel' for the flat decoration on its surface.[15] In addition to this love of variety, Geoffrey Squire sees the exaggerated independent forms of garments such as ruffs, doublets and farthingales as practising 'techniques of disintegration'. With variety, distortion, and disintegration of the whole, late sixteenth- and early seventeenth-century dress was, Squire has persuasively written, typically mannerist.[16]

For example, the stiffened and padded doublet broke away from the body beneath, and swelled into the peascod belly. This was satirized by the impassioned Philip Stubbes, who concluded that, 'for certaine I am there was never any kinde of apparell ever invented, that could more disproportion the body of a man then these Dublets with great bellies hanging down beneath their Pudenda, (as I have said) & stuffed with foure, five or six pound of Bombast at the least'.[17] Squire, interpreting this Renaissance style as a caricature of the middle-aged figure, also notes that it was, and remains, a unique fashion. 'At no other time has a distended belly been artificially suggested rather than corrected or disguised.' Furthermore, this portly mature torso was frequently set over the equally stereotyped long slim legs of youth (Figure 5).[18] These chic legs, vital to the image of a courtier, suggested 'an aristocratic elegance suitable for dancing, fencing, or riding', those most courtly of pursuits.[19] Also close fitting, and well wadded like the rest of the doublet, sleeves were cut and sewn with a pre-shaped bend at the elbow, which accommodated the inward movement of the arm without straining the seams. On the other hand, straightening the arm would have been moving against the garment's cut, and the longer outer side of the sleeve would inevitably have tightened and puckered. Thus, when not in movement, elegance and ease would enforce a stance with slightly bent arms. Such considerations add a further dimension to our understanding of the 'Renaissance elbow', that ubiquitous arms akimbo stance that set the type for male assertiveness through the Tudor and earlier Stuart years (Figures 1 to 4).[20] Whatever the origins of this form of bodily display, as with all dressed movements it worked with, not against, the material conditions of the clothing, intellectual and physical circumstance together combining to produce a behavioural result.[21]

In order to bear out their fullness trunk hose, like doublets, were padded and stuffed to glorious proportions (Figure 2). This was done either with multiple linings, or the addition of wool, hair and other suitable materials. Such width and weight about the hips clearly had its effect on stance and gait. Primarily it helped achieve the gallants' swagger, but secondly it also bore out the arms, thus further emphasizing the bent and elegant elbow. However, sartorial pride might occasion a corresponding fall. Physician and writer, John Bulwer, who in the mid-seventeenth century made a direct comparison between trunk hose and women's farthingales, also related the tale of a gentleman whose garment was stuffed with bran. A small rent was torn in his hose 'with a naile of the chaire he sat upon', so that as he gallantly entertained the ladies the bran poured forth 'like meale that commeth from the Mill'. This caused much laughter amongst the company. The gent, ascribing the mirth to his social success, was encouraged to yet more energetic efforts – 'untill he espied the heape of branne, which came out of his hose', and took a shameful and hasty departure.[22]

In the absence of belts or suspenders, all upper hose styles were held up by being attached to the doublet. This was done by lacing through holes in the breeches' waistband to corresponding eyelets at the waist of the doublet. Sometimes visible – a decorative virtue out of functional necessity – more often this line of points was hidden by tabbed doublet skirts. In the seventeenth century metal hooks and eyes took over fastening these two garments, but visible points were often retained as vestigial, but flamboyant, accessories. Providing the hose were full enough to allow for stretching and sitting, this system of fastening had the advantage of ensuring that the weight of heavy and generously tailored fabrics was carried from the shoulders, rather than dragging from the waist. However, the many eyelet holes in surviving garments suggest that lacing must have been a lengthy operation, and trussing or hooking at the back required either extreme dexterity, or more likely help in dressing. Such sartorial conditions explain the interested observation of gentleman traveller Fynes Moryson (1566–1630) that, 'the Italians clothe very little children with doublets and breeches, but their breeches are open behind, with the shirt hanging out, that they may ease themselves without helpe'.[23] It also contextualizes the precepts in conduct literature that condemn public trussing or incomplete lacing. Such behaviour or appearance could only suggest that the wearer had been occupied with bodily functions.

Of the many garments that we find it difficult to deal with from a modern perspective, one of the most obdurate is the codpiece (Figure 2). Originally a triangular flap in the hose, the codpiece improved fit and, by lacing separately, performed the equivalent function of the modern fly. As with so many other aspects of sixteenth-century dress, however, the codpiece underwent an exaggeration of form that resulted in some startling items of wear.[24] The development of Venetians, though, and of later styles of breeches thereafter, made it redundant. The longer, looser garments were made with a fly opening, and the codpiece was no longer needed to join trunk hose at the fork. It would be disingenuous to deny that the codpiece had sexual significance. French comic writer, François Rabelais (d. 1553), in describing Gargantua's enormous and exuberant codpiece – 'like to that horn of abundance, it was still gallant, succulent, droppy, sappy, pithy, lively, always flourishing, always fructifying, full of juice, full of flower, full of fruit, and all manner of delight' – makes abundantly clear its symmetry with the member it encased. Indeed, 'as it was both long and large, so was it well furnished and victualled within, nothing like unto the hypocritical codpieces of some fond wooers, and wench-courters, which are stuffed only with wind, to the great prejudice of the female sex'.[25] 'Wench-courting' was also on Wat Raleigh's mind. Poet and playwright, Ben Jonson (1573?–1637), who accompanied Sir Walter's son on a tour of France, complained of this 'knavishly inclined' youth who set 'the favour of damsels on a codpiece' – a flamboyant seventeenth-century equivalent to notches on a belt.[26] And Michel de Montaigne (1533–92), author of the famous *Essays*, engagingly called it a 'laughter-moving, and maids looke-drawing peece'.[27] However, it would be as misleading to overplay the sexual symbolism of the codpiece, as to underplay it. Firstly, there are remarkably few textual or iconographic mentions that make overt any significance of this kind; and secondly, its exaggerated form is shared by most other garments in the contemporary wardrobe. We choose to dwell on the enhanced shape of the genitals, but almost miss men's over-long legs and outsized bellies.

Having no apparent practical function, the ruff is another garment that clearly demonstrates the distance between modern and early modern dress sensibility. However, because of its portrayal in graphic and sculptural media, this icon of Tudor culture has acquired a permanence that quite belies its ephemeral nature as a garment. For rather than having an enduring form, the ruff was remade at every wash. Cleaned, and then dipped in starch, the pleats of the ruff were then shaped into 'sets' with heated metal irons called poking sticks.[28] These sets were further arranged and held in place by pinning. 'By varying the sets into which the ruff is ironed and the arrangement of the pins, a different configuration can be given to the ruff each time it is laundered.'[29] Only a very few Elizabethan ruffs survive, but the complexity, creativity and time-consuming nature of their construction has been revealed by the Globe Theatre's recreation of contemporary costume. A typical one of their ruffs was made from a strip of linen ten metres long, which was then handsewn, in hundreds of pleats, into a neckband just fifty centimetres in length. The starching, ironing and pinning of this basic linen form can then take up to five hours at every laundering.[30] Vulnerable to wind and rain, the fragile nature of the enterprise was ridiculed, like so much else, by Stubbes. 'But if Aeolus with his blasts, or Neptune with his stormes, chaunce to hit uppon the crasie bark of their brused ruffes, then they goe flip flap in the winde like rags flying abroad, and lye upon their shoulders like the dishcloute of a slut.'[31] The closed and pleated ruffs were accompanied by many other elaborate and dramatic styles: open, fan-shaped, cutwork and so on. Like the standing band, the tilt and angle of the larger varieties was achieved by pinning them to a wire frame underneath, called an underpropper or supportasse – another skilled and time-consuming technique of construction. Although structural, these frames, attached to the collars of doublet or bodice, were made decorative by cording them with silk or metallic threads. For the hundred or so years in which it held fashionable sway, the ruff was a truly privileged form of dress. The time and labour involved in its techniques of making and remaking could only be afforded by the wealthy, as could its techniques of wear. For the restriction of movement and vision, and the enforced 'proud' carriage of head and wrists surrounded by such sartorial delicacies, argues the possession of leisure, or at very least a dissociation from manual occupation.[32] What for some may have been read as excessive or inconsequent, was a serious statement of luxury, wealth and style.

For women the analogous item to the doublet was the bodice. Frequently called 'a pair of bodies', this garment had no darts to allow for either fullness at the breast or tapering at the waist. All shaping was achieved by curving the seams; and the bust, although pushed up, was also flattened.[33] This effect was increased by the busk, a removable bone or wood insert slipped into a casing sewn at the front, which further pressed against the breasts and stomach. Thus although boned, these garments produced a very different effect from the nineteenth-century tight lacing corsets with which we are familiar. The nineteenth-century varieties were much more complicated in their construction, and were already shaped into the hourglass form, which then moulded the wearer. Added to this dramatic pre-shaping, the new metal eyelets enabled a much tighter lacing than had been achievable with the weaker, more flexible sewn holes.[34] Sixteenth-century bodices shaped their wearer into a longer lined and flatter torso, rather like an inverted triangle (Figure 10). They supported the body within, too, but without exerting the level of constriction the differently shaped nineteenth-century technology made possible. In addition to a design in which the central busk was removable for comfort, it is important to remember that, because the lacing controls the tightness of fit, this was also under the wearer's control. Or perhaps it would be more accurate to say under the wearer's direction, since many bodices were back lacing and might require someone else to fasten them.

This corseted body form is echoed in the idealization of an exaggerated torso so evident in portraiture from the sixteenth and early seventeenth centuries. Whether covered in cloth or painted as exposed by the low cut bodices of the 1610s and 1620s, the early modern painterly vision elongated and enlarged this area, although still rendering it flat and without obvious signs of breasts (Figures 12 and 14).[35] This iconography argues the presence of a societal perception which registered a flat, lengthy torso as a womanly attribute. Whether the focus of desire or disapprobation (as was the case with many moral commentators whose

Figure 14 Frances Howard, Countess of Somerset (1589–1632), William Larkin. By kind permission of the Duke of Bedford and the Trustees of the Bedford Estates. © The Duke of Bedford and the Trustees of the Bedford Estates.

stock-in-trade included outrage at this display), this shaping of the female form dominated the cultural aesthetic. It is a vision of female beauty clearly distinct from the centuries preceding and following; being altogether different from the high circular breasts of medieval art, or the generous curves of eighteenth-century beauty.[36] As the disproportionately long legs in certain images of male courtiers bespoke a necessary attribute of manly elegance, so the anatomically improbable but culturally desirable long bosom was the female equivalent.

Although no sixteenth-century farthingales survive from anywhere in the world, scholars have used tailors' patterns and paintings to re-create their construction. The earlier conical Spanish variety was made by an underskirt with hoops of willow, whale bone or rushes sewn into material casings, which provided a frame for the overskirt in a very similar way to the Victorian crinoline. The hula hoop look of the later French style was achieved in two ways. Either an underframe was used, as with the Spanish variety, or a less pronounced look could be had by tying a 'bum roll' – like an oversize stuffed sausage – around the hips. The flounce of this far-thingale was achieved by pinning the very long lengths of the overskirt so that it disguised the ridge caused by the frame beneath (Figure 10). Rather like the different forms that could be created by techniques of setting and pinning a ruff, so too the flounce responded to ingenuity of styling. Variations of pleats, ruffles, gathers and tucks – although perpetuated in portraits and effigies – were transient creations lasting only while the dress was worn. 'The arrangement of the skirt worn over a French farthingale was left to the wearer and her servant, who folded and pinned the flounce to suit the size of the padded rolls or frame as required.'[37]

De rigueur in the final years of Elizabeth's reign – in 1593 Philip Gawdy sent his sister-in-law 'a fuardingall of the best fashion' – the style doggedly outlasted her.[38] This must have been at least partly due to James I's wife, Anne of Denmark, who preferred its formal (and by now increasingly old-fashioned) lines for court wear. However, by 1617 it had sunk into an irrevocable decline in England, a fashion slump witnessed by Lady Clifford, eventually to become the Countess of Dorset, and Pembroke and Montgomery. In November of that year she wrote, 'All the time I was at Court I wore my Green Damask Gown embroidered without a Farthingale.'[39] A few months before, in June, Sir Dudley Carleton (1573–1632) had written from his ambassadorial posting at The Hague. The letter, addressed to his good friend John Chamberlain, mentioned the arrival of a mutual acquaintance. It seems 'My lady Bennet' did not stay long by reason of:

> the boys and wenches, who much wondered at her huge vardugals and fine gowns, and saluted her at every turn of a street with their usual caresses of whore, whore, and she was the more exposed to view because when she would go closely in a covered wagon about the town she could not because there was no possible means to hide half her vardugal.[40]

Figure 15 Elizabeth I, Marcus Gheeraerts the Younger, *c*. 1592. By courtesy of the National Portrait Gallery, London.

While clearly out of fashion in Holland, and declining in England, the farthingale continued in Spanish-influenced areas. By 1662 the arrival of the future Queen, Catherine of Braganza, and her entourage, prompted Pepys into writing that the 'portugall Ladys . . . are not handsome, and their farthingales a strange dress'. Diarist John Evelyn (1620–1706) was more emphatic: their farthingales were 'monstrous'.[41]

It takes only a moment's reflection to realize that the spatial effects of this dramatic style must have been considerable. The wearer of the French farthingale in particular has an architectural quality, and obtrudes into social space with insistent dimensions. It is tempting to link this spatial dominance to the social dominance of the fashion's elite wearers. This was most clearly the case with the farthingale's most visible champion, Elizabeth. Emanating from the monarch, female court dress of the last decade of the reign – like royal iconography – was extreme: wheeled skirts, trunk sleeves distended with padding and wire, hanging sleeves, standing ruffs, and wired rails that framed the head in a halo of gauze and jewellery. This relationship of political and sartorial power is clearly envisaged in the Ditchley Portrait (Figure 15): Eliza, massive and encircling, standing over the realm.[42]

After Elizabeth's death, the farthingale began its slow decline. The female silhouette shrank; narrower sleeves were worn, and the more modestly proportioned bum roll supported the skirts. Although continuing as court wear, the connotations of the farthingale had changed. No longer read only as splendid and elegant (or even as proud and immoral), contemporaries began to view it as formal, old-fashioned, and even faintly ridiculous. So, well before the farthingale finally disappeared in England, perceptions had begun to change. John Chamberlain's opinions (1553–1627) are illustrative. In February 1613 this witty observer of Jacobean life wrote a long letter to Dudley Carleton's wife, Alice, describing the wedding of Princess Elizabeth to Frederick, the Elector Palatine. At the close he remembered, 'One thing I had almost forgotten for hast that all this time there was a course taken and so notified that no Lady or gentlewoman shold be admitted to any of these sights with a verdingale, which was to gaine the more roome, and I hope may serve to make them quite left of in time.'[43] Thus the reception of this fashion had moved from it being viewed as an indispensable part of the elite female form, to an inconvenient, perhaps backward-looking, waste of space.

Extremity, then, characterized fashionable clothing of this period. From the middle of the sixteenth century garments progressively swelled and ballooned in size, until by the 1620s they had reached the limits of their form. Held out by an internal framework or weighted by hidden padding, these garments suggested an angular stance that highlighted component parts of the dress, and the body. Heads were isolated by ruffs or held erect by collars; the torso was held upright in its encasing doublet or bodice; arms angled out or rested on the farthingale hoops; and hips were distended by hose or skirts. While male legs and the manly gait was highlighted by the wearing of stockings, women's perambulations were hidden entirely beneath the gliding farthingale.[44] Not only anatomically exaggerated, these styles also embodied contradiction. The paunch of the peascod belly operated in counterpoint to slender young legs, the swollen hips of men's hose presented a typically female silhouette, and the plunging but flat-chested women's bodice shaped an androgynous torso. Despite the apparent fixity of an assemblage, many of the effects were ephemeral, as ruffs, lace, skirts and sleeves might change their appearance at the next wearing. But while the effects themselves were short lived, their preparation was lengthy and complicated. With extensive lacing, pinning and buttoning, dressing was a time-consuming process requiring, for its most dramatic and complex forms, not only the wealth to afford them, but also the leisure to wear them. The complaint of dramatist Thomas Tomkis (fl. 1614) that 'a ship is sooner rigged by far, than a gentlewoman made ready' is much quoted.[45] His exasperated description of a task taking over five hours is obviously exaggerated satire, and also conveniently omits to mention that the techniques of assemblage were identical for men. It does, however, indicate that an activity our society endeavours to make increasingly rapid and simple was approached with an altogether different set of values four hundred years ago.

The extremity of dress form was matched by the extremity of its surface appearance. With a decorative abandon the dressed figure was layered in different textures and loaded with lace, jewels, chains and accessories. Garments were embroidered, slashed, pinked, puffed and paned. The few garments that remain to us are in a hugely faded and tarnished state, but portraits indicate the resplendence that was once theirs. These pictures were painted in full day and show the richness of colour and textures. Quite another effect must have obtained by candlelight glinting on jewellery and metallic thread. That the wearers were alive to their clothing's night-time possibilities is indicated by Francis Bacon's advice (1561–1626) on the costuming of masques. The future Lord Chancellor wrote in his *Essays*: 'The *Colours*, that shew best by Candlelight are; White, Carnation, and a Kinde of Sea-Water-Greene; and *Oes*, or *Spangs*, as they are of no great Cost, so they are of most Glory.' However, he warned, 'As for *Rich Embroidery*, it is lost, and not Discerned'.[46]

While Bacon was writing of the appearance of the dressed figure on a stage, the implicit notion of performance is equally applicable to the clothing worn in the theatre of everyday life. For the courtier *sprezzatura* – that nonchalant and effortless grace – was the ideal bodily comportment, and in the public spaces of the newly urban early modern world it was practised through the medium of contemporary dress. While apparently contradictory, it is the difficulties of fashion that add to the grace of its successful performance. Indeed, perhaps such an effortless ideal could only flourish among the extremity of such effortful sartorial forms. But it was a performance destined to end. Inevitably, as with all fashions, such styles reached the limits of their possibility, and when there was nowhere else to go with the old aesthetic a new look began to emerge.

Beginning around the reign of Charles I, dress came to be characterized by a new decorative restraint; instead of featuring variety and contrast, a dressed outfit was completed by matching colours and fabrics. Individual details no longer obtruded onto the eye, and parts of an ensemble were pressed into sartorial service for the good of the whole. Less strange to our eyes and contoured more to what we choose to delineate as the body's 'natural' shape, mid-seventeenth-century fashions at first sight slip through interpretation. Their relative familiarity does not provoke questioning, and commentators simply have less to say about less startling clothes. Apart from a temporary flutter into petticoat breeches, this comparative restraint was to last until the eighteenth century saw women burgeoning into enormous side hoops and panniers. However, although less remarkable at first sight, certain features of this vestimentary order do rise to the notice.

For both men and women the dressed waistline moved to higher up the body, and thus presented a new paradigm of desirability (Figures 7 and 13). But while this shortened torso contributed to an appearance of being less encased, the basic construction of the garments remained unaltered. Thus while renouncing former padding and distension in sleeves or stomach, the doublet and bodice both retained internal rigidity: the doublet with the stiffened neck and belly piece – two triangular inserts placed either side of the front opening; the bodice with the boning and busk. Being short-waisted and square-necked the bodice gave its wearer a broader, thicker appearance. Matching this look the sleeves, too, were puffy and short. Set well down on the shoulders and cut to three-quarter length, they limited vertical movement of the upper limbs and, for the first time, exposed a woman's forearm. For hundreds of years only revealed to the intimate gaze, the seventeenth century disclosed this body part to public view (Figure 13). Beneath the waistline 'puffy fluid bulk' was manifested in the voluminous folds of the skirt worn over hip pads.[47] Female beauty, in these styles, was realized as a kind of soft massivity. Less evident in men's dress the high-waisted doublets yet enabled the doublet skirts to lengthen, and hanging over full breeches the male outline thus echoed, albeit in a minor key, the broad bottom-heavy look of the women (Figures 7 and 16). At the margins of dress linen and lace maintained a constant presence, however, as with the tailored garments,

Figure 16 Endymion Porter, Van Dyck and School, 1628–32. By kind permission of the Earl of Mexborough.

the impression of rigidity had gone. Instead, 'unstarched and exploiting the natural weight of linen thread, they drooped and draped, flapping about the shoulders and wrists and over the top of boots'.[48] The dominant decorative motif were long bold slashes, through which showed either a contrasting lining fabric, or the shirt or smock; and the favoured material, particularly for women's dress, was satin. Its folds and shine made it an ideal textile for draping full fashions, and the typical Caroline portrait emphasizes the play of light sliding on its surface. In a stock pose the subject furthers this effect by lightly grasping the abundant and satiny billows.

So, our simple story of costume forms as illustrated by a doodle at the margins of a 1570s ecclesiastical register, turns out to be more complex. In his casual depiction of the jaunty Renaissance elbow, the artist unconsciously leaves us an image of a body and mentality shaped by apparel. For clothing forms helped structure both the wearer's physical behaviours, and his or her ideas. It affected stance, movement and the relationship to space; and also dramatically influenced the criteria that signified such concepts as vigour, manliness, femininity and beauty. However, so far we have considered only notional people from the past – the 'typical' Elizabethan in trunk hose or the 'average' Caroline lady in satin. It is now time to turn to actual individuals, and the experiences they recorded of the relationship between their clothing and their physical bodies. In doing so we will find that apparel impacted heavily on their sensations of health and physical well-being. It was also involved in a complex interpretation of the body, in which the boundaries between flesh and fabric merged. Finally, dress was used in both highly personal, and culturally generated ways, to help individuals create, mark and manage moments of transition in the body's journey from the cradle to the grave.

Notes

1. For further detail, see Janet Arnold, *Patterns of Fashion: The Cut and Construction of Clothes for Men and Women c.1560–1620* (London, 1985); Jane Ashelford, *Dress in the Age of Elizabeth I* (London, 1988); Karen Baclawski, *The Guide To Historic Costume* (London, 1995); C.W. Cunnington and P. Cunnington, *Handbook of English Costume in the Sixteenth Century* (London, 1954; repr. 1962); C.W. Cunnington and P. Cunnington, *Handbook of English Costume in the Seventeenth Century*, 2nd edn (London, 1966); Aileen Ribeiro and Valerie Cumming, *The Visual History of Costume* (London, 1989).
2. BIHR, Cons. AB. 33 (1570–2), fol. 13^v. There are two almost identical sketches on fols 12^v and 13^v.
3. *Letters of Philip Gawdy*, ed. by Isaac Herbert Jeayes, The Roxburgh Club, 148 (London, 1906), pp. 90–1. Gawdy wrote his letter from Greenwich on 29 August 1594.

4. David Piper, *The English Face* (London, 1957), p. 112. On the republican appropriation of Caroline portrait images see Laura Lunger Knoppers, *Constructing Cromwell: Ceremony, Portrait, and Print 1645–1661* (Cambridge, 2000), esp. pp. 31–68.

5. Lesley Edwards, '"Dres't Like a May-Pole": A Study of Two Suits *c.*1600–1662', *Costume*, 19 (1980), 75–93 (p. 84).

6. *Diary*, II, 66, 6 April 1661. Also quoted in Edwards, 'Dres't Like a May-Pole', p. 84.

7. Edwards, 'Dres't Like a May-Pole', pp. 86, 90.

8. Edwards, 'Dres't Like a May-Pole', pp. 79, 80.

9. Baclawski, *Guide to Historic Costume*, pp. 37–8. If the bodice was not boned, a corset of almost identical design would be worn beneath. The main difference between the two garments was decorative: the corset, not made to be seen, was plainer and more purely functional.

10. See Françoise Piponnier and Perrine Mane, *Dress in the Middle Ages*, trans. by Caroline Beamish (New Haven, 1997), pp. 91–2.

11. See Jane Ashelford, *The Art of Dress: Clothes and Society 1500–1914* (London, 1996), pp. 95–9. Nightgowns were for informal day wear and not, as the name might suggest, bed attire.

12. Ashelford, *Art of Dress*, p. 100.

13. Naomi Tarrant, *The Development of Costume* (Edinburgh, 1994), pp. 66, 116. See also Avril Hart, 'The Mantua: its Evolution and Fashionable Significance in the Seventeenth and Eighteenth Centuries', in *Defining Dress: Dress as Object, Meaning and Identity*, ed. by Amy de la Haye and Elizabeth Wilson (Manchester, 1999), pp. 93–103.

14. Alexandra Warwick and Dani Cavallaro, *Fashioning the Frame: Boundaries, Dress and Body* (Oxford, 1998), p. 83.

15. Christopher Breward, *The Culture of Fashion: A New History of Fashionable Dress* (Manchester, 1995), p. 67.

16. Geoffrey Squire, *Dress, Art and Society* (New York, 1984), pp. 45–69.

17. Philip Stubbes, *The Anatomie of Abuses*, The English Experience, 489 (London, 1583; repr. Amsterdam, 1972), sig. E2^v.

18. Squire, *Dress, Art and Society*, p. 55.

19. Ellen Chirelstein, 'Emblem and Reckless Presence: The Drury Portrait at Yale', in *Albion's Classicism: The Visual Arts in Britain, 1550–1650*, ed. by Lucy Gent (New Haven, 1995), pp. 287–312 (p. 295).

20. See Joaneath Spicer, 'The Renaissance Elbow', in *A Cultural History of Gesture*, ed. by Jan Bremmer and Herman Roodenburg (Oxford, 1991), pp. 84–128.

21. In 'Mode and Movement', *Costume*, 34 (2000), 123–8, Jackie Marshall-Ward – Director of the historical dance group, Danse Royale – discusses the effects of Renaissance costume on the body when performing contemporary dances.

22. J. B., *Anthropometamorphosis: Man Transfrom'd: Or, the Artificall Changling* (London, 1653), pp. 541–2.

23. Fynes Moryson, *An Itinerary*, 4 vols (Glasgow, 1907), IV, 219–20. See also G.R. Quaife, *Wanton Wenches and Wayward Wives: Peasants and Illicit Sex in Early Seventeenth Century England* (London, 1979), where the author quotes from a court case concerning homosexual assault. During the deposition a yeoman's son explained that he had gone into a field 'with the purpose to untruss his points for the easing of nature' (p. 175).

24. Grace Q. Vicary, 'Visual Art as Social Data: The Renaissance Codpiece', *Cultural Anthropology*, 4 (1989), 3–25 suggests that the later enlarged type of codpiece developed as a functional and symbolic response to the contemporary syphilis epidemic.

25. *The Works of Rabelais*, trans. by Sir Thomas Urquhart, intro. by J. Lewis May, 2 vols (London, 1933), Book 1, Chapter 8, pp. 29–30.

26. Quoted in *Advice to a Son: Precepts of Lord Burghley, Sir Walter Raleigh, and Francis Osborne*, ed. by Louis B. Wright (Ithaca, 1962), p. xxii.

27. *Montaigne's Essays: John Florio's Translation*, ed. by J.I .M. Stewart, 2 vols (London, 1931), II, 254.

28. Starch was introduced into England from the Netherlands in 1564. This technological development enabled ruffs to grow in size and complexity, see Ashelford, *Art of Dress*, p. 33; and Nancy Bradfield, *Historical Costumes of England 1066–1968*, rev. edn (London, 1970), p. 78. Interestingly, Richard Mabey, *Flora Britannica* (London, 1996) states that an alternative form of starch, particularly for ruffs, was found in the crushed roots of the wildflower Arum maculatum, or Lords-and-ladies. However, its use often caused 'severe blistering of the launderers' hands' (p. 386).

29. Jenny Tiramani (Associate Designer, Shakespeare's Globe Theatre), Information panel for 'Patterns of Fashion' exhibition, Victoria and Albert Museum, Gallery 40, 1 February 1999 – 22 August 1999.

30. Ibid. For more on the complexities of constructing ruffs, and the Globe's re-created costumes in general, see Jenny Tiramani, 'Janet Arnold and the Globe Wardrobe: Handmade Clothes of Shakespeare's Actors', *Costume*, 34 (2000), 118–22.

31. Stubbes, *Anatomie of Abuses*, [sig. D7ᵛ].

32. The argument linking restrictive clothing to economic conditions was first developed by Thorstein Veblen in *Theory of the Leisure Class* (1899). He maintained that, along with the phenomenon of conspicuous wealth, such conspicuous leisure was a condition of fashionable dress. More recent re-articulations of this theory can be found set out in Quentin Bell, *On Human Finery: The Classic Study of Fashion Through the Ages*, rev. edn (London, 1976), pp. 32–9.

33. Arnold, *Patterns of Fashion*, p. 8.

34. However, in *Patterns of Fashion* (p. 46, Figure 328; pp. 112–13, no. 46) Arnold includes detailed photographs and drawings of a sixteenth-century German bodice in which the lace holes are reinforced inside and out with metal rings.

35. As Ellen Chirelstein has pointed out in 'Lady Elizabeth Pope: The Heraldic Body', in *Renaissance Bodies: The Human Figure in English Culture c. 1540–1660*, ed. by Lucy Gent and Nigel Llewellyn (London, 1990), pp. 36–59, there are 'no known full-scale portraits from this period that depict truly rounded breasts and nipples' (p. 58). The only contexts in which such an imaging seems to have been acceptable are the bold – in every sense – illustrations in popular literature, and depictions of masque costume. The most famous of the latter are the designs by Inigo Jones, of which a number show women in topless costumes. As strict representations these drawings need to be treated with caution, for they presumably bear the same idealized relationship to the actual worn costume as do designers' drawings today. This caution is supported by the few full-length portraits that exist depicting court women in fanciful, but unexceptional, masque dress (for example, 'Lady in Masque Costume as a Power of Juno', John de Critz, 1606; 'Lucy Harrington, Countess of Bedford as a Power of Juno', attr. John de Crtiz, 1606). However, the exception to this is a miniature by Isaac Oliver ('Portrait of an Unknown Woman as Flora', c. 1610). The unknown subject wears a masque dress cut beneath the bosom, which, through transparent gauzy linen, clearly shows her breasts and nipples. Chirelstein suggests that in both 'the idealised and privileged context of the masque', and in the private, intimate world of the miniature, 'nudity' was more allowable than in portraits proper ('Lady Elizabeth Pope', pp. 56–9).

36. For the depiction of breasts in art, see Anne Hollander, *Seeing Through Clothes* (Berkeley, 1993), pp. 186–207.

37. Arnold, *Patterns of Fashion*, p. 12.

38. *Letters of Philip Gawdy*, p. 77.

39. *The Diaries of Lady Anne Clifford*, ed. by D.J.H. Clifford (Stroud, 1990), p. 64.

40. *Dudley Carleton to John Chamberlain 1603–1624: Jacobean Letters*, ed. by Maurice Lee, Jr. (New Brunswick, 1972), p. 237.

41. *Diary*, III, 92, 25 May 1662; *The Diary of John Evelyn*, ed. by E.S. de Beer, 6 vols (Oxford, 1955), III, 320, 30 May 1662.

42. Andrew Belsey and Catherine Belsey make a similar point in 'Icons of Divinity: Portraits of Elizabeth I', in *Renaissance Bodies: The Human Figure in English Culture c. 1540–1660*, ed. by Lucy Gent and Nigel Llewellyn (London, 1990), pp. 11–35.

43. *The Letters of John Chamberlain*, ed. by Norman Egbert McClure, 2 vols (Philadelphia, 1939), I, 426.

44. Squire suggests the farthingale provided a motionless counterpart to active masculinity, see *Dress, Art and Society*, p. 65.

45. Thomas Tomkis, *Lingua or the Combat of the Tongues* (1607), quoted in Arnold, *Patterns of Fashion*, p. 39.

46. Francis Bacon, 'Of Masques and Triumphs', in *The Essays*, ed. by John Pitcher (Harmondsworth, 1985), p. 176. Oes and spangs sewn on to decorate material, were small pieces of metal like sequins.

47. Hollander, *Seeing Through Clothes*, p. 106.

48. Squire, *Dress, Art and Society*, p. 78.

Addressing the Body

Outwardly for Defence . . . Inwardly for Cleanliness

Later generations tend to look back in sartorial judgement, and impute to early modern dress a negative range of values. It was surely restrictive, unhygienic, uncomfortable, unhealthy and impractical. It must have got in the way. To wear it would have needed endurance, and those who did are pitied, and wondered at. Such sentiments are found expressed in much historiographical comment. For example, G.R. Elton wrote of Tudor dress that 'the huge hooped skirts rendered movement difficult, while the tight bodices and deep stomachers squeezed vital organs in a way not exceeded by the worst Victorian tight-lacing'.[1] Similarly, a Museum of London exhibition catalogue states that: 'this extreme fashion was uncomfortable', and also that Tudor finery was 'highly impractical'.[2] A National Portrait Gallery exhibition guide says much the same thing: 'Elizabethan dress was impressive but impractical'. The text also judges certain garments to have been unhealthy, for with 'no special clothes for pregnancy, these corsets could . . . increase the risk of miscarriage'.[3] But reading the accounts left by contemporaries reveals a very different interpretation of how it felt to wear such garments. They felt their encasing dress enhanced their physical well-being and protected against ill health and misfortune. Indeed, as Anne Hollander contends, comfort in clothing is not a physical condition, but a mental one. It does not arise from particular sensations of the body, but from having a particular self-image.[4] The self-image will be a satisfying one – productive of a sense of well-being – if it conforms to the prevailing belief system. The index of well-being in dress is not the extent to which an early modern assemblage conforms to our perceptions of health and comfort, but how far it matched contemporary perceptions.

The present, however, frequently finds it difficult to take the past seriously when clothed. It seems that something fundamental to our sense of what it is to be a proper man or woman must be being infringed, for dressed figures from the past can seem less intelligent, attractive, or even less natural. For one historian, wearing the court dress of her later portraits

Queen Elizabeth 'resembles a stuffed doll'. Men, she continued, 'looked equally artificial'.[5] Again, Elton found Tudor breeches to have been 'enormous (and very unsightly)'. He went on to describe dandies wearing 'idiotically tall hats and high heels', and wrote that they 'infested' Elizabeth's court.[6] In reading these judgements, one might almost say that viewed from the perspective of our particular sartorial assumptions, the humanity of historical actors is lessened. This attitude towards dress exists in contrast to the positive response generated by many other cultural productions. In particular, music, architecture, literature and art are commonly admired and respected, often above our contemporary efforts. In these fields the endeavour and humanity of the past seems magnified. In the area of dress, as we have seen, it can appear diminished. To account for this anomaly it can only be that our body image has changed dramatically. Furthermore, this body image must be deeply implicated in what we feel it means to be a 'proper' person.

The vision of the 'proper' person revealed by sixteenth- and seventeenth-century portraits is typically one of a body enveloped. Clothing encases its wearer entirely, except for the face and the hands. Even the exposure of these features is tempered by linen at neck and wrist, by hats and beards, and by gloves. Furthermore, it is easy to discern in contemporary writings a corresponding fear of the consequences of being inadequately clothed. Having too few layers, or not being covered at all, was a continuing cause of anxiety to the writers of personal narratives, because of the danger to their health. For if inadequately covered one might catch cold, and having caught cold one might in turn be caught by illness, and even death. Ralph Josselin (1616–83), the Essex Puritan cleric, was relieved one warm June that having worn less he did not take harm: 'This day I left my head cap, and wore a thinner stomacher, I formerly left of my night wascoate, and found no damage thereby, and I hope I shall not now.'[7] Alice Thornton's (1627–1707) baby was not so lucky. In making the tragedy of this child's illness and eventual death understandable for herself, the gentry housewife explained, 'when he was about fourteen daies old, my pretty babe broake into red spots, like the smale pox, and through cold, gotten by thinner clothing then either my own experience or practice did accustom to all my children'.[8]

A similar fear recurs in Pepys's diaries. Though the cold penetrated different parts of his body, his head seemed particularly vulnerable. 'So to my office late, and home to supper and to bed, having got a strange cold in my head by flinging off my hat at dinner and sitting with the wind in my neck.' The following January brought a similar affliction. 'And then home to supper and bed, having a great cold, got on Sunday last by sitting too long with my head bare for Mercer to comb me and wash my eares.' Two months later it happened again. 'Home to supper and to bed – having got a great Cold, I think by my pulling off my periwigg so often.' It was not until the icy spring of two years later that Pepys next found himself with 'a great cold', so bad 'that I am not able to speak . . . This cold did most certainly come by my staying a little too long bare-legged yesterday morning when I rose while I looked out fresh socks and thread stockings, yesterday's having in the night, lying near the window, been covered with Snow within the window, which made me I durst not put them on.'[9]

Urban lifestyles, central heating and thermal pollution insulate us from the full effects of seasonal change, and it is hard to remember how much more intense the experience of cold was four hundred years ago. In draftier rooms warmed with nothing but an open fire, there would have been no option but to use clothing as a protection against the cold. However, the function of dress as a protection, or a sealant, seems also to argue a different understanding of the body and its workings. In the dominant tradition of humoral medicine, health was seen as the proper balance of the four internal humours: blood, phlegm, yellow bile and black bile.[10] While a balanced state brought wellness, imbalance resulted in ill health and disease. Either harmful or healthful, the environment was a powerful agent in this dynamic physical process, such things as weather, water, air, or astrological movements affecting the equilibrium of both individuals and nations. Thus cold was not just unpleasant, but the potential cause of minor or severe ailments. For example, 'whenever the skin and outer parts of the body suddenly get cold and become constricted so that the pores are blocked', then catarrh could 'ooze down', 'sometimes with great danger to the lungs'.[11] Similarly, deafness and pain in the ears 'cometh many times through cold', as also coughs and hoarseness.[12] More spectacularly, Saturn was said to govern diseases of a cold nature, such as leprosy, palsy, gout, consumption, 'and the like cold and Melancholick infirmities'.[13] In 1605 Puritan gentlewoman, Lady Margaret Hoby (1571–1633), suffered from a pain in her shoulder that came 'by reason of Could', to which same cause Pepys ascribed discomfort in urinating.[14]

Remedies for cold disorders usually involved some 'hot' application. 'Venice treacle', for example, cured 'all paines of the head in man or woman that comes through cold', while a drink of claret, spices and sugar was said to be comforting to 'a cold stomacke'.[15] The author of *The Sufficiencie of English Medicines* recommended a long list of 'hot' plants and herbs, while Thomas Bonham included in his health advice the instructions for making an oil to help cold and moisture.[16] However, in the humoral tradition prophylaxis, or prevention, was no less important than therapeutics, or the cure.[17] If Ralph Josselin felt he had caught cold in the October of 1677 by the wearing of 'thin stockens', then it made sense for him to cover up more warmly.[18] Similarly, Pepys found himself 'mighty apt to take cold, so that this hot weather I am fain to wear a cloth before my belly'.[19] Clearly in the preventative fight against cold, clothing was a key defence. However, co-existing with beliefs about humoral imbalance, early modern medicine also pictured disease as a pollutant, or external invading danger.[20] Georges Vigarello, for example, explores how contemporary physiology pictured the skin as permeable, and the body therefore as being perpetually under threat of invasion from without.[21] If this was the case, it is easy to imagine how dress could come to be seen, in part, as a carapace that covered the vulnerable flesh beneath. It is apposite to remember the Dutch humanist Desiderius Erasmus (d. 1536) here, for whom clothing was 'the body's body'.[22]

This belief in the vulnerability of uncovered skin helps us to understand certain early modern images and practices. At first reading, the Puritan John Winthrop's (1588–1649) account of his first wife's death is almost unbearably moving, but also very alien. As the account of Thomasine's last days reveals, the dying woman was swathed in numerous layers of fabric:

But on Saterday morninge she beganne to complaine of could, and a little after awakinge out of a slumber, she prayed me to sett my heart at rest, for now (she said) I am but a dead woman, for this hand (meaninge hir left hande) is dead allready, and when we would have persuaded hir that it was but numme with beinge under hir, she still constantly affirmed that it was dead, and that she had no feelinge in it, and desired me to pull off hir gloves that she might see it, which I did; then when they would have wrapped some clothes about it, she disliked it, tellinge them that it was in vaine, and why should they cover a dead hande: when I prayed hir to suffer it, she answered that if I would have it so she would, and so I pulled on hir gloves, and they pinned clothes about hir hands, and when they had doone she said O what a wretche was I for layinge my legge out of the bedd this night, for when I should pull it in againe it was as it had come throughe the coverlaye, (yet it seemed to be but hir imagination or dreame for the women could not perceive it).

As Saturday drew on Thomasine grew more feverish, and those waiting with her had to cover her hands again 'which laye open with her former strivinge'. Finally towards evening she suffered from chest pains and, it seems, had difficulty in breathing. To give her ease 'they were forced to cutt the tyeings of hir waystcote'.[23]

This image of a dying woman encased in bed linen, garments and gloves can thus become more approachable if we entertain a vision of the fragile body warmed, guarded and decorated by protective cloth. However, Margaret Pelling has made a further connection between the concealing nature of dress and early modern medical practice. Before the use of antibiotics, she notes, many accidents and diseases would have resulted in scarring and chronic failure to heal. In the crowded context of early modern urban growth, Pelling detects new sensitivity to these bodily imperfections – a sensitivity which she then links to the encasing and highly ostentatious dress. The clothes – hose, sleeves, gloves and ruffs – concealed, and the ostentation re-directed the eye from the body beneath to the fabric above.[24] Visually, blemishes and deformity were less noticeable beside the perfections of tailored fabric.

The notion of vulnerable flesh and protective apparel leads us to consider the cultural positioning of those garments that we would call underwear. In form these consisted of a shirt for men and a smock for women. Both were full T-shaped garments, long to the wrist and falling well down the lower portion of the body. Made almost always of linen, the most expensive garments used the finer grades, such as holland or cambric. These were often embroidered at neck and wrist, those points in the vestimentary topography where such undergarments were glimpsed as outer wear. The female smock (known in later periods as a shift or chemise) and the male shirt were functionally interchangeable. Lady Ann Fanshawe (1625–80), wife to diplomat Sir Richard, wrote in her memoirs that, captured by the Parliamentary forces during the Civil War, he was visited by a well wisher, Lady Denham. Sir Richard asked her if he could borrow 'a shirt or two and some handkerchiefs'. Having none of her sons' at home, she 'feched him 2 smocks of her own'.[25]

Unlike women, men also wore linen drawers.[26] For females this sartorial lack presumably conferred a freedom of leg movement beneath skirts, and ensured privacy and convenience in the context of chamber pot use. However, the absence of drawers may also have brought the sort of vulnerability experienced by Elizabeth Numan. Assaulting her, a Batcombe man 'did violently take up the clothes of Elizabeth Numan of Wanstow up to her middle and showed her nakedness to many'. Similarly, a Halse husbandman, acting as procurer to his unwilling wife, offered those present that 'for a penny a piece they should see his wife's privities'. Throwing her upon a board he 'did take up her clothes and showed her nakedness in most beastly and uncivil manner'.[27] So while encompassed – and possibly protected by – layers of linen, wool and silk, beneath them there was nothing to impede access. This is in striking contrast to the rest of the wardrobe, which had to be laced, pinned, hooked and tied into position. Gaining access to the upper body required the negotiation of vestimentary complexity, but in simply raising the skirts one immediately arrived, in John Donne's words, 'where thou' wouldst be embayed'.[28] 'Under the petticoat, fresh air', writes Daniel Roche. 'A conception of the body and of sexual relations is revealed by this convenient absence.'[29]

The practical function of shirts, smocks and drawers was twofold. They protected the wearer from their outer garments, and the outer garments from the dirt and secretions of the body beneath. Absorbing these impurities, linen underwear was changed and washed as often as personal circumstances allowed. Outer garments, although brushed and subject to other techniques of dry cleaning, were not laundered. It was only the inner layer of clothing in contact with the skin that was purified by washing and bleaching. Although the increasingly anxious standards of modern hygiene judge this practice unsavoury, it is parallel to the customs ordering the wear of a business suit. The shirt will be changed daily; the suit will be occasionally dry cleaned, but never washed.

The difference between the modern and the early modern regimen lies in the type of care bestowed on the body. The former locates hygiene in cleansing the skin of alien matter by the agency of water. The latter placed it in the removal of impurities generated from within and excreted to the body's surface. Thus shifting, or changing undergarments, constituted the 'dry wash'.[30] While necessary to health, this dry cleanliness also measured civility and good manners. Fresh linen was a sign of a refined and disciplined body, in the same way as the 'white collar' description today signifies physical restraint but mental skill, and a standard of personal grooming. It is this set of beliefs concerning physiology, hygiene and civility that contextualizes the Duchess of Newcastle's (1624?–74) description of her husband: 'He shifts ordinarily once a day, and every time when he uses Exercise, or his temper is more hot than ordinary'.[31] In contrast, it also locates Sir John Oglander's (1585–1655) contempt of an acquaintance, 'a heavy, dull, drunken fellow, slovenly and nasty, a man in wants, scarce having linen to keep him sweet'.[32] As Roche has concluded, 'Expressing a hygiene different from our own, conforming to the moral style of "good manners", suited to the technological capacity of an age when water was scarce, the invention of linen marked the apogee of an aristocratic civilisation in which appearances were all important.'[33]

Functionally hygienic and protective, these intimate linen garments were indelibly marked by their association with the body. Indeed, in this supremely cloth-conscious society, the boundaries blurred between the two, and the second skin of cloth became metaphorically indistinguishable from the body's 'natural' covering. For both, the index of beauty and desirability was fineness of texture and whiteness of appearance. It was a pretty sight watching the young Henry VIII play at tennis, 'his fair skin glowing through a shirt of the finest texture'.[34] Not literally possible, the Venetian ambassador's description invites us to participate in an economy of beauty different from our own. For Henry's manly attributes are here visualized as grace, smoothness, whiteness, warmth and wealth. The latter, naturally, was fundamental because it purchased freedom from the roughening affects of physical labour, and also the finest, most expensive of linens. In Michael Drayton's poem, 'Edward the Fourth of Mistres Shore' (1619), beautiful costly textiles and skin are merged still more markedly. 'If thou but please to walke into the Pawne / To buy thee Cambricke, Callico, or Lawne, / If thou the whitenesse of the same wouldst prove, / From thy more whiter Hand plucke off thy Glove; / And those which buy, as the Beholders stand, / Will take thy Hand for Lawne, Lawne for thy Hand.'[35]

The bodily associations carried by shirts and smocks extended to other items worn next to the skin: bands, cuffs and ruffs. Similarly, their excellence lay in the attribute of whiteness, fineness of fabric or decoration, and the elaborate care required to keep them laundered, starched and shaped. Furthermore, these garments were found at the visual borders between body and clothing, thus helping to separate public from private space.[36] Being neither wholly textile nor entirely skin, their lacy texture mediated between the two. Containing something of each, these items managed to frame both the body and its clothing; whiteness and lightness isolating head and hands, and contrasting with rich surrounding fabrics. Paradoxically, a lot of the power of these garments derived from a diminution, or even an absence in their form. For it is the space between the threads that makes the lace, and insubstantiality that renders linen so fine as to be gauzy and transparent. This airy lightness frothing abundantly at the borders of dress is fundamentally luxurious. Unlike the hidden linen of smock and shirt, the visible manifestations at neck and wrist changed form over the sixteenth and seventeenth centuries. However, while varying in shape their significance remained constant: a light, white luxury that increased the desirability of skin and cloth alike. Pepys was clear about the social and aesthetic value of linen, and its fundamental importance in presenting a well-dressed persona. 'I do find myself much bound to go handsome; which I shall do in linnen, and so the other things may be all the plainer.' Eleven days later saw him putting this sartorial plan into action. 'Got me ready in the morning and put on my first new lace-band; and so neat it is, that I am resolved my great expense shall be lace-bands, and it will set off anything else the more.'[37] Put rather cynically,

'Fine linen was a necessity if you wanted to appear other than what you were'.[38]

So, linen was intimate yet partially exposed to public view, and practical yet symbolically rich. Moreover, in the context of male tailoring and fabric supply, the production of these garments constituted a particularly female endeavour. In the domestic setting this is unsurprising as, regardless of a woman's rank, needlework was an appropriate and needful female occupation. However, in the neighbourhood networks that constituted the local marketplace, and in the large-scale trading of the city, the sewing of linen items was generally both undertaken and supervised by women. This situation is glimpsed in the account books of the Reverend Giles Moore (1617–97). Among his carefully kept records the Sussex cleric itemized the expenses incurred concerning his personal and household linen. These included regular payments to female artisans. For example, on 21 March 1663/4 Moore 'Bought of G.[oodwife] Reading 10 Ells of flaxen cloath above a yard broad' for which he paid £1 7s. 6d. Two months later he 'Pay'd the Wid: James for the whiting of it 1ˢ 8ᵈ'. Beneath this entry, though not until the following year 1665, Moore noted, 'Pay'd Rᵈ· Harlands wyfe for making mee 3 New shirts & marking Caps', a commission which cost 1s. 8d. Mistress Harland was noted on other occasions too, such as when she received payment 'for making 6 Bonds [bands] at 3ᵈ the paire 1ˢ 6ᵈ & 2ᵈ a paire for 3 paire of Cuffes 6ᵈ & Halfe a Qᵗᵉʳ of an Ell of Cloath which she bought to make stocks 6ᵈ Pay'd her at Walstead for All of Them'.[39]

The most significant market controlled by women was that of supplying linen for the monarch; or as the wage bill for Julian Elliott, seamstress to Charles I put it, for 'Makeing his higˢ Lynen for his Bodey'.[40] Royal accounts detail payments made to these women and the type of goods they supplied: shirts, bands, ruffs, night wear and stockings. The persons named in the accounts may have employed a number of needlewomen under them, and at some point towards the end of the seventeenth century the post of royal seamstress may have become more nominal – granting revenue rather than wages – than actual. The position was also combined with that of laundress to the King.[41] This dual role again reflects the fundamental importance of washing to the cultural positioning of linen, and also its situation within the confines of women's authority. Finally, along with the making of linen and its renewal through laundering, the eventual reuse of linen garments in other forms was also sited within predominantly female activities: clouts or nappies for the young, bandages for the injured and ill, 'rags' for menstrual bleeding.[42]

The bodily, and the feminized nature of linen, could give this commodity a powerful sexual aura. Lady Denham, who gave her smocks to the imprisoned Sir Richard Fanshawe, did so only because her sons were away and she had no shirts to give in their stead. Indeed, Lady Fanshawe's account has Lady Denham expressing unease at the intimacy sharing such linen implied. Having none of her sons at home she fetched Sir Richard two smocks and some handkerchiefs of her own, 'saying she was ashamed to give him them'.[43] Time and again Pepys purchased personal linen and obtained sexual attentions at the same time. For example, his long-term mistress Betty Martin (née Lane) was a linen draper by trade, and it seems their relationship began, and continued, alongside the making, inspection and purchase of intimate garments. A typical passage from his diaries reveals Pepys alert to all the possibilities held within such transactions:

So to . . . Westminster-hall – where I expected some bands made me by Mrs. Lane; and while she went to the starchers for them, I stayed at Mrs. Howletts, who with her husband were abroad, and only their daughter (which I call my wife) was in the shop; and I took occasion to buy a pair of gloves to talk to her, and I find her a pretty-spoken girl and will prove a mighty handsome wench – I could love her very well.

By and by Mrs. Lane comes; and my bands not being done, she and I parted and met at the Crowne in the palace-yard, where we eat (a chicken I sent for) and drank and were mighty merry, and I had my full liberty of towsing her and doing what I would but the last thing of all; for I felt as much as I would and made her feel my thing also, and put the end of it to her breast and by and by to her very belly . . . Here I stayed late before my bands were done, and then they came; and so I by water to the Temple and thence walked home.[44]

Daniel Roche has written that there is a long history 'associating linen and the erotic'. Samuel Pepys, it seems likely, would have agreed.[45]

So now we can appreciate the cultural practices and beliefs that lay behind Gervase Markham's advice to homemakers, with regard to the provision of apparel for physical well-being:

Our English housewife, after her knowledge of preserving and feeding her family, must learn also how, out of her own endeavours, she ought to clothe them outwardly and inwardly; outwardly for defence from the cold and comeliness to the person; and inwardly, for cleanliness and neatness of the skin, whereby it may be kept from the filth of sweat, or vermin; the first consisting of woollen cloth, the latter of linen.[46]

Bodily Transitions

As well as providing the body with protection and cleanliness, however, clothing was also used to mark transitions, or to ease and facilitate the body in its passage from one state to another. For example, both Lady Ann Clifford and Ralph Josselin marked the age and progress of their children in terms, not of the calendar, but of clothing. Josselin entered in his diary on 14 January 1663/4, that 'this day Rebekah was coated, lord clothe us with the garments of thy righteousnes in Christ Jesus'.[47] Little Rebekah Josselin had móved past the need for formative swaddling, and had been dressed in childhood coats. Likewise, in her diary entries, Lady Clifford does not mention Margaret's age. The milestones she records are sartorial ones. 'Upon the 1st I cut the Child's strings off from her Coats and made her use tags alone, so as she had 2 or 3 falls at first but had no hurt with them. The 2nd, the Child put on her first coat that was laced with Lace, being of Red Bays.' Almost two years later, 'This day the Child did put on her crimson velvet Coat laced with silver Lace, which was the 1st velvet Coat she ever had'.[48]

These parents understood developmental milestones in terms of dress, a process that had started right from, or even before, birth. When Jane Hook wrote to tell her aunt, Lady Joan Barrington (d. 1641), of her pregnancy she received in reply gifts of linen, for which she gave 'harty thankes'. Lady Joan's own daughter asked, via her husband, for a similar gift. She wished 'that shee might begg some cloutes of you, being destitute her selfe, and if you could spare her a paire of old sheetes you might doe her a pleasure'.[49] This gathering together of sheets and towels, linen for the baby, and personal linen for herself, was an almost universal activity for expectant mothers.[50] These preparations had of course a practical function, but also signalled the child's imminent arrival, and helped structure the actual experience of birth.[51] After delivery and cleansing, the new baby was swaddled, a custom that utilized the protective and sustaining properties of clothing. For the human form was thought to be especially vulnerable after emerging from the shelter of the womb. Unformed and defenceless, its pliant, malleable limbs needed to be straightened and moulded to prevent deformity and ensure healthy growth (Figure 17). In this practice, George Vigarello has written, 'the swaddling clothes themselves are endowed with corrective power'.[52]

Right from the earliest moments, then, clothing provided a way of thinking about, and undergoing, the process of maturation. Fundamental to this process was the establishment of a gendered identity. To explore this point further it is useful to adopt a distinction raised by certain feminist

Figure 17 Portrait of Cornelia Burch aged 2 Months, 1582 (oil on canvas) by Dutch School (sixteenth century). Ferens Art Gallery, Hull City Museums and Art Galleries, UK/ Bridgeman Art Library.

theorists, who clarify matters by separating sex from gender. The former is a biological given – the type and collection of physiological characteristics with which we are born. Gender, as opposed to sex, arises from how our biological bodies act in the world. It is what we do, how we behave, what we say. Gender, to use Judith Butler's term, is performative.[53] It is something we create and re-create daily; and a fundamental way in which we do this, is through dress.

The clothing of babies in pink or blue is for us a powerful ascription of gender, but it is not an act that would have been meaningful in the sixteenth or seventeenth century. Similarly, our most important signifier of gender – the wearing of skirts – was also without meaning when all children graduated from swaddling to the caps and long coats of early childhood. Boys and girls alike dressed in full skirts, so these garments imposed on the wearer a kind of neuter category of infancy (Figure 18). Instead the garments most highly imbued with gender significance for early moderns were breeches – and that item which held and shaped the female torso – the corset or stiffened bodice.

The donning of these particular garments was crucial to the performance of gender. For a child, or a child's parents, it simultaneously marked a formative moment in male or female identity, and *was* that

Figure 18 John and Margaret Russell, attributed to Robert Peake. By kind permission of the Duke of Bedford and the Trustees of the Bedford Estates. © The Duke of Bedford and the Trustees of the Bedford Estates.

identity made visible. An analogous case would be a girl's first bra. Sometimes – and most appropriately given the importance of the garment in teaching gendered identity – called a 'training bra', the AA cup is not 'needed' by the wearer for support. It is, instead, one of the ways in which femaleness is signalled and created in contemporary Western society. For

Ann Clifford the stiffened garment that her daughter first wore in April 1617 performed the same function. 'The 28th was the first time the Child put on a pair of Whalebone Bodice.'[54] Lady Margaret Sackville was two years and nine months old.

Taking place at a later age – usually between six to eight years – the breeching of boys was perhaps even more significant. It marked the transition from the female-dominated world of the nursery, to being more in men's company and tutelage. In other words, once breeched the child's social context and behaviour were expected to change. The touching and witty letters written from Lady Anne North (d. 1684) to her son help us to appreciate how important and proud a moment this could be in the early modern household. Sir Francis North (1637–85), Chief Justice of the Common Pleas and future Lord Chancellor, had been widowed with three children in the November of 1678. His mother, Lady Anne, took the children to live with her at her home, Tostock. On 10 October 1679 she wrote from there to Sir Francis, to describe to him his son's big sartorial moment. The letter, as an exceptional description of the performance of gender through clothing, is worth quoting in full:

> You cannot beleeve the great concerne that was in the whole family here last Wednesday, it being the day that the taylor was to helpe to dress little Ffrank in his breeches in order to the making an everyday suit by it. Never had any bride that was to be drest upon her weding night more hands about her, some the legs and some the armes, the taylor butt'ning and other putting on the sword, and so many lookers on that had I not had a ffinger amongst them I could not have seen him. When he was quit drest he acted his part as well as any of them, for he desired he might goe downe to inquire for the little gentleman that was there the day before in a black coat, and speak to the men to tell the gentleman when he came from school that here was a gallant with very fine cloths and a sword to have waited upon him and would come againe upon Sunday next. But this was not all, for there was great contrivings while he was dressing who should have the first salute, but he sayd if old Lane had been here she should, but he gave it me to quiett them all. They are very fitt, everything, and he looks taler and prettyer than in his coats. Little Charles reioyced as much as he did, for he jumpt all the while about him and took notice of everything. I went to Bury and bo^t everything for another suitt, which will be finisht upon Saturday, so the coats are to be quite left off upon Sunday. I consider it is not yett terme time and since you could not have the pleasure of the first sight I have resolved you should have a full relation from
> Yo^r most aff^{mate} Mother,
> A. North.
> When he was drest he asked Buckle whether muffs were out of fashion because they had not sent him one.

Lady Anne followed up this letter with another two days later, in which she wrote:

> Dear Son,
> I thank you for sending me so perticular an account of the little ones' ages, which I think as forward children for these times as can be. I gave you an account in my last that this day was designed wholly to throw off the coats and write man, and great good fortune it was to have it a fayre day. It was carried with a great deale of privacy purposly to surprise Mr. Camborne, and it tooke so well as to put him to the blush as soone as he saw him in the church, wch pleased Frank not a little.[55]

Interestingly, this loving woman did not, until informed, know the detail of her grandchildren's ages. Significant in the process of little Frank's development was not his relationship to the calendar, but his relationship to his clothes. The day he put on his breeches was the day he could 'throw off his coats and write man'.

Paul Griffiths, in his work on youth in this period, spends a section defining what contemporaries understood by this term. Part of this includes a tabulation of different descriptors used by his court sources, and the age of the subject for whom they were employed. The descriptors – lad, maid, boy, girl, wench, child, youth, infant – are thus mapped with the ages that contemporaries felt best matched this term. So, for example, all occurrences of 'infant' were for children aged three or below, and most of them occurred for children in the first year of life. Of relevance for us is the fact that, with one exception, 'boy' was used *only* of children aged eight or more. The exception is an instance where this term was applied to a child of six. Up to this age the dominant descriptive term for male and females alike is the ungendered category of 'child'. While Griffiths does not offer this as a possibility, it seems too marked for coincidence that the onset of the male identity term 'boy' occured at around the time customary for breeching. It seems probable that breeching marked out the boundaries of gender in these cases, enabling the performance of boyhood.[56]

In this cloth-conscious society so attuned to sartorial possibilities, textiles and dress were fundamentally involved in bodily transitions and rites of passage. Many of these, like little Frank and his first breeches, were private or intimate experiences only accessible to us because of the chance survival of particular documents. Some, like christenings and weddings, had a greater public impact. However, perhaps the most public event, and the one on which we are going to focus, was the rite of burial. Among the upper orders the celebration of this ritual involved large numbers of people and large amounts of money, both things that leave us with relatively full sources today. Indeed, unlike other transitions its sartorial significance was carried chiefly by others, the fact of demise rippling outwards from the deceased and involving many in the performance of mourning. Thus, in 1663, when Catherine of Braganza fell seriously unwell, Pepys found himself facing a minor crisis of sartorial etiquette and financial caution. He had ordered a new cloak, but before its completion the Queen became ill. If this distant figure were not to recover he would be unable to wear his coloured and costly garment, for mourning would be *de rigueur*. Prudently he 'sent to stop the making of my velvett cloak, till I see whether she lives or dies'.[57] In contrast to the remote social obligation felt for such a faraway figure, Frances, widow of the Duke of Richmond, was prostrate when her husband died of an apoplexy in 1624. She took it 'extreme passionatly', and 'cut of her haire that day with divers other demonstrations of extraordinarie griefe'.[58] Between these two extremes, early moderns had a large vocabulary of apparel and behaviour that they used to articulate the fact of death, and it is towards this that we will now turn. Dressed in special gowns and hoods, bearing gifts of gloves, scarves and rings, who were 'these solemne mourners araid in black', and why were they so apparelled?[59]

Clothing Grief

Although first appearing in the late fifteenth century, it was post-Reformation England that saw the height of splendour and popularity of the great heraldic funerals. These vast public affairs were organized by the College of Arms, and were only available to armigerous families.[60] Run along lines of strict protocol they were massively expensive, complicated to arrange, and involved huge numbers of people. For the former, Lawrence Stone estimates that at their height 'these ostentatious rituals' cost little less than a year's income.[61] In terms of the latter, the size of the proceedings reflected the importance of the deceased. Lady Burghley, wife of the most notable statesman of the Elizabethan age, had a funeral procession that totalled 315 mourners. Seven hundred attended the funeral of that flower of Renaissance courtiership, Philip Sidney (Figure 2). Elizabeth I had an astonishing 1600 people participating in her obsequies.[62] Clearly such vast and complex affairs took considerable time to organize, particularly because the rules of protocol decreed that the rank and sex of the deceased determined the rank, sex and number of the principal mourners. Thus only particular people could fulfil these roles and the logistics of marshalling the different participants added to the time delay between death and eventual burial. With a minimum wait for interment of several weeks after death, embalming was a necessity. Anne of Denmark's funeral was dogged by delays caused on all these fronts. Although she died on 2 March 1619, the proposed date for the ceremony was repeatedly postponed. On 24 April John Chamberlain complained at length:

> The day of the Quenes funerall is not yet set downe, though yt be more then time yt were don . . . the number of mourners and the whole charge spoken of is beyond proportion, above three times more then was bestowed upon Quene Elizabeth, which proceeds not of plentie for they are driven to shifts for monie, and talke of melting the Quenes golden plate and putting yt into coine . . . Some difficultie there wilbe to marshall the Ladies and who shalbe cheife mourner, for the Lady of Arundell professes not to geve place to the Countesse of Nottingham, that pretends yt in her husbands right . . . the Countesse of Northumberland and divers others are likewise saide to take the same exception to her, and will by no meanes go behind, so that to stint some part of the strife (yf yt be possible) the old Marchionesse of Northampton is sent for yf by any meanes she can supplie the place.[63]

The Queen was eventually buried on 13 May, over two months after her death.

The purpose of these public displays was to commemorate the deceased's role within society and to perpetuate this beyond the apparent dead end of mortality. Death disrupted the ranks of the elite; the heraldic funeral sought to seal over the rupture and smooth it into continuity. In other words, the heraldic funeral was orchestrated 'with the emphasis very much on the preservation of the social body'.[64] It was a ritual in which mourning cloth and clothing – or blacks – played a major role. The cloth from which the garments were made was supplied by the estate, and given to the mourners on the basis of their rank according to rules laid down by the College of Arms. Thus the amount, cost and quality of fabric was distributed according to the recipient's social status. For example, at the burial of a king or prince, a duke was allowed 'for his Gowne Slopp and Mantle xvi yards of x$^{s.}$ the yerde and livery for xviii servants'. Reflecting the nuances of nobility, an earl was also allowed sixteen yards of cloth, but at only eight shillings the yard, and was supplied with liveries for twelve servants. Yeomen and pages, near the bottom of the hierarchy, were presented with four yards of cloth.[65] So Phineas Pett (1570–1647), in the preparation for the funeral of Prince Henry in 1612, explained that he 'had black cloth delivered to me according to the place I was ranked in above stairs, which was a gentleman of the Privy Chamber extraordinary'.[66] When Anne of Denmark's funeral was finally staged, Chamberlain was disappointed that despite the large number of participants in the procession, the Lords and Ladies made but 'a pore shew'. This may have been in part due to the burdens, quite literally, of rank, for 'they came laggering all along even tired with the length of the way and waight of theyre clothes, every Lady having twelve yardes of broade cloth about her and the countesses sixteen'.[67]

As well as stipulating the quantity and quality of mourning cloth due to any given participant, rules also governed the eventual form and wear of the garments. A long-lived example of these were the orders proposed by Margaret Beaufort, the mother of Henry VII, regulating the mourning apparel of the ladies at Court. First issued around 1493, the provisions were repeatedly re-copied into the seventeenth century, and explained, according to rank, what garments were to be worn and how.[68] The orders operated according to the general principle that those of the most elevated ranks had garments of the greatest length. For example, the Queen was to have 'a tippet at the hoode lyenge of a goode length', whereas the King's daughters, unmarried sisters and aunts, although permitted to wear the same styles as the Queen, had 'the tippetts somewhat shorter'. Likewise, while a countess might wear her tippet more or less to the ground, those of the Queen's household gentlewomen must be only a yard long.[69] However, as well as hierarchies expressed through scale, the regulations detailed differences of textile. So if furred, the Queen's mantle used ermine, as did that of a duchess, whereas a countess had only miniver.[70] Finally, the rules prescribed the manner in which these garments had to be worn. The tippets of the most important were to hang down behind the wearer, displaying their differing lengths and widths. Those of lesser mourners such as lords' daughters and knights' wives were 'to be pynned vpon the arme'. The gentlewomen of the household had to pin theirs 'vpon the syde of the hoode', and chamberers bound theirs 'aboute their hedds'.[71] The wear of barbes, archaic head coverings derived from conventual apparel, also encoded such hierarchies. Everyone not under the degree of a baroness 'to weare a barbe about the chynne. And all other as knightes wyfes to weare it under there throates: and other gentleweomen beneath the throte goyle.'[72] In this case the more enveloping was the garment, the more elevated the estate of the wearer. This was echoed by other heraldic orders pertaining to the wearing of hoods. Lesser mourners were enjoined to carry theirs over their shoulders, while the most important participants wore theirs well forward over the head 'wth their hoods hanginge farre over their eyes'.[73]

These detailed and rule-bound provisions are hard to grasp now and, if Elizabeth Russell's enquiries are anything to go by, were also difficult for contemporaries to master. Apparently of a careful disposition and feeling her demise imminent, Lady Russell wrote to Sir William Dethick, King at Arms, to clarify the requirements for her own funeral. She wished to know 'advisedly and exactly in every particuler' the prescribed number of participants and likely costs. This included 'the number of mourners due for my callinge beinge a Viscountesse of Birth, with their charge of blackes and the number of waittinge women for my selfe and the women mourners'.[74]

The vast number of participants at heraldic funerals, all of whom needed to be supplied with appropriate mourning, explains why the greatest cost of these rituals was, in fact, black cloth.[75] At Sir Nicholas Bacon's funeral in 1578, £669 out of the total expenditure of £910, went on blacks. In 1596, £1079 was paid out for Lord Henry Hunsdon's funeral, £836 of which was for mourning cloth. Similarly, in 1604, £700 out of a total of £1060 was paid out for cloth at the Earl of Huntingdon's funeral; and eight years later at Robert Cecil, Earl of Salisbury's service, a staggering £1544 of a total £1977, was expended this way.[76]

Given the considerable proportion of the funeral costs that went on blacks, it is no wonder that one of the difficulties delaying Anne of Denmark's burial was the problem of paying for cloth. Chamberlain reported that 'the Quenes funerall is put of . . . unles they can find out monie faster, for the master of the ward-robe is loth to weare his owne credit thread-bare'.[77] It also explains the economy measures taken at the funeral of John, Earl of Rutland, in 1588. The previous Earl, his elder brother Edward, had died just the year before and the estate was still recovering from obsequies that involved about 560 people.[78] When John died so soon after, the Earl of Leicester and William Cecil wrote to the executors suggesting that 'the funeral should be hastened so as to abridge the charge of the household'. Following further advice for limiting the costs by limiting the number of mourners who needed to be clothed, they finished with the order that: 'To the intent that all superfluous charges should be spared . . . there is to be no charge of black for us or our servants'. In the event there were about 200 mourners,[79] and the blacks required still seem far from modest, including: twelve yards for the young Earl and six yards for his horse; five yards for each of eleven knights, plus thirty-three yards for their retainers; and five yards for each of six esquires. At the end of the list of male participants were the sixty yeoman ordinary and extraordinary who received a coat of a yard and a half, and thirty-six poor men who each were given a gown of three yards. Similarly, on the female side, the Countess of Rutland had an allowance of twelve yards, whereas the six chamber and laundry maids each received three yards.

However, the Earl's agent, Thomas Screven, seemed to feel the slight of straightened circumstances. 'I have provided black for the funeral, which is the best I could get at the rate set down, which was very mean, meaner than has been at any funeral for many years.'[80] As Ralph Houlbrooke suggests, underlining the funeral's function in cementing social standing, those 'which fell short of what observers thought appropriate to the status of the deceased attracted unfavourable comment'.[81]

From early in the seventeenth century the heraldic funeral began a long decline, with increasing numbers of the elite opting for 'private' rituals that were under their own control, and not that of the College of Arms.[82] Mourning cloth and clothing, however, continued to play an integral part. Certainly the wholesale distribution of blacks stopped, and full mourning became limited to the immediate family and those intimately connected with the deceased. Nevertheless, as the Isle of Wight landowner, Sir John Oglander, reminds us, it was still an important and costly matter. For when his adult son, George, died in 1632, the distraught Sir John spent thirty-eight pounds on mourning clothes – a substantially greater sum than the twenty pounds he gave to his wife 'to find her apparel and other necessaries for the whole year'.[83] However, although the distribution of full mourning was now reserved for a relatively small circle of intimates, the seventeenth century saw a massive increase in the giving out of smaller tokens of grief – wearable items such as scarves, ribbons, rings and gloves. Sometimes these gifts were a matter of bequest, stipulated by the deceased in his or her will. Such was the case of Sir William Calley (d. 1641), retired cloth merchant, who requested that rings of remembrance be made in gold and given to certain of his family and friends. The rings, in common with conventional motifs, were also to have 'deathes heades all engraven, and over that enameled to give death the more lively countenaunce'.[84] More often mourning accessories were dispensed by the executors as part of the funeral ritual, in much the same way as had governed the distribution of blacks. When Sir John Oglander's brother-in-law was buried with a great assembly of the gentry and all the town, 'gloves and ribbons' were 'given to all'.[85] As with the doling out of black cloth, mourners of more importance usually received tokens of a greater number, or better quality. Sir Ralph Verney reported that his friend and neighbour, Sir Richard Pigott, had been laid to rest honourably and at considerable charge. 'Wee that bore up the pall had Rings, Scarfes, Hat-bands, Shamee Gloves of the best fashion and Sarsanet Escutcheons delivered to us; the rest of the Gentry had Rings, all the servants gloves.'[86]

The Berkshire probate accounts also reveal this careful gradation of giving. The evidence of Lady Mary Gardner's burial in 1642 is particularly interesting. She appears to have been given the full honour due to her rank and her father, as executor, kept thorough accounts. This included five shillings for hiring black cloth to hang about the church, threepence worth of tenter hooks for fixing up the mourning cloth in the chancel, sixpence for a man 'to looke to' the mourning cloth, and a further sixpence charge for the labour of hanging it. Twenty-nine shillings went on 'mourneinge gloves at the said deceasedes funerall', and a further fifteen shillings was spent on gloves to recompense the appraisers of the estate 'for their pains'. Ribbon was also 'given to persons that were at the deceasedes funerall', in two different grades. For seventy-two yards at 12*d*. the yard, the executor paid three pounds; for sixty-eight yards at 8*d*. the yard he was charged £2 5*s*. 4*d*.[87]

The collection of probate accounts also shows the increase over the seventeenth century of this practice of giving mourning tokens. Of the accounts dated before 1600, none include the distribution of these items. There are six accounts that do so for the first fifty years of the seventeenth century, and nine mentions in the second half of the century. Of these nine, eight occur after 1680. Replacing, for the wealthier in society, the social obligation of giving black cloth, there is some evidence to suggest that the distribution of mourning accessories came to occupy a similar place with respect to the costs of funeral observances. For example, using a detailed narrative and financial account, Ralph Houlbrooke has discussed the burial of Colonel Edward Phelips of Montacute, in 1680. Of the total expenditure of just over eighty-eight pounds, more than half was due to the cost of the gloves, rings and scarves that were given.[88]

This move from heraldic to private funerals and the change from remembrance through mourning cloth to mourning accessory, did not occur in a doctrinal vacuum. Following the unleashing of Protestantism at the Reformation, the English religious landscape changed considerably and, in the seventeenth century particularly, the rise of godly Protestantism was immensely important. It would be reasonable to expect that such dramatic doctrinal shifts would be reflected in the rituals through which people expressed their grief. Certainly theologians had clear views of the subject of post-mortem remembrance. The mainstream Church of England position, although opposed to Popish ritual, had no objection to the paraphernalia of mourning. As Archbishop John Whitgift wrote, such apparel was a matter of 'civility and order', and if worn in that spirit should be commended. Moreover it might have the laudable effect of reminding us of mortality; a wearable *aide memoire* of our own death.[89] By contrast, the official statement of the Elizabethan Puritan position, *An Admonition to the Parliament* (1572), spoke unfavourably of the custom of 'straunge mourning by chaunging theyr garments, which if it be not hipocritical, yet it is superstitious and heathnish'.[90] The outspoken Thomas Cartwright advanced a further objection. If worn with a 'merry heart' mourning apparel was hypocritical, but if worn with sincerity the clothing of grief led to a treacherous excess of sentiment. 'Seeing therefore, if there be no sorrow, it is hypocritical to pretend it, and, if there be, it is very dangerous to provoke it . . . it appeareth that this use of mourning apparel were much better laid away than kept.'[91] Thomas Becon, in *The Sick Man's Salve* (1560), also repudiated the wearing of black for the souls of the faithful, since death was a joyful reunion with God, and 'they in heaven be clothed in white'.[92] In addition Puritans were anxious to diminish the scale of funerals and channel money towards charity and poor relief, 'particularly by providing gowns for the needy rather than for other mourners'.[93] Thus Becon's character, Epaphroditus, desires his family wear what garments they will at his burial, but that thirty poor men and women, and thirty children, be given 'seemly' gowns of a 'convenient colour'.[94]

The most extreme end of the spectrum was occupied by those like the Separatist, Henry Barrow. He too, when describing 'these solemne mourners araid in black, many of them with hoodes, caps, crosses and other knackes', considered them to be idolatrous and full of hypocrisy. Christians, he said, should not 'mourne after such a superstitious and prophane maner, or to have their mourning only in their garmentes'. He accused wives and heirs of but wearing 'a black attire outwardly', and the preacher of being glad that he 'hath his mourning liverie and his hire'. Finally, grieving women, Barrow implied, were most struck with the fashionable aspects of their dress, and 'have their mourneries fitted at an haire breadth'.[95] These and other scornful sentiments, expressed in *A Brief Discoverie of the False Church* (1590), earned Barrow arraignment and execution.

The theory espoused by religious leaders, however, seems to have made very little difference to actual funeral observances. As Gittings contends, 'burial practices do not reflect religious changes as closely as might possibly be expected'. Instead she stresses the importance of secular, traditional rites in what she describes as a conservative ritual more marked by continuity than change.[96] In support of this she looks at funeral costs over the first half of the seventeenth century, pointing out that if a simple 'Puritan style' burial were being widely adopted, then one would see a decline in funeral spending. On the contrary, she finds that nowhere was funeral expenditure down, and in three of the four counties she surveyed average spending actually increased.[97] She concludes that the majority, even of those who might be called 'puritans', did not opt for simple plain burials. 'It would therefore seem reasonable to suggest that the supposed drastic simplification in burial rituals is a distortion fabricated by the polemicists and perpetuated by unwary historians.'[98] What was adopted, across the religious spectrum, was a rhetoric of decency without pomp. But such seemliness existed on a sliding scale, and usually signified a send-off that was suitable to the rank and social standing of the deceased. It could, thus, be very fine indeed. In 1583 the Earl of Sussex, for example, desired a burial without pomp, but appropriate to his degree. He estimated that this would cost around £1500.[99] The Commonwealth period, during which one might expect Puritan observances to be at their most rigorous, continued to see a surprising regard for social pageantry. Even *A Directory for the Publique Worship of God*, the book of liturgical reforms introduced in 1644, maintained not to 'deny any civil respects or differences at the burial, suitable to the rank and condition of the party deceased whilst he was living'.[100] Puritanism saw no marked diminution in the lavishness of burials then, or in the remembrance of the dead through mourning adornment.

So we have evidence, that, despite political and religious upheavals over the sixteenth and seventeenth century, the importance of mourning dress remained constant. Certainly the form of memorial wear changed, moving from clothing vast numbers in styles distinguished by quantities of black cloth, to dressing of a few in full mourning and the many in a range of smaller accessories. But if the form evolved, its place within the economy of grief stayed unchanged. While arguing the transhistorical nature of emotions is always problematic, Houlbrooke suggests that 'there is no reason to suppose that the basic character of grief changed' over time. What did change was 'the means of its expression'.[101] These means of expression included the wearable tokens and garments of mourning apparel, items of material culture that were key to the performance of loss and commemoration. But it remains, however, to ask why mourning apparel was so important. From Pepys's blackening of his shoe soles at his brother's demise, to the 'laggering' countesses in their sixteen yards of broad cloth at Queen Anne's, why did early modern culture have such a complex sartorial vocabulary for articulating death, and what did it say?[102]

Firstly, as we have already noted, mourning provided a visual commemoration of the deceased's social persona, extending his or her life through memory and sartorial witness. The gradations of mourning attire also acknowledged the different degrees of relationship within the community pertaining to the deceased and the grieving family. Ralph Houlbrooke feels that the seventeenth-century tokens expressed overlapping hierarchies of status, kinship, friendship and regard even more effectively than the earlier custom of giving black cloth.[103] The provisions at Colonel Phelips's funeral show just how subtle the distinctions could be. Full mourning dress was restricted to certain family members, servants, and the pall bearers; twenty-five in total. Twenty-six rings were given to intimate equals, such as family or pall bearers. The scarves came in three different qualities. Eighteen people received the finest made of a silken fabric called 'love', including the bearers, the cleric and the man who penned the deceased's will. Nineteen, including the curate and other figures of relative importance were given scarves of broad tiffany, and twenty-five, among whom numbered servants of the family and a tenant, received narrow tiffany scarves. Five hatbands of love went to close relatives, and twenty-four hatbands of tiffany to those connected in a more distant way. Knots of ribbon were given to the female gentry and maid servants. Gloves, the most numerous of the tokens, also came in three grades. Eight shammy pairs went to kin and ninety-six of cordovan leather and kid were dispensed to friends and other relatives. Finally 118 of the coarsest grade, a sheep's leather, graced the hands of servants, tradesmen, and others.[104]

The distribution of mourning cloth and accessories must also be seen within the context of early modern gift giving. The exchange of presents was of enormous significance in this period. Sustaining intimate relationships, gift giving also played a central and defining role in community interaction and the practices of government. In a society shaped by the networks of patronage and clientage, and where the personal merged with the official, gift exchange was a strongly cohesive force. The offering and accepting of gifts both created and fulfilled obligations, and in some senses bound giver and recipient together. The giving and receiving of objects, and the objects themselves, thus gave material expression to relationships.[105] In a society well attuned to the responsibilities conferred by gifts, the distribution and wearing of black cloth and mourning garments thus sustained relationships between the deceased and his or her social circle, even beyond death.

The giving and receiving of mourning apparel also spread the loss of bereavement throughout the community. Rather than being carried exclusively by those whose pain was the greatest, sharing the clothing of grief also, to some extent, shared the burden of that grief. However, for those who continued in mourning garb after the funeral rites, their dress proclaimed their removal from normal society. Revealing their special status, it marked out a liminal time during which they were freed from the rules of polite social interaction, and given time to adjust to their loss. When

Bulstrode Whitelocke's (1605–75) first wife died 'he was so farre from any thoughts of woeing [wooing], that he went with his haire all over-grown on his face, so that he appeared as one 50 years old, his doublet was of blacke leather, his breeches of course haire stuffe, in mourning'. Meeting his future second wife he courted her, and to signal his return to normal social activities he 'cutt off his great beard, trimmed & better habited himselfe'. To his future wife his 'being trimmed and better clothed then before was not unpleasing, & and now his servants & neighbours tooke notice of his being a suitor to M[ist]ʳ[i]ˢ Willoughby'.[106]

Sometimes, as with Bulstrode Whitelocke, the sartorially defined limbo of grief, which suspended the usual mores, duties and obligations of relationship, was only temporary. In other cases it lasted much longer. A whole year after the death of Pepys's mother, he recorded his wife's attractive appearance in an outfit bought just before her mother-in-law's demise, 'and so not worn till this day'.[107] Widows, particularly, might use their mourning weeds as a way of permanently redefining their status, signalling their removal to a position independent of further marital transactions. Thus, large portions of life in early modern England could be spent in visible connection to the dead. Many of the portraits that survive picture such a relationship as the sitter – though perhaps many years after the death commemorated – chose within the frame the per-petual identity of a mourner.

Finally, the donning of mourning apparel seems to have provided a way for individuals to be assured that they were responding appropriately and with due regard for their loss. The day that he learnt of his mother's death, Pepys resolved 'to put myself and wife, and Barker and Jane, W Hewer and Tom, in mourning; and my two under-maids, to give them hoods and scarfs and gloves'. He went to his tailor to make initial arrangements for this household observance of grief, and this seemed to provide him with a certain consolation of having done what was fitting. For when he went to bed he wrote, 'my heart sad and afflicted, though my judgement at ease'.[108] The importance of fulfilling these demands of sartorial duty to the dead may explain Pepys's subsequent anger with his wife when she appeared two months later in second mourning. Most of her outfit was unexceptional: a 'black moyre waistcoat and short petticoat'. However, the quantities of silver lace on this latter garment must have appeared frivolous. The petticoat was 'laced with silver lace so basely that I could not endure to see her, and with laced lining, which is too soon'. Pepys was so 'horrid angry' that he stormed out to the office, and Elizabeth felt it necessary to send 'twice or thrice to me to direct her any way to dress her'.[109]

For those situated at the outer reaches of the ripple of grief, the observance of mourning had more to do with their connections to the living, than their relationship to the departed. In all cases, however, the clothing of grief was a mechanism for assuring the living that their response to the crisis of death was the right one. They could see themselves responding through dress, and this steered them through the shoals of mortality. Moreover, others could see their sartorial response, too. For it is clear that much of the performance of mourning was a public observance. Intimates, retinues, and even the 180 poor women hired for Anne of Denmark's funeral, had all to be seen to be in black in order for the thing to be properly done. This placement of grief within the public arena makes sense of Pepys's shoe soles, darkened so that when he knelt down even the soles of his feet displayed the correct sartorial message. It makes sense, too, of how in the midst of his grief for his mother, he could write that, 'I to church, and with my mourning, very handsome, and new periwig make a great show'.[110] The utilization of clothing, then, enabled these men and women from the sixteenth and seventeenth centuries to manage the ultimate transition in the physical process of maturation: death. However, mortality also involved social transitions, and these too were eased by the adoption of particular garments. By dressing themselves in special ways early moderns fulfilled cultural, and personal, expectations of how a bereaved person looked and behaved. In effect they created a material form for grief and made themselves a persona of loss.

Notes

1. G.R. Elton, *England Under the Tudors*, 3rd edn (London, 1991), p. 435. Subjective judgements aside, the comparison with Victorian tight-lacing is incorrect, for the structure and technology of Victorian corsets made possible a closer fit than at any time in the past.
2. Kay Staniland, 'Tailored Bodies: Medieval and Tudor Clothing', in *London Bodies: The Changing Shape of Londoners from Prehistoric Times to the Present Day*, compiled by Alex Werner (London, 1998), pp. 72–81 (pp. 75, 80).
3. *The Pursuit of Beauty: Five Centuries of Body Adornment in Britain*, text by Clare Gittings (London, 1997) [n.p.].
4. Anne Hollander, *Seeing Through Clothes* (Berkeley, 1993), pp. 315, 339.

5. Virginia LaMar, 'English Dress in the Age of Shakespeare', in *Life and Letters in Tudor and Stuart England*, ed. by Louis B. Wright and Virginia LaMar (Ithaca, 1962), pp. 383–426 (pp. 388, 389).

6. Elton, *England Under the Tudors*, p. 435.

7. *The Diary of Ralph Josselin 1616–1683*, ed. by Alan Macfarlane, Records of Social and Economic History, new ser., 3 (London, 1976), p. 170.

8. *The Autobiography of Mrs. Alice Thornton*, Surtees Society, 62 (1875), p. 166.

9. *Diary*, V, 277, 22 September 1664; VI, 21, 24 January 1665; VI, 89, 24 April 1665; VIII, 105, 9 March 1667.

10. For a survey of early modern medical practices in general, see Mary Lindemann, *Medicine and Society in Early Modern Europe* (Cambridge, 1999).

11. Richard Lower, *De Catarrhis* (1672), trans. by Richard Hunter and Ida Macalpine (London, 1963), p. 4.

12. Richard Hawes, *The Poore-Mans Plaster-Box*, The English Experience, 664 (London, 1634; repr. Amsterdam, 1974), pp. 12, 16.

13. George Simotta, *A Theater of the Planetary Houres For All Dayes of the Yeare*, The English Experience, 414 (London, 1631; repr. Amsterdam, 1971), p. 5.

14. *The Private Life of an Elizabethan Lady: The Diary of Lady Margaret Hoby, 1599–1605*, ed. by Joanna Moody (Stroud, 1998), p. 214. For an example of Pepys's trouble see *Diary*, II, 241, 31 December 1661.

15. Hawes, *Poore-Mans Plaster-Box*, pp. 7, 41.

16. Timothy Bright, *The Sufficiencie of English Medicines*, The English Experience, 854 (London, 1580; repr. Amsterdam, 1977), pp. 39–40. Thomas Bonham, *The Chyrurgeons Closet*, The English Experience, 31 (London, 1630; repr. Amsterdam, 1968), p. 178.

17. Lindemann, *Medicine and Society*, p. 10.

18. *Diary of Ralph Josselin*, p. 603.

19. *Diary*, II, 129, 30 June 1661.

20. Lindemann, *Medicine and Society*, pp. 10–11.

21. Georges Vigarello, *Concepts of Cleanliness: Changing Attitudes in France since the Middle Ages*, trans. by Jean Birrell (Cambridge, 1988).

22. Desiderius Erasmus, *De Civilitate Morum Puerilium* (1530), trans. by Brian McGregor, in *Collected Works of Erasmus* (Toronto, 1974–1997), *Literary and Educational Writings 3*, XXV, 269–89 (p. 278).

23. John Winthrop, 'Experiencia', in *Winthrop Papers Volume 1 1498–1628* (Massachusetts, 1929), pp.185–8.

24. Margaret Pelling, 'Appearance and Reality: Barber-Surgeons, the Body and Disease', in *London 1500–1700: The Making of a Metropolis*, ed. by A.L. Beier and Roger Finlay (London, 1986), pp. 82–112.

25. *The Memoirs of Anne, Lady Halkett and Ann, Lady Fanshawe*, ed. by John Loftis (Oxford, 1979), p. 134.

26. Karen Baclawski, *The Guide to Historic Costume* (London, 1995), traces the history of drawers wearing to the Middle Ages for men, and to the nineteenth century for women (p. 92). C.W. Cunnington and P. Cunnington, *The History of Underclothes*, rev. edn (London, 1981) more or less agree, describing male drawers as originally a medieval garment and stating that: 'It does not seem that Englishwomen wore drawers before the very end of the eighteenth century' (p. 36). Anne Hollander, *Seeing Through Clothes*, concurring on male wear, puts the date of women's donning of drawers even later, after about 1850 (p. 133). In a manner typical of the uncertainty and disagreements underlying dress history, however, J.L. Nevinson asserts that women *did* wear drawers, at least in the seventeenth century. Their general absence from inventories, he concludes, merely reflects their home-made status (J.L. Nevinson, entry on 'Dress and Personal Appearance', in *Diary*, X, 98–104). In part, Nevinson's evidence for this comes from Pepys's diaries, which describe his French wife, Elizabeth, as being dressed in the garment. While this is sometimes taken to indicate that Elizabeth Pepys had brought the custom with her from the continent, the historian Daniel Roche complicates the matter still further. In *The Culture of Clothing: Dress and Fashion in the Ancien Régime*, trans. Jean Birrell (Cambridge, 1996), Roche states that neither women *nor* men in France commonly wore drawers in this period (pp. 181–3). Interestingly, Fynes Moryson, *An Itinerary*, 4 vols (Glasgow, 1907), reports that Italian women 'in many places weare silke or linnen breeches under their gownes', a comment that also suggests that English women did not (IV, 222). Jenny Tiramani, 'Janet Arnold and the Globe Wardrobe: Handmade Clothes of Shakespeare's Actors', *Costume*, 34 (2000), 118–22, points out that as an alternative to wearing drawers, men might tuck their shirt tails between their legs (p. 121).

27. Quoted in G.R. Quaife, *Wanton Wenches and Wayward Wives: Peasants and Illicit Sex in Early Seventeenth-Century England* (London, 1979), pp. 167–8.

28. John Donne, Elegy 18, 'Love's Progress'. In this mock elegiac poem, Donne advises lovers against starting their amorous journey at their mistress' face. This way their progress is bound to be shipwrecked

against the hazards and delays of eyes, lips, breasts, pubic hair, and so on. Instead the poem urges the direct route from the feet up, in which few bodily – and incidentally vestimentary – features delay arrival at 'the centric part'.

29. Roche, *Culture of Clothing*, p. 182.
30. Vigarello, *Concepts of Cleanliness*, esp. pp. 17–20.
31. *The Lives of William Cavendishe, Duke of Newcastle, and of his Wife, Margaret Duchess of Newcastle*, ed. by Mark Antony Lower (London, 1872), p. 193.
32. *A Royalist's Notebook: The Commonplace Book of Sir John Oglander of Nunwell*, ed. by Francis Bamford (London, 1936), p. 69.
33. Roche, *Culture of Clothing*, p. 178.
34. Quoted in Jane Ashelford, *The Art of Dress: Clothes and Society 1500–1914* (London, 1996), p. 16.
35. *The Works of Michael Drayton*, ed. by J. William Hebel, 5 vols (Oxford, 1961), II, 247–55 (p. 249). The Pawn was the area on the south side of the Royal Exchange, which housed stalls selling items of fashionable wear. Among the retailers and artisans were haberdashers, milliners, seamstresses and starchers. For discussion of the sixteenth- and seventeenth-century fashion trade see Jane Ashelford, *Dress in the Age of Elizabeth I* (London, 1988), pp. 74–89; and Ashelford, *Art of Dress*, pp. 44–53, 76–85, 110–19.
36. Roche, *Culture of Clothing*, pp. 154, 163.
37. *Diary*, III, 216, 8 October 1662; 228, 19 October 1662.
38. Roche, *Culture of Clothing*, p. 158.
39. *The Journal of Giles Moore*, ed. by Ruth Bird, The Sussex Record Society, 68 (1971), pp. 15, 48. The professional sempstress was limited to sewing linen and dress accessories until the end of the seventeenth century (Ashelford, *Art of Dress*, pp. 115–16). For a survey of their activities before and after this point, see Naomi Tarrant, *The Development of Costume* (Edinburgh, 1994), pp. 116–24.
40. Quoted in Patricia Wardle, '"Divers necessaries for his Majesty's use and service": Seamstresses to the Stuart Kings', *Costume*, 31 (1997), 16–27 (p. 19). For information about Elizabeth's sempstresses, see Janet Arnold, *Queen Elizabeth's Wardrobe Unlock'd* (Leeds, 1988), pp. 219–27. The royal needlewomen were involved in making and embroidering linen goods. Richer work using more expensive textiles and threads was undertaken by the King's Embroiderer. In *The Subversive Stitch: Embroidery and the Making of the Feminine* rev. edn, (London, 1996), Rozsika Parker explores the historical context

in which, between the Middle Ages and the nineteenth century, decorative needlework moved from being a non-gendered artistic production for use in the public sphere, to being a domestic craft pursued by female amateurs.

41. This was the situation from at least Elizabeth to James II, the only exception being in the household administration of Charles I, see Wardle, 'Seamstresses to the Stuart Kings', p. 20.

42. As Daniel Roche points out, little is known about this aspect of female linen 'essential for a history of the body and sexuality', *Culture of Clothing*, p. 155, n. 13.

43. *Memoirs of Ann, Lady Fanshawe*, p. 134.

44. *Diary*, IV, 234–5, 18 July 1663.

45. Roche, *Culture of Clothing*, p.157.

46. Gervase Markham, *The English Housewife* (1615), ed. by Michael R. Best (Montreal, 1994), p. 146.

47. *Diary of Ralph Josselin*, p. 504.

48. *The Diaries of Lady Anne Clifford*, ed. by D.J.H. Clifford (Stroud, 1990), pp. 66, 83. Lady Clifford refers to Margaret's leading strings, which were very similar to the harness and reins used for toddlers today.

49. *Barrington Family Letters 1628–1632*, ed. by Arthur Searle, Camden 4th ser., 28 (London, 1983), pp. 174, 191.

50. David Cressy, *Birth, Marriage and Death: Ritual, Religion and the Life-Cycle in Tudor and Stuart England* (Oxford, 1997), pp. 50–1.

51. On the delivery and lying-in, including the use of linen cloths and clothing, see Doreen Evenden, *The Midwives of Seventeenth-Century London* (Cambridge, 2000), pp. 79–86; Cressy, *Birth, Marriage and Death*, pp. 80–4; Adrian Wilson, 'The Ceremony of Childbirth and its Interpretation', in *Women as Mothers in Pre-Industrial England*, ed. by Valerie Fildes (London, 1990), pp. 68–107, esp. 70–83.

52. Georges Vigarello, 'The Upward Training of the Body', in *Fragments for a History of the Human Body*, ed. by Michel Feher, Ramona Naddaff and Nadia Tazi, 3 vols (New York, 1989), II, 148–99, (p. 171).

53. Butler surveys the main theoretical positions with regard to gender, sex and identity. However, she goes much further in her understanding of performative gender, presenting the sexed body as a discursively produced entity that does not pre-exist gender, but is itself a gendered category. She thus collapses the distinction between the two, and profoundly challenges our notions of 'naturalness', see Judith Butler, *Gender Trouble: Feminism and the Subversion of*

Identity (New York, 1990), esp. pp. 1–34, 128–41. On sex and gender in the early modern period specifically, see Thomas Laqueur, *Making Sex: Body and Gender from the Greeks to Freud* (Cambridge MA, 1990).

54. *Diaries of Lady Clifford*, p. 55.

55. *The Autobiography of the Hon. Roger North*, ed. by Augustus Jessopp (London, 1887), pp. 215–16, 216.

56. See Paul Griffiths, *Youth and Authority: Formative Experiences in England 1560–1640* (Oxford, 1996), pp. 19–34.

57. *Diary*, IV, 344, 22 October 1663.

58. *The Letters of John Chamberlain*, ed. by Norman Egbert McClure, 2 vols (Philadelphia, 1939), II, 545. Letter to Dudley Carleton, 21 February 1624.

59. Henry Barrow, *A Brief Discoverie of the False Church* (1590), in *The Writings of Henry Barrow 1587–1590*, ed. by Leland H. Carlson (London, 1962), p. 460.

60. On heraldic funerals see Clare Gittings, *Death, Burial and the Individual in Early Modern England* (London, 1984), pp. 166–87; Julian Litten, *The English Way of Death: The Common Funeral Since 1450* (London, 1991), pp. 173–94; Nigel Llewellyn, *The Art of Death: Visual Culture in English Death Ritual c.1500–c.1800* (London, 1991), pp. 60–72; Jennifer Woodward, *The Theatre of Death: The Ritual Management of Royal Funerals in Renaissance England 1570–1625* (Woodbridge, 1997), pp. 15–36; J.F.R. Day, 'Death be very proud: Sidney, Subversion, and Elizabethan heraldic funerals', in *Tudor Political Culture*, ed. by Dale Hoak (Cambridge, 1995), pp. 179–203.

61. Lawrence Stone, *The Crisis of the Aristocracy 1558–1641* (Oxford, 1965), p. 575.

62. HMC, *Salisbury*, 13, p. 409. Day, 'Death be very proud', p. 181. Woodward, *Theatre of Death*, pp. 17–18, and Appendix 1.

63. *Letters of John Chamberlain*, II, 232–3.

64. Llewellyn, *Art of Death*, p. 60.

65. Bod. Lib. Ashmole MS 857, fol. 188.

66. *The Autobiography of Phineas Pett*, ed. by E.G. Perrin, Navy Records Society, 51 (1918), p. 101.

67. *Letters of John Chamberlain*, II, 237.

68. A sixteenth-century copy is to be found in BL Harley MS 6064, fols 27^r-28^r. The College of Arms has a seventeenth-century version in Vincent MS 151, fols 105–8.

69. BL Harley MS 6064, fols 27^r, 28^r, 27^v.

70. Ibid., fols 27^r, 27^v, 28^r.
71. Ibid., fols 27^v, 28^r.
72. Ibid., fol. 27^v. The seventeenth-century Vincent MS writes 'gule' for goyle', which the OED glosses as an obsolete term for gullet.
73. BL Harley MS 6079, fol. 25^v.
74. CA Vincent MS 151, fol. 325.
75. Gittings, *Death, Burial*, p. 181. Richard Greaves, *Society and Religion in Elizabethan England* (Minneapolis, 1981), p. 713. Lawrence Stone estimates that it represented about three quarters of the funeral expense, see *Crisis of the Aristocracy*, p. 576.
76. These figures, and their manuscript sources, are given in Stone, *Crisis of the Aristocracy*, Appendix 25, pp. 784–5. In addition Stone lists the funeral of the Earl of Huntingdon in 1596, for which a relatively modest amount of £532, out of £1393, was spent on blacks.
77. *Letters of John Chamberlain*, II, 224. Letter to Dudley Carleton, 27 March 1619.
78. Stone, *Crisis of the Aristocracy*, p. 573.
79. Ibid.
80. HMC, Rutland, 1, pp. 241, 242, 243. For more about this funeral see Greaves, *Society and Religion*, pp. 711–12.
81. Ralph Houlbrooke, *Death, Religion, and the Family in England, 1480–1750* (Oxford, 1998), p. 292.
82. For the differences between 'public' heraldic interments and privately arranged burials see Ralph Houlbrooke, '"Public" and "Private" in the Funerals of the later Stuart Gentry: Some Somerset Examples', *Mortality*, 1, (1996), 163–76; Paul Fritz, '"From Public to Private": the Royal Funerals in England, 1500–1830', in *Mirrors of Mortality: Studies in the Social History of Death*, ed. by Joachim Whaley (London, 1981), pp. 61–79; and Day, 'Death be very Proud', p. 183.
83. *A Royalist's Notebook*, pp. 178–81, 237, 231.
84. PRO, SP16/479/21.
85. *A Royalist's Notebook*, p. 124.
86. Frances Parthenope Verney, *Memoirs of the Verney Family*, 4 vols (London, 1892–1899), IV, 327.
87. Ian Mortimer (ed.), *Berkshire Probate Accounts 1583–1712*, Berkshire Record Society, 4 (Reading, 1999), pp. 168–9. Unfortunately, similar information is less readily available for other areas. For example, in only a few of the surviving Yorkshire probate accounts (BIHR, Prob. Ex. 1607–1646) are funeral costs itemized, and these give details of food and drink, the ringers' charges, allowances to the poor, and so on. None of the accounts mention mourning cloth, clothing or accessories.

88. Houlbrooke, 'Public and Private', p. 171; *Death, Religion, and the Family*, pp. 282–3.
89. *The Works of John Whitgift*, ed. by John Ayre, 3 vols, Parker Society, 40 (Cambridge, 1851–3), III, 368–71.
90. *Puritan Manifestoes*, ed. by W.H. Frere and C.E. Douglas (London, 1907), p. 28.
91. *Whitgift*, p. 369.
92. *Prayers and Other Pieces of Thomas Becon*, ed. by John Ayre, Parker Society, 12 (Cambridge, 1844), p. 121.
93. Greaves, *Society and Religion*, p. 717.
94. *Becon*, p. 124.
95. *Writings of Henry Barrow*, p. 460.
96. Clare Gittings, *Funerals in England 1580–1640: The Evidence of Probate Accounts* (unpublished B. Litt. thesis, University of Oxford, 1978), pp. 96, 76.
97. Ibid., p. 86; Gittings, *Death, Burial*, p. 52.
98. Gittings, *Funerals in England*, pp. 72, 93.
99. Greaves, *Society and Religion*, p. 709. The actual cost turned out to be £1629.
100. Quoted in Gittings, *Death, Burial*, p. 55.
101. Houlbrooke, *Death, Religion, and the Family*, p. 221; on early modern grief and mourning, pp. 220–54.
102. *Diary*, V, 90, 18 March 1664.
103. Houlbrooke, 'Public and Private', pp. 172–4.
104. Ibid., p. 171.
105. On gift giving see Marcel Mauss, *The Gift: Forms and Functions of Exchange in Archaic Societies*, trans. by Ian Cunnison (New York, 1967); and J.G. Carrier, *Gifts and Commodities: Exchange and Western Capitalism since 1700* (London, 1995).
106. *The Diary of Bulstrode Whitelocke*, ed. by Ruth Spalding, Records of Social and Economic History, new ser., 13 (London, 1990), pp. 90, 92, 93.
107. *Diary*, IX, 134, 26 March 1668.
108. *Diary*, VIII, 134, 27 March 1667.
109. Ibid., p. 242, 29 May 1667.
110. *Diary*, VIII, 138, 31 March 1667.

–3–

Clothes Make the Man

His Garments Helpe Him to bee Counted Such a One

Phineas Pett (Figure 6), eventually to become a master shipbuilder and naval commissioner, described his strategy for advancing his fortunes. As a young man in dire financial straits he was yet 'contented to take any pains to get something to apparel myself, which by God's blessing I performed before Easter next after, and that in very good fashion, always endeavouring to keep company with men of good rank far better than myself'.[1] Pepys was expressing something similar when he talked mightily to a colleague 'of the convenience and necessity of a man's wearing good clothes'. The short-term outlay was considerable, but outweighed by the long term advantage: 'and so to Sir W Turners and there bought me cloth, coloured for a suit and cloak, to line with plush the cloak – which will cost me money, but I find that I must go handsomely, whatever it costs me; and the charge will be made up in the fruits it brings'.[2] For these men, and many others, social advance was achieved, in part, through the medium of dress. For just as clothing articulated physical transitions, so too it was fundamental to the making and managing of the social self. In the following chapter we will explore this process encapsulated in the shrewd advice that Sir Frederick Fregoso, a character in that seminal Renaissance conduct book, *The Courtier* (1561), offered his listeners. A man, he counselled, 'ought to determine with him selfe what he will appeare to be, and in such sort as he desireth to be esteemed, so to apparrel himselfe, and make his garments helpe him to bee counted such a one'.[3] For, as we shall see, the expression of personality, the communication of political and moral beliefs, the establishment of reputation and discredit: all this created a social identity and occurred through dress and public witness.

The comments in personal narratives show how much the writers' sense of self, and their understanding of the identity of others, was governed by appearance. Frequently these passages are, for us at least, understated. We lack the contemporary understanding to make the comments entirely meaningful, but they are telling, if only in as much as showing a memory of clothing was worth recording. Lady Clifford littered her diary with such references that were clearly important for her: 'All the time I was at the Court I wore my Green Damask Gown embroidered without a Farthingale'.[4] Likewise Yorkshire Royalist Sir John Reresby's (1634–89) memoirs contain similar comments, such as noting the 'night I went to a French play, putting on a good suit of cloaths which I gott made by the French embassador's tailer at Francfort'.[5] Some writers were more loquacious and have explained more clearly the significance that their clothing held for them. For scholarly Lucy Hutchinson (1620– post-1675), her self-declared carelessness in dress expressed her indifference to certain social conventions and her stated preference for intellectual pursuits. She showed a 'negligence of her dress and habit and all womanish ornaments, giving herself wholly up to study and writing'. Lucy contrasted her own sartorial persona with that of her husband. Unlike her, the Parliamentarian leader, John Hutchinson, enjoyed dress and took pleasure in its devising and its display. He was 'very neatly habited, for he wore good and rich clothes, and had variety of them, and had them well suited and every way answerable, in that little thing showing both good judgement and great generosity, he equally becoming them and they him, which he wore with such unaffectedness and such neatness as do not often meet in one'.[6] Clothes and their wear were, for Lucy, the index of her husband's gentility and inner superiority. Another female writer from the seventeenth century constructed an entirely different identity for herself. Instead of 'neglecting' her appearance as did Lucy Hutchinson, Margaret Cavendish, the Duchess of Newcastle, dwelt on it and was 'addicted' to fashion:

> But my serious study could not be much, by reason I took great delight in attiring, fine dressing, and fashions, especially such fashions as I did invent myself, not taking that pleasure in such fashions as was invented by others: also I did dislike that any should follow my Fashions, for I always took delight in singularity, even in accoutrements of habits.[7]

In two different ways, then, both Margaret and Lucy established for themselves a position somewhat beyond the bounds of the usual. In the case of Margaret Cavendish, we have confirmation that others shared this vision of herself. John Evelyn's diary entry for 18 April 1667 described how 'I went to make Court to the Duke & Dutchesse of *New-Castle* at their house at *Clarkenwell*'. He was received with 'extraordinary kindesse' which pleased him as much as 'the extraordinary fancifull habit, garb, & discourse of the Dutchesse'.[8] According to Pepys, Evelyn was much to be

envied, for gossip was rife and many were eager to catch just a glimpse
of her. Pepys was delighted to meet Lady Cavendish by chance:

> going home with her coaches and footmen all in velvet; herself (whom I never
> saw before) as I have heard her often described (for all the town-talk is
> nowadays of her extravagancies), with her velvet-cap, her hair about her ears,
> many black patches because of pimples about her mouth, naked necked,
> without anything about it, and a black juste-au-corps; she seemed to me a very
> comely woman – but I hope to see more of her on May-day.

Alas, on the occasion of the May Day drive in Hyde Park, Pepys and
many others were destined to disappointment. There was 'a horrid dust
and number of coaches, without pleasure or order. That which we and
almost all went for was to see my Lady Newcastle; which we could not,
she being fallowed and crowded upon by coaches all the way she went,
that nobody could come near her.'[9]

This assessment of others on the basis on their clothing was naturally
not confined to an extraordinary few. Participants in any social interaction
made immediate judgements of the other party according to their dressed
appearance. As theorist Joanne Finkelstein explains, 'styles of clothing
signify fundamental statuses of gender, age and class which, in turn,
provide a basis for social engagement . . . in many ways, appearance
prescribes the manners of exchange fundamental to everyday sociation'.[10]
Thus Royalist Lady Anne Halkett (1623–99) was so agreeably surprised
by the look of Lady Anne Campbell, that she revised her opinion of the
barbarous north. 'For shee was very handsome, extreamly obleiging, and
her behavier and drese was equall to any that I had seene in the court of
England. This gave mee so good impresions of Scotland that I began to
see it had beene much injured by those who represented itt under another
caracter then what I found itt.'[11] In contrast, Sir John Reresby found his
expectations sadly awry. 'One day, walkeing over Pontneuf, and haveing
a belt with large sylver buckles, a man well dressed, as he came after me,
rubbed a little upon me as he passed by.' Discovering his belt cut and his
valuable buckle gone Reresby suspected, correctly, that it was the man just
gone before, 'though his appearance and dress (for he had a sword and a
good cloake) spoake him noe man to doe such an action'.[12]

As Pepys put it, he and his contemporaries were well aware of the
extraordinary 'power of good clothes and dress' in determining social
identity.[13] As such, apparel became a tool that could be utilized to produce
a particular impression. For example, Evelyn described the trial of Lord
Strafford for treason. He pointed out that the 'Manegers, who were to

Figure 19 Portrait of Daniel Goodricke, Unknown artist, 1634. York Museums Trust (York Art Gallery).

produce & manege the Evidence & whole processe in the name of the *Commmons* of *England*', were deliberately not dressed in their legal capacity. They 'not appearing in their gownes as Lawyers, but in their cloakes & swords, as representing the Commons of *England*'.[14] Lawyer and Parliamentarian politician, Bulstrode Whitelocke (Figure 20), chose to manipulate the sartorial code in order to make a similar point. 'He went to the Quarter Sessions att Oxford according to his engagement to the gentlemen, who putt him in the chayre though he was in coloured clothes, a sword by his side, & in a falling band, and unusuall garbe for Lawyers in those times, butt purposely used by Wh[itelocke] now to shew his sitting with them as a freeholder like themselves.' According to

Figure 20 Bulstrode Whitelocke, Unknown artist, 1634. By courtesy of the National Portrait Gallery, London.

Whitelocke he was successful in creating an image of legal competence *and* gentility, for 'they perceived that one might speake as good sence in a falling band as in a ruffe', and they treated him 'both in Court & out of Court, with extraordinary respect & Civility'.[15]

Lucy Hutchinson was not so pleased with the success of Major General Harrison's strategy for manipulating his public persona through the medium of apparel. A Spanish ambassador was to have public audience in the House: a great occasion since he was to be the first foreign delegate to acknowledge the English republic. The day before the audience, Harrison admonished the 'handsomely clad' members and urged them 'to shine . . . in wisdom, piety, righteousness and justice, and not in gold and silver and worldly bravery, which did not become saints'. When the ambassadors came the next day, Harrison urged, 'they should not set themselves out in gorgeous habits, which were unsuitable to holy professions'. Although Colonel Hutchinson 'was not convinced of any misbecoming bravery in the suit he wore that day, which was but of sad-coloured cloth trimmed with gold, and silver points and buttons', he and 'all the other gentlemen' duly appeared on the morrow 'in a plain black suit'. All the other gentlemen, that is, except Harrison himself. Harrison came that day 'in a scarlet coat and cloak, both laden with gold and silver lace, and the coat so covered with clinquant that scarcely could one discern the ground'. How easily must 'this glittering habit' have swum into sight, borne in the surrounding tide of sober black. It is impossible not to conclude with Lucy that 'his godly speeches, the day before were but made that he alone might appear in the eyes of strangers'.[16]

Alongside the armed encounters that scarred the political landscape of the 1630s and 1640s, a military motif also marked the contours of the male body. Mid-century portraits of elite masculinity characteristically represent their subject dressed in the accoutrements of combat: spurred riding boots, buff coat, and the identifying officers' sash.[17] The most valuable of these was the vastly tough and heavy leather coat, usually made of oxhide, used as protection in the field against weapons and weather. Participating powerfully in the construction of high-status manhood, such garments were vital to reputation, and self-image (Figure 19). Illustrating this significance is an event that Yorkshire gentleman John Hodgson (d. 1684), a Captain in the New Model Army, remembered with particular vividness relating to his buff coat. In 1662 Hodgson received a visit from a local official with a warrant to confiscate his arms, on the basis that Hodgson's parliamentary allegiance had rendered him suspicious to the post-Restoration regime. They took away over twenty pounds worth of 'fowling pieces, pistols, muskets, carbines and such like', and then demanded Hodgson's buff coat. He refused to relinquish it, and after heated argument the official left with the order that Hodgson must appear before the Deputy Lieutenant the following morning. Waiting on Sir John Armytage the next day, 'he threatened me, and said if I did not send the coat, for it was too good for me to keep'. Hodgson declined and the argument escalated. Sir John, 'growing into a fit, called me rebel and traitor, and said if I did not send the coat with all speed, he would send me where I would not like well'. Hodgson continued in staunch refusal eventually departing the room and, 'notwithstanding all the threatenings, did not send the coat'. The following day, however, Armytage retaliated and had delivered a letter – which Hodgson claims to quote from verbatim – again ordering that the buff coat be given up forthwith. Taking advantage of Hodgson's wife being then alone at home, the messenger hunted out the coat and took it away. Although wanting to reclaim it from Sir John, a third party advised that Hodgson settle for the four pounds financial recompense that Army-tage was offering. However, so Hodgson recounted, Sir John avoided paying and he concluded that 'I had never satisfaction'. Most tellingly, of the buff coat Hodgson wrote that 'one of Sir John's bretheren wore it many years after'.[18]

So, Hodgson took equally the confiscation of his more expensive collection of arms, but utterly refused to part with his old buff coat. For all the protagonists in the conflict this garment became a symbol and focus of their political ideology, their aggression and dislike, and their struggle for power. Waged through the medium of the coat, the struggle was uncompromisingly gendered. Quintessentially an item of men's dress it was imbued with significations of violence, vigour and manly success. Within Hodgson's story his wife was a mere cipher – an invisible presence powerless to act in the matter of such a powerfully masculine vestment. Furthermore, at the end the coat was not simply confiscated but, like a trophy, appropriated by the victor for display on the backs of his brethren. Apparently on opposite sides of a political gulf, John Hodgson and Sir John Armytage were yet united in their understanding of a vestimentary code, and its importance in issues of reputation, identity, and esteem.

These anecdotes about struggles for sartorial significance amongst Commonwealth supporters should encourage us to reconsider the stereo-type of plainly clad Puritanism. Firstly, however, we need to reconsider the term itself, for not defined by any particular belief or behaviour, 'puritan' has proved a remarkably elusive concept. Indeed, attempts to fix a meaning and a set of referent subjects 'have been going on for well over 400 years'.[19] For Patrick Collinson this quest is futile, and 'all attempts to distinguish this person, or that idea, or a certain practice or prejudice, as Puritan rather than otherwise are liable to fail'. Instead he posits Puri-tanism as being 'in the eye of the beholder': a fluid relationship formed by perceptions and self-perception.[20]

Clearly, handed down and inherited by us, the common apprehension – or stereotype – of plain, sober puritan apparel is one such perception. When used to stigmatize, it gave rise to images of 'the flatcapped, short cloked, russet clothed, and lether breeched broode of *Puritans*'.[21] Adopted by the godly themselves, it resulted in a self-image of moderate decorum. Lady Grace Mildmay (1552–1620), for one, espoused the view that women should 'array themselves in comely apparel with shamefastness and modesty, not with braided hair or gold or pearl or costly apparel'.[22]

For Alice Thornton, her moderation in matters of dress was the sign of a life lived in Christian grace.[23] Along similar lines Mary Rich, Countess of Warwick (1625?–78), considered her early delight in 'curious dressing and fine and rich clothes' as vain, idle and inconsiderate: as symptomatic, indeed, of 'being stedfastly set against being a Puritan'.[24] This repudiation of sartorial extravagance is linked, though, to the pursuit of dress in the discursive realm. Here it supplied the godly with an area of imaginative plenty and a metaphorical language of self-description. Lady Brilliana Harley's (1600–43) sartorial imagery concerned the signs of service. 'Be confident, he [God] is the beest [best] Master and will give the beest waiges, and they weare the beest livery, the garment of holynes, a clotheing which never shall weare out, but is renwed every day.'[25] Alice Thornton strove after 'the addorning of my spirritt and heart with all those Christian vertues'.[26] Grace Mildmay's mother, Lady Sharington, refused to give her daughter 'jewels and pearl and costly apparel' until 'I were furnished with virtue in my mind and decked inwardly'. Virtuously indeed, Grace shunned company least she 'be enticed and drawn away by some evil suggestions to stain mine unspotted garment'.[27] Images such as these abound in Puritan writings. In them clothing was used as a metaphor for virtuous spirituality, and a way of imagining – and hence forming – the pious self.

A further and less readily remembered labelling of Puritan behaviour concerned not excessive simplicity in dress but excessive splendour. In October 1602 Dr Dove, the Dean of St Paul's, preached against 'the excessive pride and vanitie of women in apparraile'. From the pulpit he took this opportunity to single out the female followers of Puritan preacher, Stephen Egerton. According to the Dean they 'abounded in that superfluous vanity'.[28] Similarly Matthew Sutcliffe levelled against Puritans the charge of going in 'new fashiond & conceited apparel, & are all clad in *Satin*, & *velvet*, and costly apparel'.[29] John Woolton, Bishop of Exeter, also accused the godly, or those who were 'most precise', of having 'no scruple to tumble and wallow in all kind of prodigality, as in dainty fare, in costly apparel, and sumptuous building'.[30] As far as matters of fine dress went, it seemed Puritans were damned if they did, and damned if they didn't.

For the godly, though, it was appropriate to be apparelled in a comely fashion for was not the body of God's creating? Similarly, it was necessary to dress suitably for one's station in life, for the social hierarchy was ordained by the Lord. From accounts we can see members of the Puritan elite dressing in a manner appropriate to, and unremarkable for, their station. Nathaniel Bacon, son of Lord Keeper Sir Nicholas, and half-brother to the eminent Francis, was a leading figure among the Puritans of East Anglia. A full transcription of the bills from 1588 to 1594 sent in by the two tailors who chiefly supplied Nathaniel and his wife and daughters, gives us an accurate picture of the extent and quality of his family's wardrobe. In 1590, for example, Peckover charged for making the women three gowns with fashionable 'Frenche verdeinggale Rolles' and 'verdeinggale sleves'. The next year he supplied them with garments made from fabrics such as crimson velvet, silk cypress, and different coloured satins, and trimmed with 'fine gould', 'stiffe purle gould', 'smothe purle gould', 'Rugget purle gould' and 'super fine gould oes'. It is a similar story for Nathaniel. In 1588 he had a cloak made. Along with the charge for sewing it up, the bill itemized gold lace to lay the same cloak, silk to set on the lace, and velvet for a cape for the garment. The cape had a hood which was faced in velvet, had gold buttons, and 'gould twyst to the lopes'.[31]

Lady Harley advised her son to 'to be contented with plaine clothes', yet she also – and without, one imagines, any sense of contradiction – approved of the silk chamlet chosen for his suit, and recommended him to wear Spanish leather shoes and silk stockings.[32] For the problem in judging dress lay, as so often, in the matter of view point. Although it may seem clear, the boundary between simplicity and finery is both relative and revisable, and is dependant solely upon who is judging whom. This results in a situation where the vestimentary text is read, and re-read, through the eyes of class, religious belief, political allegiance, gender and moral standpoint. Such contestation of meaning is amply illustrated in opinions concerning the length of men's hair. Stereotypically, Parliamentary supporters of the 1640s were held to have theirs close cropped – a feature of appearance that earned them the opprobrious nickname 'roundheads'.[33] For Lucy Hutchinson, however, this was an affected custom adopted only by Puritan zealots. She complained that 'roundhead' was very ill applied to her husband, who had 'a very fine thickset head of hair, kept it clean and handsome without any affectation, so that it was a great ornament to him'. But she went on to record that 'the godly of those days' would 'not allow him to be religious because his hair was not in their cut'.[34] The divisions amongst the Puritan camp were not restricted to John Hutchinson and his colleagues. Lady Harley's husband Sir Robert, Sir Francis Barrington, and Sir John Cutts all wore their hair cut short. Yet, J.T. Cliffe warns us, they 'cannot be regarded as typical', for others such as Sir Nathaniel Barnardiston, Sir Arthur Hesilrige and Sir William Armyne wore theirs long.[35] Certainly, the most extreme among the Puritans thought long hair on men ungodly, as witnessed by William Prynne's

1628 text *The Unloveliness of Love-Lockes*. With his usual vitriolic energy and repetitive outpourings, the Puritan pamphleteer used the opportunity to warn 'the Christian Reader' against the 'Womanish, Sinfull, and Unmanly, Crispnig [*sic*], Curling, Frouncing, Powdring, and nourishing of their Lockes, and Hairie excrements'.[36] However, to complicate the matter still further, Archbishop Laud – on the very opposite end of the religious spectrum to Prynne – concurred with him that long hair was unseemly and immoral, and as Chancellor of the university of Oxford tried to enforce this view.[37]

Puritan John Winthrop, in writing to Margaret Tyndal, his future wife, seemed aware of the complex judgements surrounding appearance. He warned her of the 'matter of apparrell fashions and other circumstances', for it was the subject of vain minds, and savoured too much of the flesh. However, he went on to 'confesse that there be some ornamentes which for virgins, and knightes daughters etc may be comly and tollerable'. Wisely, given the ever-shifting boundary between dressed piety and pride, he omitted to determine just what these might be. Instead he closed the subject of Margaret's bridal raiment by promising that 'I will medle in no particulars', and left the choice to her 'owne wisdome, and godlinesse'.[38]

It seems, then, that all we can say about Puritans is that they dressed – like anyone else – as they individually thought befitted their beliefs and personal circumstances. As John Winthrop advised, they made the choice of their clothing according to their 'owne wisdome, and godlinesse'. However, the notion of Puritans as a distinct group was given apparent coherence by perceptions of either mean, or lavish dressing. Although, like all stereotypes both ideas dissolve upon closer scrutiny, they do indicate the power that clothing had to affect judgements made of both others, and of the self.[39] While the significations of clothing differed depending upon who was reading the ensemble – godly, immoral, plain, or luxurious – yet still that clothing was vital to people's ideas of identity.

Sir John Oglander's wife, daughter of staunch puritan Sir George More, solved the ambivalence of apparel in a manner presumably satisfactory to herself. According to her husband, she 'never wore a silk gown but for her credit when she went abroad, and never to please herself'.[40] Her example alerts us to the importance of *ways* of wearing. When the appropriateness of any given garment was uncertain, how it was worn, and when, could matter a great deal. One area in which this was particularly crucial was hat honour. Simply put, this was the code that declared men were to remove their headwear for superiors, and to remain covered in the presence of those of a lesser status (Figure 4). Between these two actions though, lay a range of possible responses through which the hat wearer could articulate his attitudes to authority, his relationship with others, and his assessment of his own status. 'Aggression, defiance, salutation, respect, submission, entreaty, and emotion were all readily conveyed by adroit handling.'[41] According to his wife, the Duke of Newcastle's use of headgear was typical of his unassuming dignity, but it also indicates the kind of *noblesse oblige* born of unquestioned privilege. 'He hates Pride and loves Humility; is civil to Strangers, kind to his Acquaintance, and respectful to all persons, according to their Quality; He never regards Place, except it be for Ceremony: To the meanest person he'll put off his Hat.'[42]

Clearly this communication worked because all parties shared an understanding of what was meant. This enabled the Governor of Holstein to identify Bulstrode Whitelocke, despite his being plainly dressed. 'Rantzow knew not w[hi]^ch was the Am[bassadou]^r [,] he being in plain Grey gown of English Bayes till (as he said) he observed Wh[itelocke] w[i]^th his hatt on, & a great many brave fellowes standing by him uncovered'.[43] It also allowed a rather enterprising thief the opportunity to enrich himself. The teller is John Chamberlain, who wrote to both Dudley Carleton and Ralph Winwood of an affront lately done the Spanish ambassador. A trickster, riding near the ambassador's coach saluted him, and 'the Spaniard putting of his hat in requitall, had yt snatcht from him and lost yt with a rich hat-band and jewell'.[44] Despite Chamberlain's rather gleeful tone in recounting this bit of gossip, hat honour could be an extremely serious matter. The notebooks of John Finet, Master of Ceremonies to Charles I, have numerous references to the way dignitaries negotiated the hierarchies of court and personal standing through the doffing, or otherwise, of their headgear. Lapses of etiquette were remarked and censured, and skilful hat handling gained diplomatic prestige and, literally, eased international relations.

The case of Sir James Spence's audience with Charles I amply illustrates this complicated subtext. Sir James, although originally a Scot, was visiting court in the March of 1629 in the capacity of Swedish ambassador. As a private individual from Britain he obviously owed deference to Charles, but as the representative of a foreign monarch certain privilege and honour were his due. Having gained consent to an audience with both the King and the Queen, at his request Sir James was also granted a private meeting with Charles. Before this occurred, however, the Earl of Carlisle smoothed the diplomatic path by suggesting to Charles that 'thoughe the ambassador were a Scottish man borne and his natural subject, he should receyve all the honours and respects given any other ambassador, and be permitted to cover in his presence'. Accordingly Sir James, when brought before the King, 'giving no more humble respectes than an other ambassador would have, he was putting on his hat, after the fyrst invitation, but after that often putting it off and on agayne, as he was invited to it by his majesty'. Sir James then went to Henrietta Maria before whom he remained bare headed, for the good manners owed to a woman did not diminish, he said, the dignity of his royal employer. But this painstaking etiquette also earned Sir James political mileage, for he was compared with less skilled diplomats and his conduct found more gracious. But the test of Spence's *politesse* was not yet over. From the Queen he was conducted to the requested private audience with Charles. At this, and all subsequent private meetings, Sir James 'never offered, nor was invited to cover'. For out of 'publick notice' and his ambassadorial role, he was in duty bound to 'pay all dewe respectes to his naturall soverayne. These were his owne and not improper reasons'. Spence's sensitivity and skill in diplomatic affairs – of which his keen appreciation of hat honour was an example – earned him flattering notice and a successful career.[45]

Thirty years later the implications of hat honour were also to occupy Samuel Pepys, though he handled its intricacies less adroitly than did Sir James. With reference to his inferiors, lapses of respect filled him with irritation. In October 1661 he reported himself 'much offended in mind at a proud trick my man Will: hath got, to keep his hatt on in the house'. On another occasion, when meeting with a group of naval captains, he was ill-pleased to find that one 'among twenty that stood bare, stood with his hat on, a proud saucy young man'. His relationships with superiors could also cause Pepys unease. Walking along the Mall one evening, he drew near to the Duke of York. It being fairly dark Pepys and his companion continued on their way without stopping. One of James's footmen came running after them, however, and looked in their faces as if to see who they were. Pepys racked his brain to see if he had inadvertently given offence. 'What his meaning is I know not, but was fearful that I might not go far enough with my hat off, though methinks that should not be it; besides, there was others covered nearer then myself was, but only it was my fear.'[46]

The offence that a refusal to observe hat honour could give, cannot be overestimated. To witness this we must turn to the Quakers, who resolutely declined to pay this sartorial respect to persons whom, although socially superior, were equal before God. In his journal for 1649 George Fox described how 'when the Lord sent me forth into the world, he forbade me to put off my hat to any, high or low'. This, he wrote, inflamed people of all sorts; 'because I could not put off my hat to them, it sent them all into a rage'. From here it was a short step to persecution:

Oh, the blows, punchings, beatings, and imprisonments that we underwent for not putting off our hats to men! For that soon tried all men's patience and sobriety, what it was. Some had their hats violently plucked off and thrown away . . . The bad language and evil usage we received on this account are hard to be expressed, besides the danger we were sometimes in of losing our lives for this matter.[47]

Fox does not exaggerate here, for hat defiance, by refusing to acknowledge hierarchies of authority, signalled a fundamental challenge to the political status quo. Although the regime at that time was Puritan, it still upheld temporal inequality as rigorously as any monarchy; and thus the State Papers are littered with references to Quakers punished for, among other things, refusal to doff their hats. For example, three Quakers arriving in Plymouth appeared before the mayor 'with their hats on'. Two 'stood stiff in their folly and were sent to prison'. In another case a Quaker petition drew attention to the plight of Thomas Curtis and John Martindale who were, it was claimed, taken without justification as vagrants. They were 'brought up at the assize before Chief Justice Nicholas, and no charge was brought against them; yet because they would not take off their hats, he fined them 40*l.* each, and sent them back to prison, where they remain'.[48]

George Fox's stalwart refusal of hat honour, John Hodgson's attachment to his buff coat, and the Duchess of Newcastle's delight in singular fashions all helped them establish a particular persona, and place within society. Their identity, in other words, was at least partly performed through dress. In this performance the garment was vitally significant: its style, richness, colour and fabric. However, the manner of its wearing was also charged with meaning. So, in *The Winter's Tale* the disguised Autolycus is judged by the Clown to be a great courtier. Then the more percipient Old Shepard replies, 'His garments are rich, but he wears them not handsomely'.[49] Importantly, this notion of character as being performed through the medium and manipulation of clothing implies the existence of an audience. Dressed identity was validated by being observed; and it was played out in the public realm. It is to the ramifications of this that we will now turn.

To See and be Seen

'After I had furnished myself with clothes fit to walk abroad in, I went to wait on the Cardinal'.[50] As Sir George Courthop (1616–85) shows us while reflecting on the travels of his youth, much of the sartorial project was a public undertaking. Although he had arrived in the city of Rome, he could not arrive in society, or 'walk abroad', until he had fashioned a suitably dressed persona. Without it he could not enter the common domain: clothing enabled social recognition. When John Verney married Elizabeth Palmer in 1680, there was a sense in which their union only achieved validity when publicly proclaimed by their dress. They planned the ceremony itself to be almost secretive. John wrote to his father on the morning of the wedding that 'we designe to be Married . . . very privately in our old clothes, none will be at it but her father, mother, brother & Aunt'. Indeed they aimed not to tell anyone, 'keeping the news within our own doors from Thursday to Saturday'. Then, however, 'wee shall owne it publiquely by our clothes in Chelsey Church'.[51]

Samuel Pepys made a habit of trying out new clothes on friends and family before venturing into the wider public view. His colleague, John Creed, was sometimes the first audience for new purchases, as when Pepys 'put on my riding-cloth suit, only for him to see how it is, and I think it will do very well'. 'And after dinner', Pepys noted in another diary entry, 'he and I upstairs, and I showed him my velvet cloak and other things of clothes that I have lately bought, which he likes very well; and I took his opinion as to some things of clothes which I purpose to wear, being resolved to go a little handsomer then I have hitherto.'[52] Sometimes the approbation of intimates was not forthcoming, and Pepys responded with a corresponding caution. On Sunday 11 June 1665, he received a new suit of 'Colour'd Farrinden', different from the black clothing he habitually wore. He tried it on but evidently his wife did not like it, which put both her and the new suit out of favour. Pepys consoled himself with the thought that 'I think it is only my not being used to wear Colours, which makes it look a little unusual upon me'. Thus comforted, after his midday meal he ventured 'out of doors a little to show forsooth my new suit, and back again'. Gaining confidence after this public trial, the next day he wore 'my yesterday's new suit to the Duke of Albemarle'. By the end of the following month he recorded his satisfaction in his public appearance 'in my new coloured-silk suit and coat, trimmed with gold buttons and gold broad lace round my hands, very rich and fine'.[53]

The same sampling of public reaction is revealed in the gradual process by which Pepys brought himself, over the months of 1663, to wear a wig. Tired of the trouble it took to keep his hair clean, on 9 May Pepys started by trying on a number of wigs at his barber's. He left undecided, and worried about 'the trouble I forsee will be in wearing them'. His indecision continued into August, when he again mentioned the matter to his barber. At Pepys's prompting, Jervas showed him a hair piece, yet still Pepys had 'no great desire or resolution yet to wear one. And so I put it off a while.' He put it off, in fact, until October, when he realized that a perruque was necessary to be modish. Having taken this decision, accompanied by his sartorial confidant Mr Creed, he sallied forth 'to one or two Periwegg shops about the Temple . . . and there I think I shall fit myself on one very handsomely made'. Four days later he took his wife to the wig-maker's to inspect his purchase, 'and she likes it very well'. Having gained the approval of intimates, Pepys then contemplated trying his new look out on a wider public, and 'will begin next week, God willing'. Accordingly, on 3 November, he took the dramatic but necessary step for wig-wearing, of cutting off his own hair. Then trying on his wig 'I had caused all my maids to look upon it and they conclude it to become me, though Jane was mightily troubled for my parting with my own hair and so was Besse'. So, we might suspect, was Pepys. Nevertheless, the next day he ventured to the office, 'showing myself to Sir W. Batten and Sir J. Mennes'. With relief he recorded that there was 'no great matter made of my periwig, as I was afeared there would'. The final trial came on the following Sunday when he attended service. 'I found that my coming in a perriwigg did not prove so strange to the world as I was afeared it would, for I thought that all the church would presently have cast their eye all upon me – but I found no such thing.'[54] This success – unremarking public acceptance – launched Pepys onto a path of enjoyable and proud wig wearing, as testified by subsequent remarks made through the diaries. Unlike Malvolio he wished to avoid singularity, and be notable for his dress, and not notorious.

Personal narratives, then, reveal concern about who was to see one's dressed image. They also disclose a sensitivity about where the visual encounter was to take place. As the tale of Pepys's wig indicates, among the many possible sites of social engagement one of the most potent was at church. It was in this place that the whole community – or as Pepys put it, 'the world' – gathered and observed one another. The overt order of the day may have been worship, but equally important was the social agenda underlying liturgy, sermon and prayer. We are familiar with the way issues of status emerged in pew disputes, of how state edicts found promulgation via the pulpit, and how community relationships were ordered through church rituals. Less obvious to us was the use of the church gathering as a venue for displaying dress. Eyes may have been lowered in prayer, but undoubtedly were also cast in sidelong glances of appraisal, as the congregation assessed one another's garments.

In addition to recording the bare fact of her attendance at church, Lady Clifford described her appearance there, with intimations as to the public effect. 'The 28th I went to Church in my rich Night Gown & Petticoat, both my women waiting upon me in their liveries.'[55] The apparently frank disclosures made by Pepys included many descriptions of his Sunday routine. On the Lord's Day he invariably rose, dressed in his finest clothes, and went to church. 'Up, and put on my new stuff-suit with shoulder-belt, according to the new fashion, and the bands of my vest and tunic laced with silk lace of the colour of my suit. And so, very handsome, to church, where a dull sermon of a stranger.'[56] Matters of the flesh were of a more pressing nature here than possible benefits to the spirit. As well as showing himself, Pepys took careful note of others. He weighed up the visual presentation, and, comparing it with his own, was able to make a judgement. It was a complex equation in which modishness, cost and social standing all played their part:

> *Lords day.* This morning I put on my best black cloth-suit trimmed with Scarlett ribbon, very neat, with my cloak lined with Velvett and a new Beaver, which altogether is very noble, with my black silk knit canons I bought a month ago.
> I to church alone, my wife not going; and there I find my Lady Batten in a velvet gowne, which vexed me that she should be in it before my wife, or that I am able to put her into one; but what cannot be, cannot be. However, when I came home I told my wife of it; and to see my weakness, I could on the sudden have found my heart to have offered her one, but second thoughts put it by; and endeed, it would undo me to think of doing as Sir W. Batten and his Lady do, who hath a good estate besides his office.[57]

Satire and moralizing were voluble on the subject of the Sunday service as fashion parade. It is a key theme of the first chapter in particular, of the misogynous text, *The Batchelar's Banquet* (1603). The newly wed bride wishes to be dressed beautifully, and although they can't afford it, manipulates her husband into giving her a new outfit. The main thrust of her argument is that she does not wish the fine clothing for herself. Indeed, she would be content with mean apparel, only when she goes to ecclesiastical ceremonies – churchings, christenings and weddings – she is ashamed of what people say. Social credit, she impresses on her husband, is established through sartorial credit. The gullible and tender-hearted husband gives in to his manipulative and competitive wife, and buys her a new gown:

> And whereas before she vaunted, that she could find in / her heart to keepe always within doores, she will bee sure now every good day to goe abroad . . . that all may see her bravery [fine clothing], and how well she doth become

it; to which cause she also comes every Sunday dayly to the Church, that there shee may see and be seene, which her husband thinkes she doth of meere devotion.[58]

Naturally, in this moralizing tale, the couple end in penury and un-happiness, and the proper solemnity of religious ceremony is seen to be sabotaged by female pride in the display of fine clothing.

But it was not just the *wearing* of garments that was given meaning by its place within the public domain. Before mass production and anony-mous off-the-peg retailing, apparel was ordered, made and purchased with widespread knowledge and participation. The extent to which this might be the case is demonstrated by the account books of Giles Moore (1617–97). Rector of Horsted Keynes in Sussex, Moore left an exceptionally detailed record of his income and expenses, tabulated according to com-modity. It is quickly apparent that the work of acquiring and maintaining his and his family's clothing was spread amongst his acquaintances. So, on 12 October 1664, Moore paid 'young Frank West' four shillings for 'a paire of Trowses which Hee bought for Mee at London'. On 11 November he similarly reimbursed John Pelham, Richard Harland's journeyman, 'in behalfe of his master for 4 dozen of Buttons which his master bought at Lewis'. Later on in November, he recorded the sums paid to individually named merchants for cloth and trimmings, and also the sum of one shilling 'Giv'n Mr Hull's Eldest Son for going along with mee & helpe buy them'.[59] Cloth was sewn into garments by local artisans, such as the tailor, Richard Harland. But the making of linen goods and small clothes was dispersed more widely throughout the community. Generally these items passed through the hands of women. For example, under his 1666 expen-diture on holland, Moore recorded that he bought an ell from Goodwife Cranfield, which he then paid Goodwife Harland – the tailor's wife – to make into four handkerchiefs. He also paid Elizabeth Pocock for first making him three bands and three pairs of cuffs, and then later gave her six shillings 'for buying, making & sending Mee 12 paire of socks'.[60] Bearing in mind the necessity of husbanding valuable cloth resources, we also find many of Moore's entries relate to the repair and mending of apparel. In August 1667 Richard Harland sent Moore his bill 'For foo-ting & mending 4 paire of stockings 1^s 4^d halfe a Q^{ter} of silke 3^d . . . the 4 paire of stockings coast the footing 3^s 6^d which was unreasonable.' So unreas-onable, in fact, that Moore took his custom elsewhere. Entries for the next year include paying an Edward Waters and 'wateres Maid' for footing his stockings, 'mending cloaths', 'mending my Cassack' and 'mending my cloake & Gloves'.[61]

Since the nineteenth century we have used the metaphor 'washing dirty linen in public'.[62] In early modern England, when the neighbouring Widow James was paid for whiting linen, the phrase bore only a literal interpretation.[63] The state of affairs where artisans, servants, widows and housewives had intimate knowledge of the age, value and condition of others' garments argues the existence of a particular sense of self that is different from our own. It is a self defined less by independence, and more by relationship and connection. Existing not in anonymous isolation – the existential freedom 'invented' by modernity – but within a community that overlooks, the individual was metaphorically knitted into relationship just as surely as his or her stockings were physically knitted into shape.

Portraits also existed within, and contributed to, the sense of public viewing. They were expressly designed to be displayed and were hung, most generally, in public rooms 'for all to see'.[64] Strolling through the long gallery – that contemporary architectural achievement so suited to picture display – the living figure experienced a series of encounters with the painted. Down from the walls the images of the familial, famous and royal, looked out at those viewers looking at them.[65] While catering for the intimate gaze, the genre of miniature painting so popular at the time was designed, nevertheless, for display. Although, as Nicholas Hilliard described, they were 'to be weewed [viewed] of nesesity in hand neare unto the eye', yet still miniatures assumed 'a function in the public sphere'.[66] Portraits were a means of sending a particular image of self out into the world. Unlike real life originals these paintings could not themselves see but, to borrow for the author of *The Batchelar's Banquet*, they could *be* seen.

The work pioneered by Sir Roy Strong has established our under-standing of these images as painted statements of lineage and status. Noting the brilliant surface colours and comparatively flat and static rendition of the subject matter, Strong has dubbed these works English icons. This is not to say that portraits bore no resemblance to their sitters in life. However, individuality of facial detail and inscription was set within a conventionalized body pattern and background. English Renaiss-ance portraits were not unique studies of personality but images that enhanced the assertion of social role and commemorated a life's achieve-ments. This was done, in great part, through the portrayal of costume. Even the most schematic and conventionalized of faces is set above clothing rendered in tiny detail from minute observation. 'The clothes, that is, provide a specificity that the faces do not.'[67] The most famous examples of this are found in the many portraits of Elizabeth. If she sat at all – and it was a rare occurrence – she modelled only for the face and the outline of the pose. For the rest of the sittings the clothes were either worn by a stand-in, or propped up in the studio. More usually the artist painted the Queen's clothes from life, but merely copied her face pattern from another source.[68] Perhaps this concentration of painterly attention on garments was common practice for other sitters, considering Edward Norgate's advice from about 1650 that, 'for the apparrell, Linnen, Jewells, pearle and such like, you are to lay them before you in the same posture as your designe is, and when you are alone, you may take your owne time to finish them, with as much neatnes and perfection as you please, or can'.[69]

The sitter's choice of clothing for this perpetual and enduring image of self was clearly anything but casual. It was a considered presentation, taking into account the viewer's likely 'reading' of an outfit. Edward Herbert, Lord Cherbury (1583–1648) was proud of his status and appearance as a Knight of the Bath. To celebrate his achievement of the 'Robes of Crimson Taffita', he had himself painted in them, and the painting hung in his study for his frequent view.[70] Unlike Herbert, however, Pepys felt that he did not own clothing suitable for the image he wished to present in his portrait, so he hired an outfit. 'Thence home and eat one mouthful, and so to Hales's and there sat till almost quite dark upon working my gowne, which I hired to be drawn [in] it – an Indian gown, and I do see all the reason to expect a most excellent picture of it'(Figure 21).[71] Lady Sussex was also most particular about her painted image. While Pepys had remedied the deficiency in his wardrobe by hiring an outfit, she desired Van Dyck to embellish her existing apparel so that it appeared finer than in reality. To Sir Edmund Verney, who in 1639 had arranged for her to sit for the artist, she wrote: 'Put Sʳ Vandyke in remembrance to do my pictuer wel. I have sene sables with the clasp of them set with dimons – if thos that i am pictuerde in wher don so i think it would look very wel in the pictuer.' Later on, when the finished portrait was copied by a lesser artist, she continued to be aware of how subsequent viewers might interpret it. 'I am glade you have got hom my pictuer, but i doubt he hath . . . made it . . . to rich in ihuels [jewels] i am suer, but it tis no great mater for another age to thinke me richer then i was.'[72]

Portraits were a way of maximizing personal visibility through a replication of image. Visibility could also be increased by expanding that image, so that it encompassed other people. Those so subsumed were marked out by badge, colour and cloth as participants in the display of status: they wore livery. Anne Clifford was very aware that her appearance at church had added cachet due to the attendance of her two liveried followers. From minor gentry stock, Nicholas Assheton recorded in his journal his part in a similar interaction from the point of view of the

Figure 21 Samuel Pepys, John Hayls, 1666. By courtesy of the National Portrait Gallery, London.

liveried. His neighbour, Sir Richard Houghton, was due to be entertaining the King in the summer of 1617. Assheton wrote on 1 June that Sir Richard had urged both him and his brother-in-law, 'to do him such fav^r, countenance, grace, curtesie, as to weare his clothe, and attend him at Houghton, at the kings comming in August'. Assheton consented. Three months later, on 11 August, he wrote: 'My brother Sherborne his taylor brought him a suit of app[ar]all, and us two others, and a live[r]y cloake, from Sir Ric. Houghton, that we should attend him at the King's coming, rather for his grace and reput^n shoeing [showing] his neibors love, then anie exacting of mean service.' His final comment on the affair is dated 13 August. 'We that were in Sir Ric^s liv^y ', he remarked, 'had nothing to do but riding upp and downe.' However, this was enough. Wearing Sir Richard's colours their job was to advertise his standing, doing so simply by showing themselves and being seen.[73] According to Paul Hentzner (d. 1623), a German travelling as companion to a young nobleman, this display was typically English. For the English, Hentzner wrote, are 'lovers of show;

followed wherever they go by whole troops of servants, who wear their masters' arms in silver fastened to their left arms'.[74]

Pepys was not followed by a troop, but he still wished to apparel his modest retinue so as to add to his dignity. On the 16 March 1662 he reported his plans for a new livery, and a week later the designs were delivered. 'This morning was brought me my boyes fine livery, which is very handsome, and I do think to keepe black and gold lace upon gray, being the colour of my armes, for ever.' Two months later the apparelling of his servant continued to add to his own feeling of consequence: 'And after dinner . . . I walked with my wife to my Brother Toms, our boy waiting on us with his sword, which this day he begins to wear to out-do Sir W. Pens boy, who this day, and Sir W. Batten['s] too, begin to wear new liverys. But I do take mine to be the neatest of them all.'[75] Bulstrode Whitelocke also reported the pleasing spectacle of being surrounded by well-dressed subservients. 'This being the day for Wh[itelockes] last audience, his followers were in their rich liveries, his gent[lemen] in their richest habits, himselfe in plain English cloth with buttons of rubyes.'[76] The difference in Whitelocke's case, is that all sumptuousness of apparel – ruby buttons aside – has been displaced on to his followers. The social theorist Thorstein Veblen called this variation on conspicuous display, vicarious consumption. Except for the presence of discreet markers, such as Bulstrode's jewelled buttons, the signs of status are effaced from the person in whom it actually resides. Instead the burden of display is carried by dependants. Veblen and later commentators agree that the nineteenth century saw the most striking expression of vicarious consumption. The garments that gentlemen wore were sober and restrained, while their wives and servants dressed in outrageous style: crinolines, bustles and tight-lacing for women, the invention of 'upstairs downstairs' regalia for serving staff. [77]

In the sixteenth century there was resistance to what may have been the beginnings of this displacement of 'excess'. I. M., the anonymous author of *A Health to the Gentlemanly Profession of Serving-Men*, bemoaned the unfitting spectacle of the fine clothes not being worn upon the person of the fine gentleman. 'I met (not long since)', he complained:

a Gentleman in Fleetestreete, whoes lyving is better woorth then .2000. Markes yeerely, attended with onely one Man, whose apparrell was much better then his Maisters, though he was a Justice of Peace in his Countrey. But I speake not this, eyther to discommend the Gentlemans homely habite, or commende to Servingman in his excesse: but the miserie of that minde, that regarded more Coyne then his credite.

He goes on to consider the person of mean estate who swaggers in fine dress with many followers. It was impossible, he concluded, to 'discerne this difference, and know the one from the other, the Gentleman from the Swashbuckler, by his apparrel, attendants, and companie'.[78] Sixty years later, as we have seen, Bulstrode Whitelocke read a similar sartorial arrangement as meaning the complete opposite. When he walked abroad to establish credit, 'it was w[i]ᵗh state[,] his liveryes rich, his gentlemen richly habited, onely himselfe in a plain grey cloth suit, with the jewell of the Q[ueen] of Swedens picture att his breast'. Indeed, in doing so Whitelocke was identifying himself with the Queen whose portrait miniature he wore. For in the Swedish royal company all were in 'excellent order, & rich in clothes, only the Q[ueen] & P[rince] were plain in their habits'.[79] Perhaps, then, along with the slow democratization of high-status dress – I. M.'s swashbuckling upstarts possessed of excessive temerity and an excessive wardrobe – there grew up a corresponding elite appreciation of the vicarious demonstration of spectacular behaviour. Possibly I. M.'s disapproval was at the beginnings of a more modern re-coding of sartorial display, which would culminate in notions of vulgarity, restraint and discretion.

Punishment and Shame

Wealth, lineage and achievement – whether real or alleged – were asserted materially for a public audience. Less desirable status was also witnessed publicly, and also seen through the medium of dress. Early modern mechanisms for punishment illustrate this clearly. Whether judicial, ecclesiastical or popular, imposed discipline was public and shaming, and routinely used clothing in creative ways to add to the culprit's physical and emotional discomfort. For the Church courts this can most easily be seen in its 'characteristic penalty' of penance.[80] Typically the guilty were ordered to perform acts of contrition dressed in a white sheet and carrying a white rod. Usually undertaken in church, penance might also be done in other public places, as was the case with the five who 'dyd penance with shetts a-bowt them' at Paul's Cross on 4 November 1554.[81] Although penitential wear was standard – and F.G. Emmison notes that church-wardens usually kept sheets for the purpose – the ecclesiastical judges might use their discretion when deciding on penalties.[82] To increase the humiliation, for example, the offender might be ordered also to appear bareheaded, barelegged, stripped of their outer clothing or, in the case of women, with their hair loose. On the other hand, to mitigate the punishment the penitential shroud might be foregone altogether, as happened to John Munt and Grace Hubbard. Found guilty in 1600 of sexual practice before marriage, they were allowed to 'acknowledge their fault at the time of solemnization of matrimony in their ordinary apparel'.[83]

Clothing also figured amongst punitive strategies in the secular world. For example, on 9 July 1561, Henry Machyn (1498?–1563?) tells us that a pillory was set up for an apprentice. Having stolen money from his master, the apprentice had bought himself 'nuw aparell, nuw shurtt, dobelet and hose, hat, purse, gyrdyll, dager, and butes [boots], spurs, butt-hose, and a skarffe'. Incorporated into the judgement, these new garments 'dyd hang up on the pelere [pillory]'.[84] More often though, other supplementary symbols were used to advertise guilt and underscore humiliation.[85] Thus the woman punished on the 22 March 1560/1 for selling fish unlawfully, rode about 'with a garland a-pone her hed hangyng with strynges of the small fysse'.[86] On other occasions there was a more literal labelling of misdemeanours, the culprit wearing a textual description of the crime, rather than the metaphorical signal. The couple paraded through town on the 5 November 1557 suffered just this. The man was 'on horse-bake, ys fase toward the horses tail, and a wrytyng on ys hed; and he had a fryse [frieze] gown, [and] ys wyff leydyng the horse, and a paper on her h[ead, for] horwdom'.[87] The most extreme form of this 'textual' punishment was branding. For those like the maid 'bornyd in the brow' for poisoning, the sign of guilt was to be displayed for the rest of the culprit's life.[88] While these objects and textual descriptions were not apparel in the strict sense of the word, they were 'worn' by the offender. By altering the gestalt of normal appearance, they invited ridicule and social humiliation.

The ultimate disgrace, however, involved the removal of clothing. Machyn recorded two occasions where hanging the offender was not punishment enough, the extreme nature of the offence requiring some further display of disapprobation. On the 10 January 1559/60, William North and his man were hanged for killing Master Wynborne outside the west door of St Paul's. When they were cut down in the afternoon, the hangman carried them into St Gregory's churchyard, where a grave had been dug ready. 'And so they wher strypyd of all, and tumbelyd nakyd in-to the grayff'. The other incident involved two men – John Boneard and Gregory, a Spaniard – who were arraigned for attempted robbery. During the case Gregory pulled out a knife, and before the judges, stabbed a witness giving evidence against him. Boneard was burned in the hand, but Gregory's contempt of authority fared much worse. A gibbet was set up immediately, his hand was struck off and nailed to it, and 'contenent he was hangyd up . . . and Gregory hangyed all nyght nakyd'.[89]

Although embedded within the ultimate retribution of capital punishment, the juridical stripping of clothes from the condemned corpse was not trivial, or accidental. As J.A. Sharpe has written, 'public executions were carried out in a context of ceremony and ritual', and as with all ceremonies and rituals, every gesture had significance.[90] These divestitures were morally loaded, and onlookers had no doubt as to the contempt they signalled. To understand this fully we need to look back at the contemporary importance of a decent burial. Those of the very lowest status – children, the poor, and even the destitute – were extended the respect of a correct and Christian interment. Only to those who had forfeited their place in the community, only to excommunicates, suicides and some executed felons, was this denied.[91]

The punishments meted out in early modern England indicate that the inappropriate use of clothing – including nakedness – was a sign of stigma or social dysfunction. In the case of crime, this sartorial isolation was imposed on the wearer. Evidence suggests, however, that in other situations individuals might willingly engage in unacceptable dress behaviour as a way of expressing a social or mental position in some way marginal, or on the edge. We have seen how after the death of his first wife Bulstrode Whitelocke communicated his distracted state by neglecting his person, and later signalled the transformation back to his social, rational self by returning to accepted styles of dress. The characterization of melancholy, apparelled carelessly in black, loose and dishevelled, and with a wide-brimmed hat pulled low, also points to the centrality of clothing to perceptions of social fitness.[92] Interestingly, Robert Burton's advice for its cure included the reversal of sartorial negligence, indicating the agency of dress and that clothing could not only be a symptom, but also a *cause*, of mental unease. Let the melancholic be, 'neatly dressed, washed and combed, according to his ability at least, in cleane sweet linnen, spruce, handsome, decent, and good apparell, for nothing sooner dejects a man then want, squalor and nastinesse, foule, or old cloathes out of fashion'.[93] For Alice Thornton's distant forbear Christopher Wandsford, no such return to the normal was possible. He was a lunatic, 'fallinge for the moste parte once a day into a fitt of frensie or lunacie, in which fitt he used to teare his clothes frome his backe and burne theime if he were suffred'.[94] Whether Nehemiah Poole was mentally disturbed or merely socially disruptive is unclear, but on 21 January 1659 he was 'indicted for coming to the church in his shirt; and by the justices committed to the house of correction for three months'. As Henry Newcome then added, 'It is a mercy that restraint is laid on such persons as these are'.[95]

Michael MacDonald, in his moving study of mental health in early modern England, looks briefly at this relationship between clothing and madness. He concludes that the mentally disturbed were often reported as either disrobing or destroying their garments; acts that were irrational, wasteful and 'socially self-defacing'. Those who deliberately spoiled their own apparel 'repudiated their social pretensions'. Indeed, MacDonald writes, it was a kind 'of social suicide'.[96] It is no accident that at the point at which Lear and Edgar lose their capacity for rational speech, they also lose their clothing.[97] Naked they are less than human, a sentiment echoed in real life by Joachim Hane. A German employed by the Interregnum government as an engineer and a spy, Hane recorded in his journal the occasion when his clothing had been stolen. To cover himself he was forced to put on the thieves' discarded garments 'of thin canvis ragged and torne'. Hane described this episode in terms if a fundamental shift of social status. 'I was now become a worme and no man, a scorne to all that saw me.'[98]

A Very Good Fancy in Making Good Clothes

Joachim Hane and his contemporaries read the inappropriate use of apparel as a typology of a dysfunctional personality, but in fact they understood all aspects of social role through the medium of clothing worn within the community view. Success, power, wealth, guilt and madness were all focused in the public eye and carried in some way on the person. However, the fundamental relationship that clothing and identity have in every society was rendered more binding in early modern England by methods of production. Before off-the-peg retailing all new garments were ordered by and made for a particular individual. He or she had power, not merely in the selection of a garment as today, but over its design and appearance. In a world of unique garments, responsibility for dressed image was located much more personally. So important was the consumer to the process of constructing apparel, that to Lucy Hutchinson's mind her husband bore the active and creative part, rather than the tailor. The Colonel was 'genteel in his habit, and had a very good fancy in making good clothes'.[99]

Bearing in mind how much appearance was a self-creation, it is easier to understand how dress became such a potent tool in the courtly struggle for advancement. Robert Carey (1560–1639), eventually created the Earl of Monmouth, believed he owed part of his preferment to his skill in dressing. The establishment of Charles I's household as Duke of York led to inevitable jostling for precedence amongst the courtiers eager to secure a position. Carey apparently found favour with the Lord Chamberlain, whom he reported as speaking to the King in the following terms. Robert Carey:

> carried himself so as every honest man was glad of his company. He ever spent with the best, and wore as good clothes as any, and he exceeded in making choice of what he wore to be handsome and comely . . . sure I am, there is none about the Duke that knows how to furnish him with clothes and apparel so well as he; and therefore in my opinion, he is the fittest man to be Master of the Robes.

As Carey wrote, 'this cast the scales', and with days 'I was sworn chief Gentleman of the Bedchamber, and Master of the Robes'.[100] Similarly, it was not just James I's penchant for handsome young men that led Lord Thomas Howard to advise Sir John Harington in 1611, that if he were to succeed at court he must:

> be well trimmed; get a new jerkin well borderd, and not too short; the King saith, he liketh a flowing garment; be sure it be not all of one sort, but diversly colourd, the collar falling somewhat down, and your ruff well stiffend and bushy. We have lately had many gallants who failed in their suits, for want of due observance of these matters.[101]

In such a climate no wonder a man might 'lie ten nights awake carving the fashion of a new doublet'.[102]

This more active involvement of the individual with the creation of his or her clothing required a complex and largely forgotten expertise. Without the coercive influence of mass production and ubiquitous fashion images, the early modern consumer had to make a whole range of choices concerning the colour, fabric, cut, style, cost and fit of each garment. In order to do so successfully, he or she needed a particular set of skills and body of information: observations about fashionable dress, a certain knowledge of garment construction, the ability to imagine the finished item, and the vocabulary with which to communicate ideas to the tailor. Furthermore, material was often obtained separately by the customer and given to the tailor for making up. In these cases a knowledge of textile properties was essential, along with the ability to judge its quality and to estimate the amount each garment would need. Lady Judith Barrington's instructions to her steward regarding a stepson's outfit, illustrate the financial and aesthetic judgements that such an ordinary undertaking required:

Heer is a patern of a good colerd cloth and lace for a suite for Jack Barrington. My French taylor last week tooke heer measure of him, and I hope it will fitt him better then Pickering did; worss hee cannot. 3 laces in a seame I heer now is the best fashion, except we would bestow all lace, which wee will not, and besides that is to costly. Thear needs no buttons on the armes or back for this winter, and the sooner he hath itt the better, for you know his need.[103]

This dress awareness was not limited to women like Lady Judith. It was equally – if not more so – the province of men. At a time when women from the middling and upper sort led relatively privatized lives with limited access to commercial and public spheres, men were involved in making sartorial provision for themselves, and their households. As such, expertise in clothing and textiles was somewhat differently gendered than now, when cultural norms declare fabrics and fashion to be a largely female concern.

In the Calley household we can see seventeenth-century gentlemen making such informed decisions. After the Calleys' friend and former steward Richard Harvey left their service in 1635, they continued to use him as agent for their London business. In this capacity Sir William frequently sent to Harvey with detailed instructions regarding textiles. The letters both reveal the writer's specialist knowledge, and imply a similar expertise on the part of the recipient. On Calley's part this may have been gained in the course of his former profession as a cloth merchant. For Richard Harvey such ability is harder to account for, except as the knowledge appropriate to a well-informed seventeenth-century consumer. Thus, on 14 November 1640 Sir William wrote:

I wish these percelles of Linen bought & sent downe soe conveniently as you may viz:

63 elles of flaxen cloath or fine Rhoane Canvas that is somewhat more then ell broade of aboute ii s. per ell, but not above ii s.-vi d. per ell at the uttermoste.

54 elles of Rhoane Canvas of full yeard broade of xvi d. or xviii d. per ell at the uttermoste.

54 elles of strong Canvas yeard broade at xi d. or xii d. per ell at the moste.

20 elles of shippers holland of iii s.-iiii d., or iii s.-xi d. per ell at the moste.

Sixe dozen of holland diaper Napkins of 13 to the dozen & aboute xviii d. or xix d. per Napkin, & nine elles of diaper of the same sort for tabling which is to bee three tymes the breadth of the Napkins.

40 or 50 elles of strong narrow Slesia cloath of 6d. or 7d. per ell or there aboutes.[104]

Three weeks later Calley's requested cloth had arrived, and he reported to Harvey on the extent to which the fabrics met with his approval. The detail of his letter shows how active and critical was his role as a textile consumer.

> To tell you how I like the cloath I will as neare as I can; The holland diaper both Napkins & Tabling hold out measure, but I could have beene content the Napkins had beene all in one, and not two pieces, otherwise I like the price and cloath well enough and soe I doe all the rest for the prices, but especially the flaxen cloath had it beene in one piece or in more pieces soe they had fallen out fitte for the use I intended them and with all not wanted measure, but in stead of 63 elles I wrote for, you mention but 62½ elles to bee sent, and of this there wantes; for in the greater piece there is just 52½ elles a fitte patterne, and the other piece is but 7½ elles at most which should have beene 10½ elles and then it had beene right, but I would have you forbeare questioning the draper for his want of measure till you heare from mee againe, because I will cause it to bee measured over once more though it was measured at first as soone as it was opened. [105]

However the amount does seem to have been correct, for Sir William wrote again two weeks later. 'I caused my sonne to take exact notice of the measure of the flaxen Cloath, & now finde the same to bee 62½ elles as much as you sent it for, though there wants half an ell of what I wrote for.' [106] Note that it was his son to whom Sir William deputed authority in this matter of textiles, and not his wife or daughter-in-law.

Sir William's orders to Harvey also concerned clothes for himself, his household, and his adult son (also William). He was as knowledgeable and as particular in matters of dress as of cloth, and once again his agent needed similar judgement:

> Richard harvey
> My last sent you was of the 21th [*sic*] instant which was written late in the night with somwhat distempered mynde, whereby I fow[nd] I did not expresse my selfe in divers perticulers soe plainely as had beene fitte; for whereas I wrote you to buy 12 yardes of broade black perpetuana to make 3 suites for servantes I did not then expresse what you shoulde doe with yt; which 12 yardes I woulde have sent downe unmade up, for they that shall have yt, shall make yt up heere, as themselves liste; William Calleys new doublett coller was made an ynche to highe, and 2 ynches to narrow, and therefore the taylor shoulde have sent downe some peeces of the same cloth as allsoe of my coate & suite, to have amended any thinge which might have beene amisse, which [procure] him to doe [per] the nexte . . . Allsoe I desire you to buy mee a verry sad embrodered tawney girdle to suite with my last clothes you sent mee . . . For my mourninge cloth suite, I desire the doublett shoulde bee lyned with scarlett bayes, and the hose with white fustian; Allsoe I pray you buy a payre of very

good silke stockins for William Calley, to bee of suche cullor as may matche
with his laste suite, as you and the taylor shall thinke fitte.[107]

At the same time as this the capable Richard Harvey was also corresponding with William Calley junior, again with regard to Calley's own
clothing, and also that of his dependants:

> Concerning your patternes of kersey I cannot except against them unless it bee
> they are hardly fine, but rather then I wilbe unfurnished that shalbe noe
> hinderance; for my self I choose the patterne soe written xxxv as much as will
> make mee a large Coate & suite to which I would have pointes at the knees,
> buttons for both, & silke sowing & stithing [sic], and of leather linings a payre
> ready made; I purpose to have these thinges made up in the Cuntrey, Mr
> Davison shall make fine worke when I have it; one thing I had almost forgotten
> which was as much white thread shagge as will line my doublett; and this for
> my self is all; For my three sonnes as much of this patterne or of some neare
> the Colour of this [Span]ish cloath if you can gett any as will make them
> doubletts and breeches; which these appurtenances, Lambe skinnes for the
> linings of theyre breeches fustian for theyre doubletts, silke sowing & stitching
> and buttons at least fower dozen more then will serve turne; and this for them
> is all; now that you may knowe how much kersey will serve them; aboute
> Christmas last I made them & my self suites of one Cloath of sixe [ ] broade,
> wherein there was just 8½ yeards whereby Mr Davison can easily guesse what
> will now bee sufficient for them, allowing a yeard over & above for theyre
> growth since that tyme, for I had rather leaven then lacke.
> [Marginal note] Taffata for the facing of my doublett & pocketts.[108]

Perhaps most surprisingly for us, both William Calley senior and junior
also commissioned Richard Harvey to buy clothing and cloth for their
wives. While the women had stipulated what they wanted, Harvey had not
only to obtain this choice but also to decide, with the tailor, on styles,
fabrics, accessories and size. 'My Wiffe', wrote Sir William, 'desires you
to buy her as muche of the verry beste and Richest black flowred Satten,
of the beste worke, yett fitte for an antient wooman, as will make her a
straite boddied gowne . . . the laste boddes you sent her were verry fitte.'[109]
William Calley junior had further requests: 'a blacke sattaine gowne for
my wife, or a petticoate and wascoate which is most warne . . . but most
especially I intreate you not to referre the choosing of the sattaine to the
Taylor . . . alsoe a sett of knotts as may bee most suteable for a blacke
sattaine gowne'.[110]

Half a century earlier Philip Gawdy, residing in London, had similarly
supplied his mother, father, brother and brother's wife. Along with search-
ing out fabrics, trimmings and garments as requested, he offered his

opinion as to the quality of the purchases, and his observations of current fashionable trends. For example, to his sister-in-law Anne, for whom in 1587 he was procuring material, he wrote that, 'I can assure yow that bothe the quene, and all the gentlewomen at the Courte weare the very fashion of yo' tuff taffata gowne with an open wired sleve and suche a cutt, and it is now the newest fashion. For cappes and french hoodes I fynde no change in the world all whatsoever els you shall undoubtedly be provided of'. A year-and-a-half later, though, he had different news about court styles:

> I have sent yow downe according to your request half an ell of blacke velvett, half a quarter of white satten, and a paire of truncke sleeves. The pryce yow shall knowe hearafter. I have bought them as well and as good cheape as my skill might afford me, for the manner of wearing their hoodes as the courte. Some weare cripins some weare none. Some weare sattin of all collors with their upper border and some weare none. Some one of them weares this daye with all theise fashions, and the nexte daye without. So that I fynd nothing more certayne then their uncertaynty, which made me forbeare to sende yow any thing further of myne owne devise untill I heare further from yow.[111]

These letters from the Calley and Gawdy families, then, although unremarkable at the time, reveal a great deal of knowledgeable activity concerning dress. Far from being an area limited to or controlled by women, it seems that men participated with equal – if not greater – freedom and power. To do so they needed skills that most consumers today no longer have. The expertise required for the selection of fabrics, the devising of garments and the observation of fashionable styles also helps explain the power of clothing, in early modern society, to assert personality and character. When an individual's dressed image directly reflected his or her skills and creativity, it is no wonder that reputation was lodged so firmly in appearances.

In sixteenth- and seventeenth-century England, the phrase 'clothes make the man' was more than a rhetorical flourish. Individuals materialized an identity through the medium of dress, and this identity gathered meaning through being seen in the public domain. From our historical and cultural distance, it is easy to underestimate the seriousness of this proposition. To appreciate it more fully we need now to turn to the law. Through the almost forgotten acts and proclamations of apparel, early modern authority attempted to control access to appearances, and police the protean power of clothes.

Notes

1. *The Autobiography of Phineas Pett*, ed. by E.G. Perrin, Navy Records Society, 51 (1918), p. 6.
2. *Diary*, V, 269, 12 September 1664; V, 302, 21 October 1664.
3. Baldassare Castiglione, *The Book of the Courtier* (1528), trans. by Sir Thomas Hoby (1561), Everyman Library (London, 1928), pp. 117–18.
4. *The Diaries of Lady Anne Clifford*, ed. by D.J.H. Clifford (Stroud, 1990), p. 64.
5. *Memoirs of John Reresby*, ed. by Andrew Browning (Glasgow, 1936), p. 18.
6. *Memoirs of the Life of Colonel Hutchinson*, ed. by N.H. Keeble (London, 1995), pp. 51, 49–50.
7. *The Lives of William Cavendishe, Duke of Newcastle, and of his wife, Margaret Duchess of Newcastle*, ed. by Mark Antony Lower (London, 1872), pp. 303–4.
8. *The Diary of John Evelyn*, ed. by E.S. de Beer, 6 vols (Oxford, 1955), III, 478.
9. *Diary*, VIII, 186, 26 April 1667; VIII,196, 1 May 1667.
10. Joanne Finkelstein, *The Fashioned Self* (Cambridge, 1991), pp. 150–1.
11. *The Memoirs of Anne, Lady Halkett and Ann, Lady Fanshawe*, ed. by John Loftis (Oxford, 1979), p. 51.
12. *Memoirs of John Reresby*, pp. 20–1.
13. *Diary*, VII, 329, 18 October 1666.
14. *Diary of John Evelyn*, IV, 227.
15. *The Diary of Bulstrode Whitelocke*, ed. by Ruth Spalding, Records of Social and Economic History, new ser., 13 (London, 1990), pp. 99–100.
16. *Memoirs of Colonel Hutchinson*, p. 243.
17. Penelope Byrde, *The Male Image: Men's Fashion in England 1300–1970* (London, 1971), p. 68.
18. *Autobiography of Captain John Hodgson, of Coley Hall, near Halifax; His Conduct in the Civil Wars, and his troubles after the Restoration*, ed. by J. Horsfall Turner (Brighouse, 1882), pp. 57–8.
19. Christopher Durston and Jacqueline Eales, 'Introduction: The Puritan Ethos 1560–1700', in *The Culture of English Puritanism 1560–1700*, ed. by Christopher Durston and Jacqueline Eales (Houndmills, Basingstoke, 1996), pp. 1–31 (p. 1). This essay surveys recent attempts to adequately identify and define Puritanism.

20. Patrick Collinson, *The Puritan Character: Polemics and Polarities in Early Seventeenth-Century English Culture* (Los Angeles, 1989), p. 15.
21. Matthew Sutcliffe, *An Answere to a Certaine Libel Svpplicatorie* (London, 1592), p. 134.
22. *With Faith and Physic: The Life of a Tudor Gentlewoman Lady Grace Mildmay 1552–1620*, ed. by Linda Pollock (London, 1993), p. 45.
23. *The Autobiography of Mrs. Alice Thornton*, Surtees Society, 62 (1875), p. 270.
24. *Autobiography of Mary Countess of Warwick*, ed. by T. Clifton Croker, Percy Society, 22 (1848), pp. 4, 21.
25. *Letters of The Lady Brilliana Harley*, ed. by Thomas Taylor Lewis, Camden Society, 58 (London, 1854), p. 16.
26. *Autobiography of Alice Thornton*, p. 270.
27. *Lady Grace Mildmay*, pp. 28, 34.
28. *The Diary of John Manningham of the Middle Temple 1602–1603*, ed. by Robert Parker Sorlien (Hanover NH, 1976), pp. 114–15.
29. Sutcliffe, *An Answere to a Certaine Libel*, p. 108 (irregular pagination).
30. John Woolton, *The Christian Manual*, Parker Society, 41 (Cambridge, 1851), p. 90.
31. The transcription is included in Elizabeth Stern, 'Peckover and Gallyard, Two Sixteenth-Century Norfolk Tailors', *Costume*, 15 (1981), 13–23. Cypress was a very thin, gauze-like cloth; purl, a narrow lace made of silk with gold or silver thread; and oes were small rings of metal.
32. *Letters of Lady Brilliana Harley*, pp. 16, 50. Chamlet was a soft fabric whose silk weave included threads of a fine fleece such as chamois.
33. For the origins of the term, see Jacqueline Eales, *Puritans and Roundheads: The Harleys of Brampton Bryan and the Outbreak of the English Civil War* (Cambridge, 1990, pp. 143–7.
34. *Life of Colonel Hutchinson*, pp. 86–7.
35. J.T. Cliffe, *The Puritan Gentry* (London, 1984), p. 57.
36. William Prynne, *The Vnlouelinesse of Love-Lockes* (London, 1628), sig. A3ᵛ. Almost twenty years later Prynne again capitalized on the emotive pull of such issues in his political tract *A Gagge for Long-Hair'd Rattle-Heads who revile all civill Round-heads* (London, 1646).
37. Cliffe, *The Puritan Gentry*, p. 57.
38. *Winthrop Papers Volume 1 1498–1628* (Massachusetts, 1929), p. 227.

39. For discussions of the way appearances were used to identify and lambast other political and religious groups, see Tamsyn Williams, '"Magnetic Figures": Polemical Prints of the English Revolution', in *Renaissance Bodies: The Human Figure in English Culture c. 1540–1660*, ed. by Nigel Llewellyn and Lucy Gent (London, 1990), pp. 86–110; and David Cressy, 'The Adamites Exposed: Naked Radicals in the English Revolution', *Travesties and Transgressions in Tudor and Stuart England: Tales of Discord and Dissension* (Oxford, 2000), pp. 251–80.

40. *A Royalist's Notebook: The Commonplace Book of Sir John Oglander of Nunwell*, ed. by Francis Bamford (London, 1936), p. 241.

41. Penelope Corfield, 'Dress for Deference and Dissent: Hats and the Decline of Hat Honour', *Costume*, 23 (1989), 64–79 (p. 68).

42. *Lives of Duke and Duchess of Newcastle*, p. 189.

43. *Diary of Bulstrode Whitelocke*, p. 380.

44. *The Letters of John Chamberlain*, ed. by Norman Egbert McClure, 2 vols (Philadelphia, 1939), I, 375, 376–7. Letter to Sir Ralph Winwood, 10 August 1612 and Letter to Sir Dudley Carleton, 11 August 1612.

45. *Ceremonies of Charles I: The Note Books of John Finet 1628–1641*, ed. by Albert J. Loomie (New York, 1987), pp. 57–8.

46. *Diary*, II, 199, 20 October 1661; VI, 339, 26 December 1665; IV, 252–3, 27 July 1663.

47. *The Journal of George Fox*, ed. by John L. Nickalls (Cambridge, 1952), pp. 36–7. For further Quaker writings on the subject, see William Penn, *No Cross, No Crown: Or Several Sober Reasons against Hat-Honour* (London, 1669), esp. pp. 7–15.

48. *CSPD 1655*, p. 183, 25 May 1655; *CSPD 1657–8*, p. 156, 10 November 1657.

49. William Shakespeare, *The Winter's Tale*, IV, 4, 744–5.

50. 'The Memoirs of George Courthop', in *The Camden Miscellany 11*, Camden Society, 3rd ser., 13 (London, 1907), p. 135.

51. Frances Parthenope Verney, *Memoirs of the Verney Family*, 4 vols (London, 1892–9), IV, 249–50.

52. *Diary*, III, 116, 21 June 1662; IV, 357, 31 October 1663.

53. *Diary*, VI, 125, 11–12 June 1665; VI, 175, 31 July 1665. Ferrandine was a silk and wool mix.

54. *Diary*, IV, 130, 9 May 1663; IV, 290, 29 August 1663; IV, 343, 21 October 1663; IV, 350, 26 October 1663; IV, 357, 30 October 1663; IV, 358, 31 October 1663; IV, 362, 3 November 1663; IV, 363, 4 November 1663; IV, 369, 8 November 1663.

55. *Diaries of Lady Clifford*, p. 65.
56. *Diary*, IX, 201–2, 17 May 1668. All too often the apparent immedi-
    acy and candid nature of Pepys's diaries lure scholars into treating
    these sources as transparent recordings of the 'truth'. For an essay that
    helpfully reminds us that the diaries are consciously crafted texts, and
    subject to all the opacity that this entails, see Mark S. Dawson,
    'Histories and Texts: Refiguring the Diary of Samuel Pepys',
    Historical Journal, 43 (2000), 407–31.
57. *Diary*, IV, 400, 29 November 1663.
58. *The Batchelar's Banquet: or A Request for Batchelars: Wherein is
    prepared sundry daintie dishes to furnish their Table, curiously drest,
    and seriously serued*, in *The Non-Dramatic Works of Thomas Dekker*,
    ed. by Alexander B. Grosart, 5 vols (New York, 1963), I, 164. The text
    has been mis-attributed to Dekker.
59. *The Journal of Giles Moore*, ed. by Ruth Bird, Sussex Record Society,
    68 (1971), p. 119.
60. Ibid., p. 48.
61. Ibid., pp. 122–3.
62. *The Oxford Dictionary of English Proverbs* dates the phrase from
    1815.
63. *Journal of Giles Moore*, p. 27.
64. Patricia Fumerton, '"Secret" Arts: Elizabethan Miniatures and
    Sonnets', *Representations*, 15 (1986), 57–97 (p. 60).
65. The display of portraits in the long gallery and the composition of
    picture collections is discussed by Roy Strong in *The English Icon:
    Elizabethan and Jacobean Portraiture* (London, 1969), pp. 43–50.
66. Nicholas Hilliard, *A Treatise Concerning the Arte of Limning*, ed. by
    R.K.R. Thornton and T.G.S. Cain (Ashington, 1981), p. 86. John
    Peacock, 'The Politics of Portraiture', in *Culture and Politics in Early
    Stuart England*, ed. by Kevin Sharpe and Peter Lake (Houndmills,
    Basingstoke, 1994), pp. 199–228 (p. 211). Patricia Fumerton has
    addressed the ambiguity of the private/public nature of miniatures
    in 'Secret Arts'. On the political uses of portraits and their role
    in representing power and status, see Peacock, 'The Politics of
    Portraiture'.
67. Peter Stallybrass and Ann Rosalind Jones, *Renaissance Clothing and
    the Materials of Memory* (Cambridge, 2000), p. 38.
68. Janet Arnold, *Queen Elizabeth's Wardrobe Unlock'd* (Leeds, 1988),
    p. 15.
69. Edward Norgate, *Miniatura or the Art of Limning*, ed. by Martin
    Hardie (Oxford, 1919), p. 38.

70. *The Life of Edward, First Lord Herbert of Cherbury, Written by Himself*, ed. by J.M. Shuttleworth (London, 1976), p. 38.

71. *Diary*, VII, 85, 30 March 1666.

72. *Memoirs of the Verney Family*, I, 257, 258.

73. *The Journal of Nicholas Assheton*, ed. by F.R. Raines, Chetham Society, 14 (1848), pp. 7–8, 32, 34.

74. 'Extracts form Paul Hentzner's Travels in England, 1598', in *England as Seen by Foreigners*, ed. by William Brenchley Rye (London, 1865), p. 10.

75. *Diary*, III, 47, 16 March 1662; III, 50, 23 March 1662; III, 77, 4 May 1662. Despite Pepys's protestations that he would keep this livery for ever, time showed that even servants' garb was subject to the vicissitudes of fashion. In November 1668 he ordered another design of green lined with red, 'and it likes me well enough' (IX, 372).

76. *Diary of Bulstrode Whitelocke*, p. 361.

77. Thorstein Veblen, *The Theory of the Leisure Class* (New York, 1899), pp. 126–8; Quentin Bell, *On Human Finery: The Classic Study of Fashion Through the Ages*, rev. edn (London, 1976), pp. 138–54.

78. I. M., *A Health to the Gentlemanly Profession of Serving-Men 1598*, ed. by A.V. Judges, Shakespeare Association Facsimiles, 3 (1931), sigs D3^r–D4^v, D4^v.

79. *Diary of Bulstrode Whitelocke*, pp. 374, 363.

80. Martin Ingram, *Church Courts, Sex and Marriage*, p. 3.

81. *The Diary of Henry Machyn: Citizen of London, 1550–1563*, ed. by John Gough Nichols, Camden Society, 42 (London, 1847), p. 73.

82. F.G. Emmison, *Elizabethan Life II: Morals and the Church Courts* (Chelmsford, 1973), p. 282. Flora Johnston has written a fascinating article detailing the appearance and history of a penitential, or 'sack-cloth' gown in the collection of the Museum of Scotland. It belonged to the parish of West Calder, a small community in West Lothian, and appears to date from 1646, see Flora Johnston, 'Jonet Gothskirk and the "Gown of Repentance"', *Costume*, 33 (1999), 89–94.

83. Emmison, *Morals and the Church Courts*, p. 282.

84. *Diary of Henry Machyn*, p. 262.

85. The use of symbols in popular shaming practices such as charivari was also common. See, for example, Martin Ingram, 'Ridings, Rough Music and the "Reform of Popular Culture" in Early Modern England', *Past and Present*, 105 (1984), 79–113, esp. pp. 86–90.

86. *Diary of Henry Machyn*, p. 253.

87. Ibid., p. 156.

88. Ibid., p. 236.

89. Ibid., pp. 223, 122. Françoise Piponnier and Perrine Mane point out the potency of medieval punishments that inflicted a state of undress, see *Dress in the Middle Ages*, trans. by Caroline Beamish (New Haven, 1997), pp. 102–3.

90. J.A. Sharpe, '"Last Dying Speeches": Religion, Ideology and Public Execution in Seventeenth-Century England', *Past and Present*, 107 (1985), 144–67 (p. 146).

91. Clare Gittings, *Funerals in England 1580–1640: The Evidence of Probate Accounts* (unpublished B. Litt. thesis, University of Oxford, 1978), pp. 129–34.

92. See, for example, Roy Strong, *English Icon*, pp. 21, 35–7, 352–4; Bridget Gellert Lyons, *Voices of Melancholy: Studies in the Literary Treatments of Melancholy in Renaissance England* (London, 1971), p. 22; Michael MacDonald, *Mystical Bedlam: Madness, Anxiety and Healing in Seventeenth-Century England* (Cambridge, 1981), p. 130.

93. Robert Burton, *The Anatomy of Melancholy*, 6 vols (Oxford, 1989–2000), II, 238.

94. *Autobiography of Alice Thornton*, p. 319.

95. *Autobiography of Henry Newcome*, II, 299–300. The shirt was an undergarment generally only to be seen at the decorative edging of neck and wrist, or glimpsed through slashes in outer garments.

96. MacDonald, *Mystical Bedlam*, pp. 130, 131.

97. John Broadbent, 'The Image of God, or Two Yards of Skin', in *The Body as a Medium of Expression*, ed. by Jonathan Benthall and Ted Polhemus (London, 1975), pp. 303–26 (pp. 303–4).

98. *The Journal of Joachim Hane*, ed. by C.H. Firth (Oxford, 1896), pp. 40, 41.

99. *Memoirs of Colonel Hutchinson*, p. 19.

100. *The Memoirs of Robert Carey*, ed. by F.H. Mares (Oxford, 1972), pp. 70–71, 72.

101. John Harington, *Nugae Antiquae: Being a Miscellaneous Collection of Original Papers*, ed. by Thomas Park, 2 vols (London, 1804), I, 391–2.

102. William Shakespeare, *Much Ado About Nothing*, II, 3, 17–18.

103. *Barrington Family Letters 1628–1632*, ed. by Arthur Searle, Camden 4th ser., 28 (London, 1983), p. 252.

104. PRO, SP16/471/67.

105. PRO, SP16/473/56.

106. PRO, SP16/473/91.

107. PRO, SP16/458/10.

108. PRO, SP16/400/62.
109. PRO, SP16/392/15.
110. PRO, SP16/392/16.
111. *Letters of Philip Gawdy*, ed. by Isaac Herbert Jeayes, The Roxburghe Club, 148 (London, 1906), pp. 28, 49.

-4-

None Shall Wear

On 11 January 1591/2, an attorney by the name of Kinge appeared before the Privy Council. Kinge was 'presumptuous' and presented himself before their Lordships 'in apparrell unfitt for his calling, with a guilt rapier, extreame great ruffes and lyke unseemelie apparrell'. Presumably arrayed in his best, the unfortunate – or foolish – Kinge had dressed without regard for the acts and proclamations of apparel, and was in breach of the law. The Privy Council recommended that he be dismissed from his office and lose his job.[1]

Such regulation by law of what a person may or may not wear is, within the broad outlines of 'decency', today in the West considered an unacceptable infringement of individual rights. Yet from the fourteenth to the seventeenth centuries in England this legal constraint was deemed both necessary and desirable.[2] During the Tudor regime, especially, the regulatory project was pursued with particular energy, until by Elizabeth's reign we have reached 'an era of unprecedented activity in the history of restraints on apparel'.[3] However, in 1604 after the accession of the first Stuart king, all laws were repealed. Why, then, was there this particular trajectory to the control of dress in England, and what were the reasons behind Parliament and monarch so vigorously seeking to regulate its consumption and display?

Owing, perhaps, to the perceptual gulf that lies between modern and early modern thought on this matter, the historiography surrounding the official control of dress through sumptuary law is slight and, on occasion, slighting. G.R. Elton discussed two measures concerning apparel. The first he termed 'very peculiar' and 'a quirky little piece of paternalism'. The second, a statute making compulsory the wearing of caps for those under the rank of gentleman, he described as 'extraordinary'.[4] Similarly Lawrence Stone turned his attention to a bill concerning apparel debated in the Commons in 1614, which he described as 'absurd'.[5] Even N.B. Harte, who advocated the re-examination of the role of the acts of apparel in the pre-industrial economy, called this body of laws 'one of the most curious of all episodes in the history of social organisation'.[6]

Despite a recent trend towards the uncovering of early consumer culture, then, the attempted regulation of the consumption of apparel has, by and large, been overlooked. Indeed, if anything dress control has been dismissed as a false start on the march to modernity – an enterprise that, if only historical actors had the benefit of hindsight, they would have agreed was 'curious', 'absurd' and 'extraordinary'. However, firmly entrapped by their present, contemporaries regarded sumptuary legislation as a serious and sensible matter. So firstly, what were these laws, that though of serious intent at the time have been so relegated to the back-waters of historiographical interest and understanding? Secondly, why was this legal activity focused on clothing and, with a marked increase in urgency over the sixteenth century, seeking to regulate its display? Finally why, after such legislative commitment, was the project apparently abandoned so abruptly after 1604?

Dress and the Law

From the fourteenth to the seventeenth century there were nine major statutes relating to apparel.[7] The first appeared in 1337 and prohibited all but the most elevated of ranks from wearing fur and foreign cloth. In 1363 a more detailed act expanded on this theme, listing a greater number of social estates or occupations, and a larger number of prohibited textiles. Thereafter legislation became evermore complex, each act specifying more precise gradations in the social hierarchy and a more comprehensive schedule of disallowed fabrics. After 1363 a long legislative pause followed until major acts of apparel were passed in 1463 and 1483. Then came a flurry of Henrician regulatory activity with legislation in 1510, twice in 1515, and again in 1533. This last statute remained in force until its repeal in 1604 and, along with an additional act of 1554, became the backbone of a remarkable burst of Elizabethan regulatory fervour.[8] Elizabeth and her Privy Council's contribution to the control of apparel came chiefly through proclamation. Whereas Henry had issued five of these orders, Elizabeth issued a total of twelve, several of which instituted fundamental changes.[9] Elizabeth, however, was not the only Tudor monarch to show such an interest in the dress laws. Henry was personally responsible for portions of the second 1515 law,[10] and in 1552 Edward wrote a draft bill for apparel which probably provided the text for the measure introduced to the parliament of the same year.[11] Apparel was important business, and appropriate for the attention of the legislative assembly, and the crown.

Given the contemporary view that proclamations carried less weight than statute law – only fulfilling the legal equivalent of emphatic reminder or emergency measure – Elizabeth's rule of apparel by proclamation is extremely important. Since all the official attempts to obtain parliamentary legislation in this area failed, it might reasonably be assumed that the government had no choice but to turn to repeated proclamations. However, it seems from the chronology that the explanation is not this simple. In all but one of the cases, the proclamations pre-date the relevant bill, not the other way round.[12] It is more likely, therefore, that the government envisaged the proclamations as a preparation for statute law – a temporary measure to be strengthened by parliamentary authority.

Nor was the regulation of apparel by royal proclamation simply a de facto situation arising from the failure of proposed statutes. On at least two occasions the Crown sought to strengthen its legislative authority in this area by proposing proclamation as a *replacement* for statute law. In February 1576 a bill for the reformation of excess in apparel was introduced into Parliament. Notwithstanding the expressed concern that 'disorder of apparrell is very greate in this tyme', the bill met with strong resistance in the Commons.[13] There were five objections to the measure, the chief of which concerned the legislative power it would give the crown. For 'th'effect of the bill was that the Quene's Majestie from tyme to tyme might by her proclamacion appoynt what kynde of apparrell every degeree of persons within the realme should weare'. While the speakers judiciously pointed out that such a gracious sovereign would never offer an injustice, this 'might prove a dangerous precedent in tyme to come'.[14] The bill was rewritten and returned to the Lords, where it foundered apparently through lack of approval and time. The second attempt to extend royal prerogative came in 1604, when a bill was again sent from the Lords to the Commons. This measure contained the repeal of all former apparel laws, and the provision for the King to rule by proclamation. Such was the opposition to this provision, that it was rejected in the first reading. As a result the bill was rewritten, and only the clause rescinding dress control survived to become law. The accepted view is that the disappearance of clothing regulation was thus a reflection of political manoeuvring, and not a planned change of legislative direction.[15] That the regulation of dress was linked to matters of prerogative and constitutional power may be read as evidence of its contemporary seriousness. Certainly both Elizabeth and James sought personal control over this area, and just as certainly sections of the Commons resisted any inroads on their authority in this matter. To repeat, apparel was important business.

Economic Regulation

The first justification for the regulation of dress was economic. The motivations were paternalistic and sought to secure the financial health of both the realm and the individual. Legal restraints aimed to ensure that English wealth did not leave the country in exchange for foreign textiles and garments. Moreover, by placing limits on allowable personal expenditure, individuals would be less tempted to over-indulge in finery and thus better able to live within their means. This justification was frequently repeated. All the Henrician statutes made reference to 'the greate and costly array and apparrell used wythin this Realme', which has been 'the Occasion of grete impoverisshing of divers of the Kings Sugiects'.[16] Elizabeth's orders continued in the same vein. The argument was put most clearly in a proclamation from 1574:

> The excess of apparel and the superfluity of unnecessary foreign wares thereto belonging now of late years is grown by sufferance to such an extremity that the manifest decay not only of a great part of the wealth of the whole realm generally is like to follow (by bringing into the realm such superfluities of silks, cloths of gold, silver, and other most vain devices of so great cost for the quantity thereof as of necessity the moneys and treasure of the realm is and must be yearly conveyed out of the same to answer the said excess) but also particularly the wasting and undoing of a great number of young gentlemen . . . who allured by the vain show of those things, do not only consume themselves, their goods, and lands which their parents have left unto them, but also run into such debts and shifts . . . whereby they are not any ways serviceable to their country as otherwise they might be.[17]

A further economic argument concerned the protection of home industries. By outlawing the wearing of foreign fabrics and dress accessories the apparel laws aimed to manipulate consumer desire, and channel spending towards locally produced garments. If wearing imported dress was illegal, the demand for clothing could only be satisfied by home-grown fashions. A typical injunction, for example, forbade that any man 'under the Estate of a Duke Marquise Erle and their Children . . . weare in any parte of his apparell any Wollen Clothe made oute of this Realme of England Irlande Wales Calice Berwike or the Marches of the same, Excepte in Bonnettes only'.[18] It seems that campaigns to 'Buy British' have a long established precedent.

The economic beliefs behind all these measures are generally given the name of mercantilism.[19] This theory posits a model for fiscal health that would not be unfamiliar to Mr Micawber. To paraphrase the latter, if annual exports bring in reserves of bullion and currency, and annual imports do not expend it, then the result is happiness. To ensure this favourable balance of trade with more money flowing into the realm than out, a range of regulatory laws were passed, including those controlling dress. Later mercantile tracts came increasingly to advocate consumption as a key to prosperity, but sixteenth-century articulations of this theory were much less prepared to endorse its merits. The first of these, *A Discourse of the Commonweal of This Realm of England*, appeared in 1549. In this text attributed to Sir Thomas Smith, the author made a clear distinction between locally produced items of necessity, and foreign luxuries made 'to serve pleasure'.[20] Fine clothing, naturally, fitted squarely into the second category. Items such as perfumed gloves had to be eschewed because they cost 'inestimable treasure',[21] because they occasioned the decay of domestic industry, and because excessive apparel was morally corrupting. For Smith, 'suffering for fashion' would conjure not physical discomfort, but economic and spiritual peril. Written some eighty years later, although not published until 1664, was Thomas Mun's *England's Treasure by Forraign Trade*. Mun retained the distinction between foreign and domestic products, but separated the economic and moral argument. Advising that we 'soberly refrain from excessive consumption of forraign wares in our . . . rayment', Mun called for 'such good laws as are strictly practised in other Countries against the said excesses'.[22] If, however, the said excesses were the product of local labours, the situation was reversed: 'and if in our rayment we will be prodigal, yet let this be done with our own materials and manufactures, as Cloth, Lace, Imbroderies, Cutworks and the like, where the excess of the rich may be the employment of the poor'.[23]

For the next generation of mercantilists active in the 1680s–90s, even that distinction between foreign and local wares was spurious. All consumption was positive because it stimulated growth in the economy. It was morally bad for an individual to seek material increase, but it was economically good and, moreover, of benefit to society as a whole. In this context Sir Dudley North stated that sumptuary laws were harmful and rendered their nations poor, since 'Men by those laws are confin'd to narrower Expence than otherwise they would be'.[24] Entrepreneur, Nicholas Barbon, even identified fashion as being the chief promoter of the mercantile economy. It was 'the Spirit and Life of *Trade*' because 'it occasions the Expence of Cloaths, before the Old ones are worn out'.[25] While the call for renewed dress restrictions continued into the eighteenth century, the changing climate of economic opinion probably served slowly to isolate this view as old-fashioned and impractical. In the gradual acceptance of a developing mercantile theory that consumption promoted prosperity, laws restraining excessive apparel would appear as increasingly misguided, if not downright harmful.

Moral Regulation

Concomitant with these mercantilist concerns for economic well-being was a fear of the moral results of financial hardship. The legislation constructed the perils of impoverishment in two ways. Firstly – and with more than an echo of the modern hostility towards drug culture – it was feared that individuals who overspent on clothing would be forced to crime to support their 'habit'. So, those of the King's subjects who were ruined by their expensive apparel were 'provoked meny of them to robbe and to doo extorcion and other unlawfull Dedes to maynteyne therby ther costeley arrey'.[26] Sir Thomas Elyot, in his political treatise *The Governor*, evidently shared this concern. 'Howe many semely personagis', he asked, 'by outrage in . . . excess of apparaile / be induced to thefte and robbry / and some tyme to murdre / to the inquietation of good men / and finally to their owne destruction?'[27] In Elizabethan proclamations this complaint resurfaced. The 'pride that such inferior persons take in their garments' drive many 'for their maintenance to robbing and stealing by the highway'.[28]

While the inferior sort turned to crime to relieve their financial necessity, this same proclamation constructed a different response for their betters undone by excessive tastes in clothing. To them the measure attributed the second danger in impoverishment: 'the decay and lack of hospitality' so frequently bemoaned in the sixteenth and seventeenth centuries. A common topos in conduct literature, liberality was the duty and the sign of nobility. A Christian virtue, generosity had very practical application, providing for all and cementing together the different orders of society. But, according to the same texts, the generous host was an increasingly rare breed.[29] Proclamations are not the only sources in which a perceived decline of hospitality was linked to a perceived rise in ostentatious dressing. Smith's mercantilist tract of 1549 described the elaborate wearing of servingmen who 'go more costly in apparel . . . than their masters were wont to do'. This extravagance was not restricted as it should have been, but rather their masters vied to see whose retinue could be clothed most lavishly. Through such excesses 'they are fain all the rest of the year to keep the fewer servants'.[30] The author of *A Health to the Gentlemanly Profession of Serving-Men* felt similarly. 'Trust me,' he proclaimed:

> I holde this excessive costly Apparrell, a great cause why Gentlemen cannot maynteyne their wonted and accustomed bountie and liberalitie in hospitalitie & house-keeping: for when as the Mercers book shall come, *Item* for so many yardes of Cloth of Golde, of Silver, Velvet, Sattin, Taffata, or such lyke ware: the Goldsmithes *Debet*, for Chaynes, Ringes, Jewels, Pearles, and precious Stones: the Taylors Bill, so much for such a Sute of laced Satten, and such lyke superfluous charges, amounting in one yeere to more then the revenues of his Landes, the charge of house-keeping, and other necessaries undefrayde, how can he then chose but eyther make others Gentlemen by possessing his Inheritaunce, or els betake him to London, or some other sanctuarie, where he may lyve private so many yeeres, as he is runne overshooes, that debtes thereby may be payde, and defectes supplyed.[31]

Thus, the broadly economic cluster of beliefs thus shaded into concerns about crime and luxury. Lying behind the acts of apparel there also existed, however, a set of discourses which articulated moral values more overtly. In order to understand these it is necessary to look at wider contemporary views of the origins and purpose of dress. Clothing, or so received opinion ran, was necessary to hide nakedness. Moreover, this nakedness was not so much physical as spiritual. Early modern discovery of the New World had led to a burgeoning anthropological interest in which the apparel of indigenous people was noted keenly.[32] Despite what might be inclement conditions, sixteenth-century observers saw natives in simple and minimal dress.[33] This anthropological observation strengthened the pre-existing religious belief that clothing was a direct result of the Fall. Adam and Eve's nakedness first became apparent to them because of their sin, and clothing was thus a sign of our moral imperfections; a result and daily reminder of spiritual weakness. As legal student John Manningham reported, writing down the gist of a zealously delivered public sermon he heard: 'Pride in apparell is pride of our shame, for it was made to cover it, and as yf one should embroyder a sheete wherein he had done pennaunce, and shewe it in bragging manner.'[34] A proof of this was the 'noble savage', who existed in a pre-lapsarian and minimally clothed innocence. As Walter Hammond, in his description of the inhabitants of Madagascar wrote in 1640: 'Sin and apparel entered both together . . . it was our evil custom that cloathed us, and their Innocency and Freedom of Nature that keeps them naked.'[35]

The wearing of fine apparel was thus a two-fold immorality. It was not only evidence of pride – the chief of all vices – but it was taking pride in our morally flawed state. In this way vanity opened the well-dressed path to all sorts of graver sins: pride of apparel was the slippery slope to damnation. Thus a case of demonic possession that occurred in a gentry family was described in sartorial terms. Gripped by the spirit of pride, a thirteen-year-old girl expressed 'the proud women of our times: who can not content themselves with anie sober or modest attire, but are ever readie to followe every newe and disguised fashion'. Addressing the spirit, Margaret (or the narrator of these events), ran through the most flagrant forms of an aristocratic woman's wardrobe. In a catalogue of detail over two pages long, her demands included garments of silk and velvet, trimmed lavishly with gold lace; a farthingale 'low before and high behinde, and broad on either side'; a bodice stiffened with horn 'to keepe in my belly'; sleeves set out with wire; a rebato starched blue; orange hose; and 'corke shoes of redd spanish leather'.[36]

These beliefs in the immorality of fine clothing help explain certain recurring motifs in the dress laws. The statute of 24 Hen. VIII, c. 13 stated that excessive apparel led to the 'undoyng of many inexpert and light persones inclyned to pride moder of all vices'. It also provided a further link between excessive expenditure on clothing and crime, for the moral weakness of the one led to the depravity of the other. Thus, 'the pride that such inferior persons take in their garments driving many for their main-tenance to robbing and stealing by the highway'.[37]

Social Regulation

If the first reason for clothing was to cover physical and spiritual shame, its second purpose was, in Bourdieu's terms, distinction. In his critique of the social construction of aesthetics, Bourdieu maintains that 'taste' both makes different socio-economic categories distinct, and in modern society marks the bourgeois class as possessing distinction.[38] Clothing, in the early modern period, was expected to function in the same way. Apparel simultaneously defined the difference between certain groups and con-ferred the distinction of high status. In the words of Restoration author and Anglican cleric Richard Allestree, an 'end of Apparel is the distinguishing or differencing of persons'.[39]

The two key axes along which dress operated in a classificatory fashion were rank and gender. To take the latter case first: 'Our Apparell was given us as a signe distinctive to discern betwixt sex and sex, & therefore one to weare the Apparel of another sex, is to participate with the same, and to adulterate the veritie of his owne kinde'.[40] The biblical passage that the puritan Philip Stubbes draws on here is the Deuteronomic injunction so frequently quoted by contemporary polemicists. 'The woman shal not weare that which perteineth unto the man, nether shal a man put on womans raiment: for all that do so, *are* abominacion unto the Lord thy God.'[41] However – and this is of key importance – this particular belief about clothing is entirely absent from the acts of apparel.

Despite an increasingly virulent debate that developed from the latter part of the sixteenth century about the effeminating or masculinizing nature of certain modes of dress, the laws controlling clothing make no mention of it. No legislation prohibits articles of dress to either sex. This is not because transvestitism was so shocking as to be unthinkable. As we shall see in the following chapter, cross-dressing in the theatre was standard practice, and a standard target for anti-theatrical polemics. Furthermore, gendered change of apparel was a stock motif in many plays, and common in popular literature. It was even alluded to occasionally in real-life practice, perhaps most famously in James I's 1620 order to the London divines to preach against women dressing in mannish fashions. However, the laws and orders relating to dress reveal no concern about the role of clothing as a signal for gender. While early modern regulation of apparel did scrutinize certain social distinctions, it was *not* an apparatus for policing gender difference. Despite the language of fervent outrage employed by the polemicists, early modern civil authority did not perceive transvestism as such a danger to the social order.

The second operation of distinction worked along lines of rank:

> But then, Secondly, there is also a distinction of quality to be observed in apparel: God hath placed some in a higher condition than others; and in proportion to their condition, it befits their clothing to be, Gorgeous apparel, our Saviour tells us, *is for kings courts.*[42]

At this point we reach the heart of early modern control of dress. From the 1533 statute onwards, a central message of the legislative preambles is that the abuse of apparel has caused 'the subvercion of good and politike ordre in knowelege and distinccion of people according to their estates, pre-emynences dignities and degrees'.[43] While referring back to this statute, succeeding Elizabethan proclamations also made clear their hierarchical aims. To excessive apparel was due 'the disorder and confusion of the degrees of all estates (wherein always diversity of apparel hath taken place)'.[44] It has caused 'the confusion of degrees of all estates, amongst whom diversity of apparel hath been always a special and laudable mark'.[45] Again, sartorial indulgence has led to 'the confusion also of degrees in all places being great where the meanest are as richly appareled as their betters'.[46] Along with the economic and moral concerns over excessive apparel, this belief in its 'correct' social usage continued long after the disappearance of the acts and proclamations themselves. Thus, as late as 1668 the Lords' committee considering 'Sumptuary Laws, and the Fashions of Apparel', were also ordered to bear in mind 'the Distinction of Degrees of Persons by Habits'.[47]

However, even more noteworthy than this overt justification is the structure and content of the actual provisions. All legislation of this sort orders prohibited dress according to status. The Henrician statute that formed the basis of all sumptuary legislation until 1604 starts its provisions with the injunction that: 'No person or persones of whate estate dignitie degree or condicion so ever they be . . . use or were in any manner their apparell . . . any silke of the Collour of Purpure, ne any Clothe of Golde of Tissue, but onely the Kinge, the Quene, the Kinges Moder, the Kinges Children, the Kinges Brethern, and Systers and the Kinges Uncles and Auntes'.[48] Having started at the top of the social and textile hierarchy, the statute goes on to list increasingly inferior ranks and fabrics. Near the bottom of the provisions comes the order that: 'no husband man . . . weare in his hoses any Clothe above the price of the yarde, two Shillinges, or any Clothe in his gowne above the price of foure Shillinges the brode yard . . . . nor in his doublett any other thing than is wrought within this Realme, fustian and canvas onely excepted, nor any manner of furre in any his appareill'.[49] Alan Hunt, a legal scholar who has addressed sumptuary laws as legislative projects of governance, has called this ranking of social status 'appearential ordering'. In the increasingly urban and mobile societies of early modern Europe there was a perceived need to bring social appearance under control. In the anonymity of high population density and less rigid class boundaries, early modern lawmakers saw a threat to established order. The response was an attempt to fix individual identity, and make social appearance and social role conterminous. Given the dramatic changes to English social structure in the sixteenth and seventeenth centuries – with movement between social groups becoming increasingly easy and common, and the growth in the proportion of those belonging to the upper orders – this is certainly a powerful explanation for the energetic dress control of the period. As one scholar has written, 'the various Tudor sumptuary laws attempted to freeze into place the signs that established status and social identity'.[50]

The social milieu productive of a desire for appearential ordering is consistent with that which has been described as necessary for the development of fashionable dress. The classical definition of fashion describes it as a vestimentary system characterized by change. Far from being historically universal, it seems to be a phenomenon peculiar to Europe from about the fourteenth century onwards.[51] One explanation for the systemic nature of fashionable change derives from the theories of Thorstein Veblen, who analysed dress as an expression of pecuniary culture.[52] To summarize his argument, the leisure class wear clothing that, motivated by the canons of conspicuous waste and leisure, demonstrates their privileged status. According to the principle of Conspicuous Waste fashionable garments are rich and sumptuous; according to the principle of Conspicuous Leisure their design is in some way unsuitable for work activity. Thus, Veblen announces, the leisure class neatly displays its wealth and its exemption from labour. However, motivated by competitiveness, those from below seek to emulate the upper classes. In turn the upper classes, finding their sartorial customs copied, introduce a vestimentary change. Thus the fashion cycle turns, and in a society in which a rising middle class challenges the dominance of the group above, turns perpetually.

The trickle-down theory, then, explains fashion as the joint expression of status aspiration and status assertion. While the early modern apparel orders are informed by a number of economic and moral concerns, their desire to have people dressed 'correctly' according to their degree, is a response to Veblen's emulative struggle. While we might term it 'keeping up with the Joneses', in a sixteenth-century anecdote the antiquarian, William Camden (1551–1623), called it a 'proud humour . . . to be of the Gentlemen's cut'.[53] During the reign of Henry VIII, Sir Philip Calthrop bought some fine 'French tawney Cloth', and sent it to the tailor to be made into a gown. John Drakes, the town shoemaker, visiting the same tailor saw Calthrop's fabric. Liking it well he 'caused the Taylour to buy him as much of the same cloth and price to the same intent, and further bad him to make it of the same fashion that the Knight would have his made of'. Calthrop, returning to the tailor's for a fitting, saw Drakes's fabric lying ready and asked whose it was. 'Quoth the Taylour, It is John Drake's [*sic*], who will have it made of the self same fashion that yours is made of.' At this point Sir Philip ordered the tailor to slash his gown 'as full of cuts as the sheers can make it'. This ruse to depress pretensions was more effective than any act of apparel. The hapless John Drakes, when he finally saw his own gown in ribbons, cried that 'I will never wear Gentleman's fashion again'.

Deformity and Change

It seems then that state regulation of dress in England developed alongside the growth of elite fashion, both of them arising out of a particular social context. Indeed, close attention to the apparel orders reveals a developing awareness of fashion as a general phenomenon. The statute of 1463 was the first in which the general terms of the early modern ordinances was established. Excessive dress had become the focus of censure and the familiar moral and economic arguments invoked. The year 1463 also saw the first mention of a specific style, for no one under the estate of gentleman was to wear 'any gown, jacket, or coat, unless it be of such length that the same may cover his privy members and buttocks'.[54] In 1562 a proclamation protested at 'the use of the monstrous and outrageous greatness of hose, crept alate into the realm'.[55] The next year, and again in 1571, bills were brought to Parliament for the punishment of such as shall make or wear great hosen. The proclamation of 1562 also disapproved of 'the outrageous double ruffs which now of late are crept in'. Eighteen years later the complaint against ruffs continued, but this time was joined by a stricture against cloaks. Together, these items of dress were the focus of a separate section of the proclamation of 1580. This time a point of origin for the offending fashion was identified, albeit one that is difficult to reconcile with the proclamation that was issued eighteen years previously. Excessive cloaks and ruffs are both castigated as a 'monstrous manner of attiring' that 'had not been used before two years past'.[56]

The terms in which these complaints about fashionable dress were cast reveal two underlying cultural concerns: the distrust of novelty, and a fear of deformity. Firstly, this manner of attiring had 'not been used before two years past' – in other words, it was new and it represented change. In her study of clothing regulation in England, Frances Baldwin briefly advanced the proposition that one motivating factor was simply conservatism and dislike of novel styles.[57] As far as it goes this may have been true, for throughout the centuries representatives of the established order have looked askance at new, 'shocking' modes and methods of wear. A structuring element in the process of fashion, resistance – and sometimes outrage – accompany the introduction of a new style. Moreover, it is this initial resistance which defines novelty, for it signals a break with that which has gone before. In Elizabethan society, however, change could have more serious implications. In a world created by an Unmoved Mover, inconstancy only entered after the Fall. Representing sin and decay, 'the ever-whirling wheele / Of *Change*' governed a world spinning further and further from God's purpose.[58]

The place of origin for these new, offending styles was always sited at a distance. They were foreign and 'other'; they had but 'crept alate into the realm'. Crediting – or blaming – foreigners for the invention of fashion fitted very neatly with mercantilist fears of the loss of domestic wealth.

Luxury items of dress, for which good English currency was exchanged, come from overseas. For evidence of this one had only to look at the names of the newfangled devices: Spanish farthingales, Venetian hose, Dutch slops, French hoods. Of course, by implication the morally suspect inventiveness of foreigners was matched by an equal moral laxity on the part of the English. Foreign fashions only entered the realm because, so every commentator maintained, the English were slavish copiers of trifling frivolity. As the writer Henry Peacham mused: 'I have much wondered why our English above other nations should so much dote upon new fashions, but more I wonder at our want of wit that we cannot invent them ourselves.'[59]

The second fear that the prospect of newly styled ruffs and hose awoke was the spectre of deformity. These outrageously large garments were a 'monstrous manner of attiring' that altered the body's 'true' and God-given shape. The early modern horror at (and almost prurient interest in) deformity, was the counter-image of the pursuit of moderation. Entering Western culture with classical writers, the ethic of moderation and pro-portion was a touchstone of sixteenth- and seventeenth-century thinking. The definition of physical beauty, proportion was also the rule of virtuous living; and in a period in which there was held to be a sympathy between physical and moral qualities, the one reinforced the other. For, 'The Affections of the Mind are made known by nothing so well, as by the Body.'[60] Conversely the same held true for the body and soul deformed. 'Well did *Aristotle* . . . call sinnes Monsters of nature, for as there is no Monster ordinarily reputed, but is a swelling or excesse of forme, so is there no sinne but is a swelling or rebelling against God.'[61] Naturally it was easy to forge a link between deformity and clothing, for not content with God's workmanship, the fashionable dresser 'hast contended, to bee a more beautifull Creator and repolisher of thy selfe, then hee'.[62] Thus, in a neatly circular model excessive clothing deformed the body, which in turn indicated spiritual malaise, which unhealthily hankered after exces-sive clothing. For the puritanical Stubbes, fashionable apparel actually dehumanized the wearer: 'For most of our novell Inventions and new fangled fashions, rather deforme us then adorne us: disguise us, then become us: makyng us rather, to resemble savauge Beastes and stearne Monsters, then continent, sober and chaste Christians'.[63] While undoubt-edly a powerful metaphor, at its most extreme early modern thought literalized the link between fashion and monstrosity. In 1617 William Jones, in warning his readers, related the tale of a pregnant woman given to wearing ruffs. Afterwards she gave birth to a child with 'a peece of flesh of two fingers thicke round about, the flesh being wonderfully curled like a Gentlewomans attire'.[64] Also from James I's reign comes a ballad entitled 'Pride's Fall', another cautionary tale. The narrator's whole passion and desire is for fine clothing but to her horror, when brought to bed of a child, 'my swelling womb / Yielded up nature's due, / Such a strange monster then, / Surely man never knew.' The baby had two elegantly painted and coiffured heads, held in its hand a mirror, had feet decorated with pinking and rosettes like fancy shoes, and about its neck flaunted a ruff. In short, 'From the head to the foot, / Monster-like was it born, / Every part had the shape / Of fashions daily worn.'[65]

However, despite physical and moral drawbacks the blandishments of fashion were too seductive, and the apparel proclamations acknowledged the inevitability of change and innovation in dress. While summarizing and repeating the 1533 statute, three of the Elizabethan regulations admitted that some of the original provisions had become inappropriate due to the passage of time. Therefore her Majesty:

> hath not only added by these presents such favorable tolerations and quali-
> fications to such points of the former laws now standing in force as by altera-
> tion of time may seem in some part hard to be exactly observed, but also hath
> commanded the due execution of those parts of those laws that be most
> agreeable to this time and easy and necessary to be observed.[66]

Moreover, sartorial change was not merely a consequence of the passing of time, but could be introduced by such individuals as 'devise any new kind or form of apparel'.[67] The proclamation was quick to point out that if the new fashion was 'at greater charge than appertaineth to his degree' then the offender would be in contempt of the law 'as if the said garment or garnishes had been especially prohibited'.[68] However, if the change was appropriate to an individual's rank then a certain licence of innovation was permissible. 'And if any person should be disposed for his ability to cut and garnish the outside of his hose with anything that he may lawfully wear, for the plucking out betwixt the panes and cuts, he shall be so suffered to do.'[69] Whether flouting the laws or remaining within them, it seems that by the end of Elizabeth's reign changing fashionable dress was an accepted – though not necessarily desirable – inevitability.

Far from being perverse or unreasonable, then, the Tudor apparel orders were a response to underlying concerns about economic hardship, social dysfunction and immorality. In passing such laws, early modern government hoped to right the balance of trade and sustain home industry, and simultaneously keep society well ordered and the streets safe to walk. Moreover, by asserting a visual control over its members the community at large might be protected from duplicitous individuals who seemed – or dressed – to be other than they were. Returning for a moment to the hapless attorney Kinge, his 'guilt rapier' and 'extreame greate ruffes' did not merely represent sartorial misjudgement. Rather they raised before the Privy Council the spectre of poverty, lawlessness, monstrosity and social chaos. Moreover, this was a spectre that continued to haunt early modern consciousness long after the apparel orders disappeared from the statute books.

Discipline and Display

The acts and proclamations of apparel and the reasoning behind them, however, represent only part of the story of dress control. A closer look at the wording of the apparel orders clarifies their intent still further. It was not sumptuous dress *per se* that was prohibited, but its display. The rubric of the proclamations did not forbid the owning of rich apparel. Instead the constantly reiterated injunction orders that 'none shall *wear*' (my emphasis). Excess of apparel was construed as a public offence. In this section, then, we will move in from the contexts to reinterpret the texts themselves, in order to discover just whose display of clothing was under surveillance, and where. In doing so, it becomes apparent there is a certain disjunction between the overt aims of the orders and their actual provisions. Three of the Elizabethan proclamations state that abuse of apparel is found mostly among 'the meaner sort'.[70] Yet despite this clear identification of the offending sector of society, the proclamations all but ignore the lower orders in their prescriptions. Instead they clarify, summarize and repeat the provisions of 24 Hen. VIII c. 13 for those near the top of the social hierarchy. Anyone interested in more detailed information is merely referred to the 1533 statute. Despite a rhetoric castigating the socially inferior, the chief legislative target – and site of sartorial struggle – was located within the upper orders.

More specifically still, Elizabeth's proclamations of 1574 and 1588 both made reference to the young as being most liable to extravagance in apparel. The former stated that excessive expenditure on clothing had caused 'particularly the wasting and undoing of a great number of *young* gentlemen'.[71] The latter preamble was even more pointed. The Lord Chancellor commanded 'the heads, ancients, and principals of houses of court and Chancery' to see to execution of the order because the 'excess was noted to be more largely of late years spread amongst the youth there than in any other place of England'. Further down, 'the two universities of Cambridge and Oxford, where this infection was seen to have made entry amongst the youth', shared the opprobrium.[72] It is helpful to read this identification of young men and specific sites of infringement in conjunction with observations about the universities and Inns of Court. By the latter part of the sixteenth century most of the gentry sons were sent to either or both of these institutions. Attendance was a necessary step for social advancement, and not only because of the formal curriculum. Rather, it offered the means 'to those who sought to achieve for themselves the styled identity specific to the governing class'.[73] In these 'finishing schools' for the court and positions of influence, self-presentation was serious business. The wearing of fine apparel was simultaneously 'proof' of high status and an indicator of aspiration towards it. Young men attended these places of education in part – to put it crudely – to learn how to dress. Cleric and scholar William Harrison, in his survey of contemporary England felt justified in complaining that, 'being for the most part either gentlemen, or rich mens sonnes, they oft bring the universities into much slander, for standing upon their reputation and libertie, they ruffle and roist it out, exceeding in apparell, and banting riotous companie'.[74]

Innumerable contemporary texts made very clear the discursive link between aspirant young men and their clothing. Satire scathingly described gallants and roaring boys as vain, shallow youths who owed their standing to the unremunerated skill of their tailor. Thomas Nashe, in *The Anatomie of Absurditie* (1589), criticized youths who frittered away their patrimony, 'casting that away at a cast at dice, which cost theyr daddes a yeares toyle, spending that in their Velvets, which was rakt uppe in a Russette coate'.[75] In his collection of character sketches published in 1628, John Earle was more cutting still. An idle gallant:

> Is one that was born and shaped for his clothes: and if Adam had not fallen, had lived to no purpose. He gratulates therefore the first sin, and fig leaves that were an occasion of bravery [fine clothing]. His first case is his dress, the next his body, and in the uniting of these two lies his soul and its faculties . . . He is one never serious but with his tailor, when he is in conspiracy for the next device.[76]

Nor is this linkage of youth and fine clothing found only within satirical contexts. Religious advice and conduct manuals frequently warned of the sartorial temptations to which young men typically succumbed. Yet despite the censure of such conduct, advice books also stressed the importance for them of appropriate clothing. While eschewing excess, they should dress with propriety and 'comeliness' as befitting their station. James Cleland, the author of *The Institution of a Young Nobleman*, modestly advised that, 'in your garments be proper, cleanely, and honest, weareing your cloathes in a carelesse, yet a comelie forme'.[77] The influential conduct book *Galateo* urged its readers, within the constraints of rank and current fashion, to make the most of their garments and find a personal style:

> Your apparell must be shaped according to the fashion of the time . . . Every man may applie those fashions, that be in common use, the moste to his owne advantage, that he can . . . But, whatsoever it be thou wearest, let it be fit and well made for thy bodie: least thou seme to brave it, in another mans cloathes. But with all, thou must in any case respect thy condition or estate.[78]

Baldassare Castiglione's classic work on courtiership proposed an even more self-conscious manipulation of the dressed image. As we saw in the preceding chapter, a courtier 'ought to determine with him selfe what he will appeare to be, and in such sort as he desireth to be esteemed, so to apparrel himselfe, and make his garments helpe him to bee counted such a one'.[79] This somewhat contradictory set of ideas regarding 'appropriate' apparelling, indicates the existence of a belief that it was young men particularly who dressed for success/excess.

In so far looking at the provisions of dress legislation we have been considering those who were the target of regulatory activity. However, along with prohibitive injunctions the acts of apparel also listed categories of people exempt from such provisions. As with every other aspect of these laws, the appended provisos grew increasingly minute and complex. Certain categories of licence were expanded, others were newly created, and some slipped from the status of exemption to become the focus of surveillance. What can a look at those people placed at least partially outside the regulatory reach tell us about the early modern desire to control clothing?

The first category of person to which the laws on apparel gave complete licence were ambassadors and those foreign nobles on a short visit to the realm. Clearly the latter were outside the normal bidding for influence and favour – the sort of power brokerage in which dress played an indeterminate, but nonetheless vital part. The former, as representatives of foreign princes, embodied the status of that monarch and had therefore to dress accordingly. As author Thomas Nashe put it: 'If any Noble-man (though never so high discended) should come alone to a King or Queene in Embassage, without pompe, without followers, or the apparraile of his state, who woulde receive him, who woulde credite him, who would not scorne him?'[80] In a symbolism of simultaneous exchange, then, the glory of royalty required the ambassadors to clothe richly; the rich clothing in turn conferred glory. The partial exemption for officials and those engaged in duty operated in a similar way. Obviously it was the position and not the individual person for which the dispensation was granted, a dispensation with which even Stubbes agreed:

> The majestrats also, & Officers in the weale publique, by what tytle soever they be called (accordinge to their abylities) may were (if the Prince, or Superintendent do Godly commaund) costlie ornaments and riche attyre, to dignifie their callings, and to demonstrat and shewe forth, the excelency, and worthines of their offices, and functions.[81]

Those who participated in the pageantry that helped define and cement the upper echelons of Tudor society, were also exempt from sartorial prohibition. Clearly if 'any Henche man, Herald, or Purcevaunt at Armes, Mynstrels, Plaier in interludes sightes revels justes turneis bariers solempne Watches or other marciall feates or disguysinges' were denied elaborate dress, then the whole ritual would fail.[82] In all the above cases the utilization of sumptuous dress was necessary to the established order, and not a threat.

The other major area of licence – those engaged in war – provides an unexpected moment of slippage in the official controls on apparel. Although men, particularly in their youth, were the chief target of dress regulation, here is a situation in which their indulgence in this vanity was not only tolerated, but thought appropriate. As Sir Edward Coke argued in the debate concerning the 1628 bill of apparel, 'That the soldier, whose bravery [fine clothing] is his honor, may be excluded', and 'let him be gallant'.[83] In his study of art and war in Renaissance Europe, J.R. Hale spends some time exploring the iconography of the soldier. In northern European art particularly, the standard image played with flashy dress worn extravagantly. In the absence of uniform, clothing of this sort operated as the young fighter's identifying characteristic, 'and no other costume was regularly portrayed with such care and glee as the deliberately provocative and rakish garb of the soldier'.[84] Early sixteenth-century England's involvement with this image was not expressed through graphic art, but in stylized pageantry – the sort of occasion so famously portrayed at The Field of Cloth of Gold. By Elizabeth's reign such tourneys and 'war theatre' had become highly ritualized – and politicized – sites of display. At the Accession Day tilt of 1590, for example, George Clifford took over from Sir Henry Lee as the Queen's Champion. He was dressed for the occasion as the Knight of Pendragon Castle. An account of the tournament described him as, 'woorthie Cumberland / Thrice noble Earle, aucutred as became / So greate a Warriour and so good a Knight'.[85] In conjunction with a surviving portrait almost certainly depicting his costume for this event, we can glimpse the early modern gallant in his 'marciall disguysinges' (Figure 22). It is an image in which self-conscious sartorial

Figure 22 George Clifford, 3rd Earl of Cumberland, George Perfect Harding (1781–1853), after Nicholas Hilliard (1547–1619), *c.* 1590. By courtesy of the National Portrait Gallery, London.

display is paramount, illustrating the accepted view that 'decent apparell, and fit ornaments of body, do become all military commanders'.[86]

However, it is possible to push the texts further on this matter of who was, and was not, implicated by the acts of apparel. The most obvious point – but virtually overlooked – is that unlike European clothing regulations, the core provisions of the Tudor dress laws applied only to men. The earlier acts of 1337, 1363 and 1463 had all included women under the regulations for their husbands and fathers. The act of 1483 mentioned only the wives of servants and labourers. By dramatic contrast the first Henrician statute (1510) repealed all former acts, and specifically exempted women. When repealed in its turn the overt freedom of women disappeared, however the superseding statutes maintained a tacit exemption. The 1533 law (as also those of 1515 and 1510) expressly ordered that no *man* under any given estate was to wear or use a particular type of fabric. The use of 'man' is not generic, for it contrasts with the one differently worded clause that did mention women. The provision opens with the order that no 'person' is to wear royal textiles except the King and the King's family. The itemized list of royal relations includes the Queen, and the King's mother, sisters and aunts. No other clause mentions women, and no other clause has a gender-inclusive preface. Despite the contemporary presence of a moralizing discourse that overwhelmingly associated luxury with the feminine, the laws regulating luxurious dress concerned men.[87] The disjunction of the two positions is considerable. How are we to reconcile the female object of moral debate about luxury with the juridical identification of men as the transgressors? It seems that this targeting of the male must be viewed as an aspect of the regulatory desire to control clothing in the public sphere.

Surprisingly, to date no more detailed explanation has been offered. While it may have been acceptable in 1970 for Stanford Lehmberg to presume that not even a Tudor parliament 'dared interfere with so delicate a subject as feminine fashion',[88] clearly more recent historiography requires a different story. Alan Hunt comes closer to the issue by suggesting 'it could just have been that it was quite literally men's conspicuous consumption that was conceived of as "the problem"', but shies away again by continuing, 'there is no direct evidence to support this interpretation'.[89] Hunt is right that there is very little information about the marginal position of women in the English dress laws, but such a striking omission so at odds with wider cultural attitudes can not be glossed over. According to the interpretation I am offering, in the legislative sphere male and female use of dress was in some way deemed to be different. My contention is that this perceived difference did not reside in how clothing was used, but where. The early modern acts of apparel were concerned with the manipulation of dress in public and predominantly male sites of influence: the Inns of Court, the universities, and that most important of spheres where the elite vied for standing, the court. However, in 1574 an Elizabethan proclamation changed the situation entirely. Suddenly, and without explanation, women were included in apparel regulations.[90] Moreover, rather than being merely subsumed under the equivalent male status category, female dress was given its own separate and itemized schedule. Thereafter all Elizabethan regulation was extended to cover women as well. Why should there have been this dramatic change in policy?

Firstly, Elizabeth's passion for dress was constantly noted by contemporaries and has been commented upon by every succeeding generation. As the cleric, Thomas Fuller, announced looking back a half-century later, 'She much affected rich and costly apparel; and if ever jewels had just cause to be proud, it was with her wearing them'.[91] Aside from undoubted personal pleasure, Elizabeth also gained political mileage from her fashionable magnificence. In her construction of the image of queenship, clothing was fundamental.[92] In putting Elizabeth's personal utilization of dress together with the female composition of her court, we may come close to the agenda of the later dress orders. Discussing the Elizabethan royal household, Pam Wright has concluded that the role of women was different in the court of a regnant queen.[93] Due to their access to the monarch, the female members of Elizabeth's Privy Chamber had a greater power than would normally be the case. These female courtiers did not take direct part in high politics, but had close contacts with those who did. Their importance in matters of patronage and favour was greatly increased. Simon Adams, in his study of Elizabethan court politics, comes to a very similar conclusion. Furthermore, he cites ambassadorial comments on the prominence of women at diplomatic receptions, and suggests that this might possibly have been a result of the monarch's gender.[94] It was in the Elizabethan court, then, that women were enabled access to the spheres of influence for which men dressed to succeed. It seems likely that competing in the same stakes, they should have been subject to the same rules.

This inclusion of the clothing of elite women within the scope of legal surveillance did not occur immediately. Rather it appeared towards the middle years of Elizabeth's reign, in the middle years of her life. Always pronounced, her sensitivity to rivals of all sorts was becoming extreme. By the 1570s her opposition to the marriage of her intimate circle was well known, an attitude that has led subsequent commentators to note her 'vanity' and 'sexual jealousy' almost as often as her penchant for extra-vagant dress. Self-consciously attired to be the symbolic centre of a predominantly male court, Queen Elizabeth was highly attuned to the political/sartorial threat of a younger generation:

> The Queen hath of late much annoyance from the Lady Mary Howard, one of her ladies-in-waiting . . . The Lady Howard hath offended also in attiring her own person overfinely, which is rather to win my Lord of Essex than of good will to her Mistress. The lady is possessed with a rich border powdered with gold and pearl, and a velvet suit belonging thereto which hath moved many to envy; nor hath it pleased the Queen who thought it exceeded her own. Where-fore the Queen sent privately and got the lady's rich vesture, which she put on herself and came among the ladies. The kirtle and border were far too short for her Majesty's height and she asked everyone how they liked her new fancied suit. At length she asked the Lady Mary herself if it was not made too short, and ill-becoming; to which the poor lady did consent. 'Why then,' quoth the Queen, 'if it become not me as being too short, I am minded it shall never become thee as being too fine; so it fitteth neither well.' By this sharp rebuke the Lady Howard is abashed and hath not adorned her herewith sithence.[95]

Perhaps most importantly, this period also saw the emergence of other techniques of political control. In the face of the increasing unlikelihood of Elizabeth marrying, or at least producing heirs, 'political stability and confidence required some definition of the attributes of female monarchy and representation of the focal issues of loyalty'.[96] The iconization of Elizabeth had begun. The strategies of production for the cult of Gloriana are familiar: poetics, pageants and portraiture. No longer appearing in realistic surroundings, Elizabeth starred in such allegorical roles as imperialist ruler, vestal virgin, or classical goddess.[97] The official image was also replicated for the wider public – approved woodcuts and engravings in which Elizabeth was for ever youthful.[98] This, in stark contrast to the edict that made mass produced portraits of the nobility illegal – a strategy for maintaining political dominance through dominance of representation.[99] If, for policy's sake, the presentation of the graphic image was more closely controlled, why should the second half of Elizabeth's reign not also have witnessed an equivalent watch over the sartorial image?

Looking at the inclusions and exclusions of the apparel orders, tells us then about the regulatory project's desire to control the display of clothing in the public realm. In the targeting of young men we can see the import-ance of dress as a commodity rich in cultural capital, manipulated by aspirant youths of the upper orders on the road to advancement. Similarly the exemption of those who, like heralds and soldiers, participated in the theatre of state, brings into focus the way the established order also utilized dress as an expression and assertion of power. The 1574 shift in which women were gathered into the regulatory reach was thus clearly more than a crude equation of femininity with fashion. Instead, linked to the strategies of representation of the ageing regnant Queen, it was a ploy in a power struggle waged through court politics. However, one problem remains. If, even in the early Elizabethan parliaments, the control of dress was more approved of in principle than in practice, how effective was this legislation? Were the acts of apparel obeyed and enforced, or were infringements a matter of tacit acceptance? In short, what was the authoritative status of the early modern laws controlling dress?

Doomed to Failure?

It is a truism amongst scholars that sumptuary legislation was not effective. Indeed, as the historiographical comment at the beginning of this chapter suggests, there is a 'persistent Whiggish presumption that sumptuary law was "doomed to failure", that it was unenforceable and indeed was not enforced. In the simplest terms the conventional view is that sumptuary laws were essentially silly and deserved to fail, and provide subsequent commentators with a means of feeling superior that today we know better and no longer try to regulate such matters.'[100] However, in fairness to such latter-day commentators, many early moderns also remarked on the ineffectiveness of dress controls. As an epigram of Sir John Harington quipped: 'Our zealows preachers that would pride repress / Complain against Apparrells great excess; / For though the lawes against yt are express, / Each Lady like a Queen herself doth dress, / A merchaunts wife like to a barronness.'[101] Or in the words of Bishop Latimer, one such 'zealous preacher': 'There be lawes made and certaine statutes, how every one in his estate shall be apparelled but God knoweth the statutes are not put in execution.'[102] There are two observations that lie behind the modern dismissal of apparel orders. The first is a marked lack of evidence of enforcement.[103] The second observation concerns the wording of the acts and proclamations, and their constant repetition. For in their preambles these orders bemoan the continuing abuse of apparel and the non-compliance of the population in defying earlier laws; and the frequency with which new orders appeared, and repeated themselves, contains a tacit admission of failure.[104]

Tempting as it is to accept this at face value, Hunt, from his revisionist position, warns us against such easy assumptions. To think so is to fall into the trap of equating the enforcement of a law with its validity and significance.[105] Bearing this in mind, let us return to the dress laws and consider their main techniques of discipline. Firstly, JPs, sheriffs and other legal officials were empowered, and urged, to administer and enforce the law. Secondly, the offending apparel was to be forfeit to the crown, and in addition a system of fines imposed. Half of this revenue was to go to the state, and the other half either to the enforcing officers, or any informing individual who had brought information against the offender. Thirdly, the laws made clear the responsibility that all those in authority had over their subordinates in this matter. This was particularly true for heads of households, who were enjoined to regulate the clothing of their dependants. In the case of masters turning a blind eye to apparel abuses committed by their servants, then the former were liable for an extra fine. Fourthly, a system of watchers was to be imposed in wards, suburbs, towns and institutions. These 'substantial and well-meaning men' were to survey the dress of the population, and arrest those clothed contrary to the laws.[106] Lastly, tailors and hosiers were to enter into a bond. Subject then to regular searches, if they were discovered supplying abusive styles, they forfeited their money.

From these provisions certain implications are immediately apparent. For a start, most of them rely on there being a widespread knowledge of fabrics and fashion styles among the community at large. To sum up the costume of a servant, neighbour or passer by, and assess it as to value and composition, would necessitate a very particular awareness. Not only for arresting officials would this knowledge be requisite, but also for heads of households, legal officers and informing individuals. This 'dress competence' is matched by the imposition of a system of surveillance, whereby citizens monitored not themselves but each other. Sumptuary regimes rested on 'a strong sense that one's neighbour's business was one's own'.[107]

Implicit, however, within such overlooking is a problem of status. Given especially that the dress laws were aimed primarily at abuses of apparel in the upper orders, a situation develops in which relatively lowly officials had to challenge, and possibly seize, those of a more elevated rank. Contemporaries were aware of this, and many were unhappy about it. As we have seen, the House of Commons, for example, objected repeatedly to proposed statutes that gave power to any officer 'were he never so inferior', and saw in such provisions a threat to their own privilege. Moreover, this manner of execution, Sir Walter Mildmay objected, would prove 'comberous and quarrellous, and sometymes injurious'. For officers could easily light on men 'though unknowne to them' yet of sufficient standing to wear 'thoes garmentes as they challenge', and this 'must of necessity breed great contention and strife'.[108] Their concerns about violent altercations ensuing from such a clash of authorities seem to have been well founded, for the Earl of Surrey's brother is reported to have drawn upon the watchers who challenged him for wearing a ruff of excessive dimensions.[109] In the midst of tangled and competing lines of influence, regulation of the appearance of the elite was never likely to prove successful. As scholar Roger Ascham, at one time tutor to the Queen, sadly remarked: 'I know, som greate and good ones in Courte, were authors, that honest Citizens of London, should watche at everie gate, to take misordered persones in apparell. I know, that honest Londoners did so: And I sawe, which I sawe than, & reporte now with som greife, that som Courtlie men were offended with these good men of London.'[110]

The House of Commons was also uneasy about the honesty of enforcing JPs, worrying at a tendency to corruption and self-interest that led to the unjust prosecution of some cases, and the equally unjust dismissal of others.[111] As early as 1531 Sir Thomas Elyot had argued along similar lines. Speaking of, among other laws, those for 'reducinge apparaile to convenient moderation and temperance', he asked 'howe many p[ro]-clamations thereof have ben divulgate / and nat obayed? Howe many commissions directed / and nat executed?' For which he blames those in authority who, when they 'beholdeth the transgressor, a seemly personage, also to be his servant, acquaintance, or a gentleman born . . . preferreth the offender's condition or personage before the example of justice, condemning a good and necessary law, for to excuse an offense pernicious and damnable'.[112] In those instances of prosecutions that have come to light, these concerns would seem to have been well founded. Despite the main thrust of the orders being directed against the gentry classes, it was against those of a lower estate that proceedings seem most often to have been taken. Thus Richard Bett, a tailor of Stanford Rivers in Essex, was fined in 1565 for using 'his hose with great slops contrary to the proclamation'. In 1568 three tailors from Great Dunmow, also in Essex, were similarly charged.[113] Again, offending by wearing 'a very monsterous and outraygous greate payre of hose', London servant Richard Walweyn was arrested in 1565.[114] When those of a more elevated status were apprehended, both Wilfred Hooper and Frederic Youngs have noted that they tended to be treated more leniently and that punishments – like garments – were tailored to the offender's rank.[115]

In addition to these implications of knowledge, surveillance and dispute, the laws embodied internal inconsistencies that gave their provisions a paradoxical nature. Thus the impetus behind the apparel orders came from the court, but so did the power play and social advancement that fuelled escalating dress display. Elizabeth, particularly, was concerned to reform abuses in apparel, but Elizabeth, particularly, was also determined to harness its powerful potential. Although beyond dress regulation herself, the statutes and proclamations also enabled the monarch to suspend the laws for individuals, by giving them either garments or licensing dispensations. The Privy Council's order of 1559 for the reformation of apparel even explicitly excused gentlemen and servants if they wished to wear their unlawful garments 'wythin the gates of the Courte'.[116] This problem of clothing regulation and clothing display emanating from the same centre was, as so much else, recognized by perceptive individuals at the time. Burghley, although committed to reform of apparel abuses, towards the end of his career acknowledged that, 'I doubt much that the length of all these commandments and provisions will hardly be executed abroad until there be some good example in the Court and the city.'[117] Roger Ascham remarked similarly. 'And . . . surelie the misorder of apparell in mean men abroade', he wrote, 'shall never be amended, except the greatest in Courte will order and mend them selves first.'[118]

Likewise the perpetual reiteration of the orders and their provisions acted as a reminder of prohibition, but also published a recurring catalogue of pleasures. By disallowing certain modes and appearances, the laws also opened up a channel for illicit desire. Like all forbidden fruit, it was the sweeter for being withheld.[119] Montaigne's analysis of sumptuary legislation made just this point. 'As for example, to let none but Princes . . . weare velvets, and clothes of Tissew, and interdict the people to doe it, what is it but to give reputation unto those things, and to encrease their longing to use them?'[120] Advertising alluring sartorial display, acts of apparel end by proliferating the very abuse they sought to curb.

Finally, supporting dress control in principle did not necessarily equate with approving of it in practice. Indeed, such regulation may have had the passive agreement of most of the population, but almost always as something applied to *others*.[121] For wearing fine clothing can only be unwarranted on someone else; for oneself having rich garments is the tautological proof of deserving them. Thus, in the relativity of sartorial judgement, clothing that is excessive, abusive and flaunting when viewed by the subject, might become comely and appropriate when the object of wear. Along these lines Hunt points out that the paradox at the heart of the sumptuary project is that, although supported by the majority, it was impossible to enforce compliance with its provisions. 'Indeed enforcement always ran the risk of alienating the broad consensus that favoured the existence of such laws.'[122]

Broadly speaking then, dress control in any long term, systematic sense *was* doomed to failure. This was not, though, because it was inherently foolish as an idea, or out of keeping with broader cultural issues or societal consensus. While certain implications in its provisions made compliance problematic, it was the contradictions at the centre of the apparel orders that finally rendered enforcement impossible. However, this is not to say that the legal regulation of dress was not effective in different terms. As Hunt suggests, we might usefully consider the concept of 'symbolic legislation' here – a body of laws whose existence, rather than whose enforcement, is the significant factor. For these measures successfully articulated a statement of desired intent, expressing therein a governmental and cultural preference for a particular ordering of society. Furthermore, they acknowledged and addressed widespread underlying anxieties, that ranged from moral degradation to social and financial chaos. Perhaps, in meeting these concerns head on, the acts and proclamations of apparel helped alleviate them.[123]

The ability that, as we have glimpsed, clothing had to disturb, or cement, social relationships should not be underestimated. A century after the repeal of the dress laws a disagreement as to the suitableness of raiment still soured relations between Evelyn and his local cleric. The Doctor preached a sermon on 'the pride & Luxury of Apparell' which, as 'there being none in all the Parish . . . but meane people', Evelyn decided 'could be applyed to none save my Wife & Daughter'. Feeling that his family were only dressed as befitted their station, he spoke to the Doctor who took the reproof amiss, and instead fell 'into a very furious passion'. Indeed, Evelyn complained, 'he hardly spake to me of some days, but preach'd the very same Sermon this day'.[124] But clothing could be utilized in ways that did more than just ruffle the surface of community good will. Dress, as the apparel laws attest, could be used to make false claims about status and wealth, and these false claims were felt to be a threat to the status quo. However, the use of apparel to completely misrepresent identity and forge a new persona was even more fundamentally subversive. In the next chapter we will explore this by looking at the practice of disguise.

Notes

1. *APC*, 1591–92, p. 175.
2. Laws controlling consumption date back to Classical Greece and Rome, and were also found in early Chinese and Japanese cultures. During the medieval and early modern periods many European countries other than England also instituted legislation of this type.
3. Wilfred Hooper, 'The Tudor Sumptuary Laws', *English Historical Review*, 30 (1915), 433–49 (p. 436).
4. 5 Eliz. I, c. 6 (1563) and 13 Eliz. I, c. 19 (1571). G.R. Elton, *The Parliament of England 1559–1581* (Cambridge, 1986), pp. 273, 67, 253.
5. *Proceedings in Parliament 1614*, ed. by Maija Jansson (Philadelphia, 1988), p. 78. *CJ*, I, 464. Lawrence Stone, *The Crisis of the Aristocracy 1558–1641* (Oxford, 1965), p. 566.
6. N.B. Harte, 'State Control of Dress and Social Change in Pre-Industrial England', in *Trade, Government and Economy in Pre-Industrial England*, ed. by D.C. Coleman and A.H. John (London, 1976), pp. 132–65 (p. 133).
7. There were also minor laws passed in 1355, 1364, 1420 and 1477. In addition to this legislative activity, the Commons unsuccessfully petitioned the Crown for sumptuary regulation in 1402 and 1406. Frances Baldwin gives a detailed account of all of this in the first four chapters of *Sumptuary Legislation and Personal Regulation in England* (Baltimore, 1926).
8. 11 Edw. III, c. 2 and c. 4 (1337). 37 Edw. III, c. 8–c. 14 (1363). 3 Edw. IV, c. 5 (1463). 22 Edw. IV, c. 1 (1483). 1 Hen. VIII, c. 14 (1510). 6 Hen. VIII, c. 1 (1515). 7 Hen. VIII, c. 6 (1515). 24 Hen. VIII, c. 13 (1533). 1 & 2 Phil. & Mary, c. 2 (1554). 1 Jac. I, c. 25 (1604).
9. Proclamation 6 June 1516, 8 Hen. VIII (79.5). Proclamation 19 February 1517, 8 Hen. VIII (80). Proclamation February 1534, 25 Hen. VIII (143). Proclamation 27 May 1534, 26 Hen. VIII (146). Proclamation February 1536, 27 Hen. VIII (163). Proclamation 21 October 1559, 1 Eliz. I (464). Proclamation 6 May 1562, 4 Eliz. I (493). Proclamation 7 May 1562, 4 Eliz. I (494). Proclamation 7 May 1562, 4 Eliz. I (495). Proclamation 7 May 1562, 4 Eliz. I (496). Proclamation 12 February 1566, 8 Eliz. I (542). Proclamation 15 June 1574, 16 Eliz. I (601). Proclamation 16 February 1577, 19 Eliz. I (623). Proclamation 12 February 1580, 22 Eliz. I (646). Proclamation 13 February 1588, 30 Eliz. I (697). Proclamation 6 July 1597, 39 Eliz. I (786). Proclamation 23 July 1597, 39 Eliz. I (787). See *Tudor Royal*

Proclamations, ed. by Paul Hughes and James Larkin, 3 vols (New Haven, 1969). All subsequent references to Tudor proclamations will be from these volumes. In addition, the Privy Council published the order *Articles Agreed upon by the Lordes . . . for a Reformation of their seruauntes in certayne Abuses of Apparell*, (20 October 1559) STC 7903.

10. Hooper, 'Tudor Sumptuary Laws', p. 434.
11. *Literary Remains of King Edward VI*, ed. by J.G. Nichols (London, 1857; repr. New York, 1964), pp. 495–8. For W.K. Jordan, Edward's interest in the bill of apparel is further evidence of Edward's concern with 'social and economic dislocations', see W.K. Jordan, *Edward VI: The Threshold of Power* (London, 1970), p. 26, also pp. 421–2. Loach, however, is more cautious. She sees this, and other documents in Edward's hand as evidence of interest in state affairs, but thinks they may have been copied or written with assistance, see Jennifer Loach, *Edward VI*, ed. by George Bernard and Penry Williams (New Haven, 1999), pp. 98–100.
12. The exception being the proclamation issued 16 February 1577 (623), the year following the bill for regulating apparel introduced into the Lords.
13. *Proceedings in the Parliaments of Elizabeth I*, ed. by T.E. Hartley, 3 vols (Leicester, 1981–95), I, 454.
14. Ibid. The recollections of this bill are possibly Sir Walter Mildmay's (p. 423). He did not record the identity of individual speakers.
15. Hooper, 'Tudor Sumptuary Laws', p. 449; Harte, 'State Control of Dress', p. 148; Joan Kent, 'Attitudes of Members of the House of Commons to the Regulation of "Personal Conduct" in Late Elizabethan and Early Stuart England', *Bulletin of the Institute of Historical Research*, 46 (1973), 41–65 (pp. 56–7).
16. 1 Hen. VIII, c. 14, 1510. The statutes of 1515 are very similarly worded. The 1533 statute makes reference to 'the utter impoverysshement and undoyng of many inexpert and light persones', see 24 Hen. VIII, c. 13.
17. Proclamation 15 June 1574 (601).
18. 24 Hen. VIII, c. 13.
19. 'The mercantile system' and 'system of commerce' were phrases used in 1766 by Adam Smith to describe contemporary economic theory and practice. The term 'mercantilism' was adopted by economic historians late in the nineteenth century to refer to the political economy existing between the medieval period and the emergence of *laissez-faire* doctrines.

20. *A Discourse of the Commonweal of This Realm of England*, ed. by Mary Dewar, The Folger Shakespeare Library (Charlottesville, 1969), p. 68.

21. Ibid., p. 63.

22. Thomas Mun, *England's Treasure by Forraign Trade* (Oxford, 1959), p. 7.

23. Ibid., p. 9.

24. Sir Dudley North, *Discourses upon Trade* (1691), in Richard Grassby, *The English Gentleman in Trade: The Life and Works of Sir Dudley North, 1641–1691* (Oxford, 1994), p. 298.

25. Nicholas Barbon, *A Discourse of Trade*, (1690; repr. Baltimore, 1905), p. 33.

26. 1 Hen. VIII, c. 14.

27. Sir Thomas Elyot, *The Book Named the Governor* (1531, repr. Menston, 1970), fol. 128^r.

28. Proclamation 6 July 1597 (786).

29. For a full discussion see Felicity Heal, 'The Idea of Hospitality in Early Modern England', *Past and Present*, 102 (1984), 66–93; and Felicity Heal, *Hospitality in Early Modern England* (Oxford, 1990).

30. *A Discourse of the Commonweal*, pp. 81, 82.

31. I.M., *A Health to the Gentlemanly Profession of Serving-Men*, sig. H2^v.

32. Margaret Hodgen, *Early Anthropology in the Sixteenth and Seventeenth Centuries* (Philadelphia, 1964), addresses European interest in the New World, including the related fashion for collecting curios and exotica. Diana de Marly, 'Pepys and the Fashion for Collecting', *Costume*, 21 (1987), 34–43, looks in detail at the habit of collecting prints of foreign and fancy costume. For a further contribution to the topic see *Constructing Race: Differentiating Peoples in the Early Modern World*, a special edition of *The William and Mary Quarterly*, 3rd ser., 54, no. 1 (1997), esp. the article by Karen Ordahl Kupperman, 'Presentment of Civility: English Reading of American Self-Presentation in the Early Years of Colonization', 193–228.

33. For example, see 'Of the Use of Apparell', in *Montaigne's Essays: John Florio's Translation*, ed. by J.I.M. Stewart, 2 vols (London, 1931), I, 232–5.

34. *The Diary of John Manningham of the Middle Temple 1602–1603*, ed. by Robert Parker Sorlien (Hanover, NH, 1976), pp. 189–90, February 1602.

35. Walter Hammond, 'A Paradox: Proving the Inhabitants of the Island, called Madagascar, or St. Lawrence (in things temporal) to be

the happiest People in the World', in *Harleian Miscellany*, 8 vols (London, 1744–46), I, 256–57. However, early modern thought was not always so well disposed towards indigenous peoples. As well as seeing the 'primitive' as possessing human nature untainted, contemporary belief also could construct this category as irrational and barbaric – as less than fully human. In this latter view complexity of cultural forms were taken as an index of civilization, and thus minimal clothing indicated, ultimately, diminished humanity, see Anthony Pagden, *The Fall of Natural Man: The American Indian and the Origins of Comparative Ethnology* (Cambridge, 1982).

36. George More, *A True Discourse Concerning the Certaine Possession and Dispossessi of 7 Persons in one Familie in Lancashire* (London?, 1600), pp. 26–8. A rebato was a large standing collar, wired and starched to maintain its shape.

37. Proclamation 6 July 1597 (786).

38. Pierre Bourdieu, *Distinction: A Social Critique of the Judgement of Taste*, trans. by Richard Nice (London, 1984). See also Alan Hunt, *Governance of the Consuming Passions: A History of Sumptuary Law* (London, 1996), pp. 68–69, 108–09.

39. Richard Allestree, *The Whole Duty of Man* (London, 1671), p. 194.

40. Philip Stubbes, *The Anatomie of Abuses*, The English Experience, 489 (London, 1583; repr. Amsterdam, 1972), sig. [F5^{v}].

41. Deut. 22. 5. Facsimile edition of the Geneva Bible (1560).

42. Allestree, *Whole Duty of Man*, p. 210.

43. 24 Hen. VIII, c. 13.

44. Proclamation 12 February 1566 (542). Here 'diversity' means a quality of difference or distinction.

45. Proclamation 13 February 1588 (697).

46. Proclamation 6 July 1597 (786).

47. *LJ*, XII, 228.

48. 24 Hen. VIII, c. 13.

49. Ibid.

50. William C. Carroll, *Fat King, Lean Beggar: Representations of Poverty in the Age of Shakespeare* (Ithaca, 1996), p. 5. Works that present social mobility as a structural feature of early modern society include: Lawrence Stone, 'Social Mobility in England, 1500–1700', *Past and Present*, 33 (1966), 16–55; Keith Wrightson, *English Society 1580–1680* (London, 1982); and Frank Whigham, *Ambition and Privilege: The Social Tropes of Elizabethan Courtesy Theory* (Berkeley, 1984), pp. 1–31.

51. Recently there have been revisionist moves to redefine fashion, in order to wrest it from the historical grasp of Western capitalism. For example, Valerie Steele, in the inaugural editorial of the quarterly *Fashion Theory: The Journal of Dress and Body Culture*, 1, no.1 (1997), p. 1 describes fashion as 'the cultural construction of the embodied identity'. Clearly such a definition has universal application, covering practices as diverse as Chinese footbinding, and the showing of seasonal collections by the great couturiers. Valuable as such a redefinition is, it nevertheless obscures a qualitative difference between cultures in the historical habits of elite dress. Certainly change is to be found in the vestimentary systems of every culture, but it seems that European society from the late medieval period was unique in that the primary characteristic of its clothing code was successive but unitary stylistic development. In the latter part of the twentieth century the unitary fashion cycle appears to have splintered into a qualitatively different phenomenon characterized by pluralism, see Fred Davis, *Fashion, Culture, and Identity* (Chicago, 1992), esp. pp. 157–8, 187–8.

52. Thorstein Veblen, *The Theory of the Leisure Class* (New York, 1899). For an investigation which complicates the model of social emulation, see Patricia Allerston, 'Clothing and Early Modern Venetian Society', *Continuity and Change*, special issue on clothing and social inequality, 15 (2000), 367–90.

53. William Camden, *Remains Concerning Britain* (London, 1870), p. 219. All the following quotations are from pp. 219–20. This text was first published in Latin as *Britannia sive florentissimorum regnorum Angliae, Scotiae, Hiberniae . . .* (1586).

54. 3 Edw. IV, c. 5.

55. Proclamation 6 May 1562 (493).

56. Proclamation 12 February 1580 (646).

57. Baldwin, *Sumptuary Legislation*, p. 10.

58. Edmund Spenser, *Two Cantos of Mutabilitie*, Stanza 1 (1609), in Edmund Spenser, *The Faerie Queene*, 2 vols, facsimile edn (London, 1976), II.

59. Henry Peacham, *The Truth of our Times* (1638), in Henry Peacham, *The Complete Gentleman and Other Works*, ed. by Virgil Heltzel (Ithaca, 1962), pp. 201–2.

60. I. H. Æ., 'The Mirrour of Worldly Fame' (1603), in *Harleian Miscellany*, VIII, 31–46 (p. 39).

61. Thomas Nashe, *Christs Teares Over Jerusalem* (London, 1593; repr. Menston, 1970), fols 40^r-40^v.

62. Ibid., fol. 75^r.
63. Stubbes, *Anatomie of Abuses*, sig. [B7^v].
64. William Jones, *A Wonder woorth the reading* ... (1617), quoted in M.A. Shaaber, *Some Forerunners of the Newspaper in England 1476–1622* (Philadelphia, 1929), p. 155. For a discussion of monstrous births, including a list of published cases, see David Cressy, *Travesties and Transgressions in Tudor and Stuart England: Tales of Discord and Dissension* (Oxford, 2000), Chapter 2, pp. 29–50.
65. 'Pride's Fall: Or a Warning for all English Women by the Example of a Strange Monster lately Born in Germany, by a Merchant's Proud Wife, at Geneva', in *Satirical Songs and Poems on Costume*, ed. by Frederick Fairholt, Percy Society, Early English Poetry, Ballads, and Popular Literature of the Middle Ages, 27 (London, 1849), pp. 106–14.
66. Proclamation 13 February 1588 (697). Similar provisions are found in Proclamation 15 June 1574 (601) and Proclamation 6 July 1597 (786).
67. Proclamation 12 February 1580 (646).
68. Ibid.
69. Proclamation 12 February 1566 (542).
70. Proclamation 6 May 1562 (493) and Proclamation 7 May 1562 (494). In Proclamation 12 February 158 (646) the wording is 'the inferior sort'.
71. Proclamation 15 June 1574 (601). My emphasis. Paul Griffiths also identifies contemporary concerns about youth and excessive apparel, discussing in particular guild and corporation attempts to regulate the dress and appearance of apprentices, see *Youth and Authority: Formative Experiences in England 1560–1640* (Oxford, 1996), pp. 222–32.
72. Proclamation 13 February 1588 (697). At Cambridge the university issued apparel orders in 1560, 1578 and 1585. Similar regulations were passed at Oxford in 1564 and 1576, see Hooper, *Tudor Sumptuary Laws*, p. 464. Hooper also states that the Inns of Court and Chancery repeatedly ordered the reformation of apparel, and that these orders were just as repeatedly ignored (p. 447).
73. Whigham, *Ambition and Privilege*, p. 16.
74. Raphaell Holinshed, William Harrison and others, *The First and Second Volumes of Chronicles* (London, 1587), pp. 149–50.
75. Thomas Nashe, *The Anatomie of Absurditie*, in *The Works of Thomas Nashe*, ed. by R.B. McKerrow, 5 vols (repr. Oxford, 1958), I, 1–49 (p. 33).

76. John Earle, *Microcosmography or a Piece of the World Discovered in Essays and Characters*, ed. by Harold Osborne (London, n.d.), p. 46.
77. James Cleland, *The Institution of a Young Nobleman* (1607; repr. Bristol, 1994), p. 215.
78. John Della Casa, *A Treatise of the Maners and Behauiours*, trans. by Robert Paterson, The English Experience, 120 (London, 1576; repr. Amsterdam, 1969), pp. 108–9.
79. Baldassare Castiglione, *The Book of the Courtier*, trans. by Sir Thomas Hoby (London, 1928), pp. 117–18.
80. Nashe, *Christs Teares*, fol. 3^r.
81. Stubbes, *Anatomie of Abuses*, sig. C2^r.
82. 24 Hen. VIII, c. 13.
83. *Proceedings in Parliament 1628*, ed. by Mary Frear Keeler, Maija Jansson Cole and William B. Bidwell, 6 vols (New Haven, 1978), IV, 92, 98.
84. J.R. Hale, *Artists and Warfare in the Renaissance* (New Haven, 1990), p. 63.
85. George Peele, *Polyhmnia*, in *The Life and Minor Works of George Peele*, ed. by David Horne (New Haven, 1952), p. 232.
86. William Segar, *Honor Military, and Ciuill, contained in Foure Books* (London, 1602), p. 27 (irregular pagination).
87. The partial exception to this was the Marian statute (1 & 2 Phil. & Mary, c. 2) prohibiting both men, and women, from the wearing of silk. However, the prohibition was in three ways considerably less severe than at first appears. Firstly, the statute only concerned accessories such as hats, hose and shoes. Secondly, it did not apply at all to the elite, restricting only those under the degree of a knight's son or daughter, or those whose goods valued less than two hundred pounds. Thirdly, those women of the lower and middling sort whom the law did target, were specifically exempt in the matter of caps, hats, girdles and hoods – in other words, in most of their dress accessories. For the historical tendency to equate luxury with femininity see John Sekora, *Luxury: The Concept in Western Thought, Eden to Smollet* (Baltimore, 1977), pp. 43–4.
88. Stanford E. Lehmberg, *The Reformation of Parliament 1529–1536* (Cambridge, 1970), p. 173.
89. Hunt, *Governance of the Consuming Passions*, p. 309.
90. The first intimations of this actually came eight years earlier in the unsuccessful 1566 bill for apparel, which apparently included women in its provisions, see Elton, *Parliament of England*, p. 271.

91. Thomas Fuller, *The Holy State and the Profane State* (1642), ed. by James Nichols (London, 1841), p. 298.

92. Andrew Belsey and Catherine Belsey partly address this in 'Icons of Divinity: Portraits of Elizabeth I', in *Renaissance Bodies: The Human Figure in English Culture c. 1540–1660*, ed. by Nigel Llewellyn and Lucy Gent (London, 1990), pp. 11–35.

93. Pam Wright, 'A change in direction: the ramifications of a female household, 1558–1603', in *The English Court: from the Wars of the Roses to the Civil War*, ed. by David Starkey (London, 1987), pp. 147–72.

94. Simon Adams, 'Eliza Enthroned? The Court and its Politics', in *The Reign of Elizabeth I*, ed. by Christopher Haigh (Basingstoke, 1984), pp. 72–4.

95. G.B. Harrison, *The Elizabethan Journals*, 3 vols, rev. edn (London, 1938), II, 188–9. John Harington, *Nugae Antiquae: Being a Miscellaneous Collection of Papers,* ed. by Thomas Park, 2 vols (London, 1804), I, 232–4, 361–2.

96. Christopher Haigh, 'Introduction', in Haigh (ed.), *The Reign of Elizabeth I* (Basingstoke, 1984), p. 4.

97. See, for example, Belsey and Belsey, 'Icons of Divinity'; Roy Strong, *Gloriana: The Portraiture of Queen Elizabeth I* (London, 1987); Frances Yates, *Astraea: The Imperial Theme in the Sixteenth Century* (London, 1975); Susan Frye, *Elizabeth I: The Competition for Representation* (Oxford, 1993).

98. Haigh, 'Introduction', p. 4.

99. *APC*, 1600, p. 619.

100. Hunt, *Governance of Consuming Passions*, p. 340.

101. *The Letters and Epigrams of Sir John Harington*, ed. by Norman Egbert McClure (New York, 1977), 'Against excess in Womans Apparrell', no. 364, p. 296.

102. Quoted in Hooper, 'Tudor Sumptuary Laws', p. 447.

103. Tracing instances of apparel prosecutions is very confusing: the evidence is piecemeal, enforcement erratic, and the different jurisdictions in which cases might appear, numerous. The vast systematic study required to establish an accurate idea of frequency – or infrequency – has so far defeated historians, but the overwhelming view is that 'it seems unlikely . . . that many people were actually brought before the law courts for wearing fabrics or garments made illegal by the Acts of Apparel or the subsequent Proclamations' (Harte, 'State Control of Dress', p. 147).

104. Harte, 'State Control of Dress', pp. 147–48; Baldwin, *Sumptuary Legislation and Personal Regulation*, p. 167; Hooper, 'Tudor Sumptuary Laws', p. 447.

105. Hunt, *Governance of Consuming Passions*, p. 325.

106. Proclamation 6 May 1562 (493).

107. Hunt, *Governance of Consuming Passions*, p. 193.

108. *Proceedings*, ed. by Hartley, I, 455; Kent, 'Attitudes of the House of Commons', pp. 54–5.

109. Cited in Frederic Youngs, *The Proclamations of the Tudor Queens* (Cambridge, 1976), p. 169.

110. Roger Ascham, *The Scholemaster* (1570), English Linguistics 1500–1800 Facsimile Reprints, 20 (Menston, 1967), fol. 22^r.

111. Baldwin, *Sumptuary Legislation and Personal Regulation*, p. 240.

112. Elyot, *The Governor*, fols 128^r-128^v.

113. F.G. Emmison, *Elizabethan Life I: Disorder* (Chelmsford, 1970), pp. 30, 33. It is unclear from this whether the tailors were being accused of wearing or, more likely, making these garments.

114. Hooper, 'Tudor Sumptuary Laws', pp. 441; also cited by Youngs, *Proclamations of the Tudor Queens*, p. 165.

115. Ibid.

116. *Articles Agreed upon by the Lordes*, STC 7903.

117. Quoted in Whigham, *Ambition and Privilege*, p. 161.

118. Ascham, *Scholemaster*, fols 21^v-22^r.

119. Hunt, *Governance of Consuming Passions*, pp. 102–4.

120. 'Of Sumptuarie Lawes, or Lawes for Moderating of Expences', in *Montaigne's Essays*, ed. by Stewart, I, 301.

121. Hunt, *Governance of Consuming Passions*, p. 328–9.

122. Ibid., p. 355.

123. Ibid., pp. 355–56.

124. *The Diary of John Evelyn*, ed. by E.S. de Beer, 6 vols (Oxford, 1955), V, 542, 18 July 1703.

–5–

Them and Us, He or She?

On 22 February 1623, John Chamberlain wrote his friend Dudley Carleton a letter full, as usual, of the latest political gossip. He described the departure of Prince Charles on what was to have been a secret trip into Spain, for the purpose of forwarding marriage negotiations with the Infanta. The Prince, the then Marquis of Buckingham and Sir Francis Cottington journeyed to Dover where, joined by some other attendant gentlemen, they sailed to Dieppe.[1] For the heir apparent to go journeying in this manner was felt to be a highly risky business – 'all concurre that yt is a very costly and hasardous experiment'. As Chamberlain added, 'certainly there be daungers enough every way and I can hardly conceave how they should passe thorough Fraunce undiscovered'. In order to further the secrecy of the mission, therefore, Charles, Buckingham and Cottington put on false beards. Unfortunately, their disguise was both inadequate and incompetent, and people began to question their identity. Chamberlain's account can not be bettered: 'But their faire riding coates and false beardes (wherof on fell of at Gravesend) gave suspicion they were no such manner of men'. This almost overset their plans, for having been thus taken for 'suspicious persons' the trio were pursued by official enquiry. They only 'untwined themselves' from this interference by giving 'some secret satisfaction'.[2]

So what was going on in this episode described by Chamberlain? To us the inept clothing and false beards seem like the stuff of bad farce, but was it meant seriously by those involved? If it were, then what kind of understanding of identity must they have had to guide their choice of garb or, more fundamentally, to have enabled them to attempt a disguise in the first place? In other words, was it a 'good' idea, and if so, why? Finally, with their disguise but not their identities exposed, why were these men so questionable that their movements had to be marked and controlled? Until 'suspicion' was allayed by 'satisfaction', what was so transgressive about not being as they seemed?

To answer these questions, it is necessary to explore further certain issues that we have already encountered within the context of sumptuary legislation. In part, the acts and proclamations of apparel gave voice to concerns about identity. More specifically, these measures were, among other things, a legislative attempt to close the gap between the sartorial performance of rank and its actuality: a gap that, so many contemporaries felt, threatened to engulf the certainty of an ordered estate. By legally soldering rank and appearance into a truthfully referential whole, it was hoped that sartorial deceit would have no room for play. A labourer and a husbandman might be known by their garb and, more to the point, so might the different degrees of gentility. But the counterfeiting of appearances in the quest for social mobility was not the only sartorial dislocation to be feared. Despite an apparent desire for a simple transparency of self-presentation, early moderns were acutely aware that 'seeming' might not be the same as 'being'. Clothes had the potential to disguise the wearer, and deceive and mislead the viewer. This disguise and deception was usually suspicious and, it was felt, very often dangerous.

In this chapter I am going to explore the mistrust of sartorial counterfeit within two contexts: that of social exclusion, and of gender. In both parts of this discussion the 'unhinging of apparel from the categories of "truth"' will be found to be inflected by class.[3] The context in which the masquerading figure appears, and this figure's relation to the mechanisms of power, was of overwhelming importance in deciding the manner in which his or her disguise was read. The more marginal the individual the more disturbing, as we shall see, was their disguise. And the more disturbing the disguise, the more completely was the perpetrator enmeshed in the imputed motivations of deceit and duplicity.

The Rogue

A powerful image of exclusion, and of a dangerous marginal lurking on the fringe of decent society, is represented in the figure of the vagabond or wandering rogue. Roaming beyond normal geographic and social boundaries, the rogue embodied the breakdown of good order. Undo the ties that bound family, household and commonweal, and the rogue emerged in dangerous isolation, potentially criminal, but in essence offending simply by existing. 'Vagrancy is perhaps the classic crime of status, the social crime *par excellence*. Offenders were arrested not because of their actions, but because of their position in society.'[4] In real life the Tudor and Stuart landscape was to be seen as increasingly peopled by the rootless poor. The primary social and economic conditions leading to this have been well documented: rapid population increase; long-term inflation;

changing patterns of land use and ownership. Some estimates have it that in the century between 1541 and 1651 the population nearly doubled, and with an annual rise of food prices of four per cent, real wages fell by up to a half. Enclosure of common land and the swallowing of small holdings by larger and more prosperous owners, contributed to the tide of rootless folk. So, too, the decline of feudal retainership and the monastic dissolution released large numbers, previously incorporated into households, to wander in search of a living.[5]

The organizing principle applied to the poor was, in theory, a simple one. They were divided into two main types: the impotent, who through misfortune were unable to maintain themselves; and the sturdy, who since able to get a living must, the logic dictated, be therefore unwilling. William Harrison, in his description of English society, gives us a typical account:

> With us the poore is commonlie divided into three sorts, so that some are poore by impotencie, as the fatherlesse child, the aged, blind and lame, and the diseased person that is judged to be incurable: the second are poore by casualtie, as the wounded souldier, the decaied householder, and the sicke person visited with grievous and painefull diseases: the third consisteth of thriftlesse poore, as the riotour that hath consumed all, the vagabund that will abide no where, but runneth up and downe from place to place (as it were seeking worke and finding none), and finallie the roge and strumpet which are not possible to be divided in sunder, but runne too and fro over all the realme.[6]

Having thus created a typology of need, all that remained was to sort individual cases and treat them accordingly. The deserving – that is to say the impotent, or in Harrison's words 'the true poore' – were to be pitied and provided for. By contrast, the undeserving able-bodied and idle were to be punished, for 'punishment is farre meeter for them than liberalitie or almesse'.[7] It can be seen that between these two states, therefore, lay the crucial activity of diagnosis, or the matter of correctly identifying those 'genuinely' in need from those who shammed poverty.

Around the figure of the sturdy beggar was hung the weight of innumerable social ills. Wandering rogues were seen as a 'social danger of unlimited proportions'.[8] Idle, criminal, violent, threatening and subversive, the catalogue of characteristics descended even to the subhuman or bestial. Kent JP, William Lambarde, in addressing a jury at the Maidstone Sessions of the Peace in 1582, urged that they 'rid our gaol and country of a many of mighty, idle and runagate beggars wherewith we are much pestered, and also to rid and deliver themselves from that evil mind which they carry about with them'. The metaphorical and literal remedy, said Lambarde, was 'to kill and cut off these rotten members that otherwise would bring peril and infection to the whole body of the realm and commonwealth'.[9]

However, despite the strength of the sentiment and virulence of its expression, recent scholars have suggested that the threat the rogue posed to the social order was more imagined that real. Scrutinizing court records reveals a very small proportion of indictments were actually concerned with the crime of wilful vagrancy and rogue begging. 'The inescapable conclusion is that Tudor authorities feared vagrants far out of proportion to their actual menace.'[10] Yet the sturdy beggar had a cultural visibility that belied his or her minimal intrusion into 'real' life. The object of projected fears and anxieties, the rogue loomed large in the mental world of the sixteenth and seventeenth centuries. This included an energetic literary portrayal of the wandering criminal. Frequently turning up in dramatic contexts – often as minor figures, like the cutpurse Ezekiel Edgeworth in *Bartholomew Fair*, but sometimes, as with the cheating Autolycus of *The Winter's Tale*, centre stage – rogues were also the subject of a distinct genre of books and pamphlets. The popularity, and presumably the profitability of these texts, can be traced from their rapid succession and multiple reprintings.[11]

Appearing in fiction, the target of rigorous juridical intent and of social reform, the able-bodied beggar thus roamed freely in discursive space. But from where did the dangers attributed to the rogue spring? What made this character so threatening? Primarily, it was because the sturdy beggar was seen as the embodiment of deception, 'by definition a paradox of deceit'.[12] He was able to work yet feigned an inability to do so. He misused the signs of apparel to present a ragged self in need and penury. He marked his body to counterfeit piteous disfigurement and disease. Under the cover of this persona of deception, the rogue then crept among decent folk to cheat them of pity and alms, or more seriously, violently to steal prized possessions or life. Counterfeiting was thus inherently suspicious. No honest purpose would disguise itself. One of the earliest of the rogue pamphlets warned, 'the first and original ground of cheating is a counterfeit countenance in all things, a study to seem to be, and not to be in deed . . . the foundation of all those sorts of people is nothing else but mere simulation and bearing in hand'.[13]

The motif of counterfeit and its inherent dishonesty finds an echo in people's personal experiences. In his commonplace book, Sir John Oglander related an anecdote concerning the murder of a neighbour's great grandfather. It being known that he was returning home with money, two of the gentleman's tenants disguised themselves and waited in ambush. 'Being alone, they set upon him, wounded him in many places and one of them imagining him to be dead, would have thrown him to be devoured by his own hogs.' In common with the rogue, these wrongdoers were 'hoping their disguise would have cloaked their villainy'.[14] John Clavell (1601–43), a reformed highwayman, wrote a verse recantation of his past ways. In it he repeatedly described how inseparable from deception was the criminal life. In a literal vein he ordered the 'Knights of the Road' to: 'First plucke off your visards, hoods, disguise, / Masks, Muzels, Mufflers, Patches from your eyes, / Those Beards, those Heads of haire, and that great Wen / Which is not naturall, that I may ken / Your faces as they are.' More metaphorically he then accused: 'That your worthlesse spirits cannot rise / In any course that walkes without disguise, / For bred on dunghills, if unmask'd, you feare / You shall too much in your owne filths appeare.'[15]

It can be seen that in Clavell and Oglander's terms, if we are to be safe then disguise must be unmasked and deception recognized. And this point returns us to the taxonomy of the poor for it operated in the same way. Sorting the sturdy from the impotent depended upon correct identification and a skilful reading of the signs. So crucial was this, that much of the discursive treatment of the rogue was concerned with how it might be achieved. For the genre of rogue literature the answer was textual inscription. Within the pages the reader was educated into how the rogue dressed, talked and behaved in order that these techniques of deception could be correctly identified for what they were. The confidence trickster who fleeces the unwary at dice or cards would be 'apparelled like honest civil gentlemen or good fellows with a smooth face, as if butter would not melt in their mouths'.[16] By contrast the trickster who begs for alms would tear his clothes and roll in the mire, apply substances to bring up welts on his skin, chew soap that he might foam madly at the mouth, or even feign being dumb. Along with minute details of appearances the pamphlets, borrowing heavily from one another, also reproduced classificatory systems. With pseudo-scientific precision the rogues were sorted into complicated sub-groups, each of them named and explained. Some of the texts even glossed their supposed speech, giving translations of thieves cant to reveal all of the rogue's secrets. Like insect specimens they were labelled and described, pinned to the page by the sharpness of textual observation. As pamphleteer Thomas Harman wrote, 'Now, me thinketh, I se how these pevysh, perverse, and pestilent people begyn to freat, fume, sweare, and stare at this my booke, their lyfe being layd open and aparantly paynted out.'[17]

If in the literary world the answer to correct identification was textual inscription, then the juridical solution was to inscribe the body. Local and national government waged 'a war of signs against the country's vagrants and criminals before the audience of the general populace'.[18] Firstly the *bona fide* needy were badged or licensed, so they could legally beg for charitable aid. Any then found begging in contravention of the terms of their licence, or without a licence at all, were rightfully deserving of punishment. The penalties were public and corporal. In 1530/1, a statute laid down that any able-bodied person taken in begging or vagrancy be tied naked to the end of a cart, and be whipped throughout the market town 'tyll his Body be blody by reason of such whyppyng'.[19] Five years later more disciplinary measures were added. As a first offence sturdy beggars were whipped. As a second, they were whipped again, and bored through the ear, so that the inscription of their 'true' identity be made permanent. The offender 'shall have the upper parte of the gristell of his right eare clene cutt of, so as it may appere for a perpetuall token after that tyme'. Being found guilty of a third offence – so proven by the evidence of his or her previous mutilation – the rogue shall be executed as a felon.[20] Subsequent laws continued the corporeal nature of these punishments, threatening the guilty with burning holes through the gristle of the ear, enslavement, transportation, and branding.[21] The intent was that inscriptions of pain 'be seene and remaine for a perpetuall marke upon such Rogue duringe his or her life'.[22] In practice the whipping of the poor was not so very common, and the prosecution of rogues and vagabonds – with the attendant punishments of branding, burning and death – was rare.[23] However, the legal intent is made repeatedly clear, and the attraction of such techniques of unmistakable and permanent identification, meant it lived with potent force in the legal imagination. Justices of the Peace, when taking depositions, examined suspects' bodies for telltale marks.[24] And Thomas Harman, author of the seminal rogue pamphlet *A Caveat* was also a JP, with a self-confessed purpose in writing his identification manual being the education of Justices, sheriffs, and other officers of the law.[25]

Being and Seeming

Clearly, these attempts to fix the external signs into a pattern of 'truth', arose from a fear of the possible disparity between outer appearance and inner reality, or between being and seeming. The desire to make internal truth visible, is manifest in other sociological phenomena of the sixteenth and seventeenth centuries. The search for damning marks on the bodies of witches, was a strategy for combating the terror of the threat that cannot be recognized. If good and evil look the same, how can we possibly proceed? Diligent search *must* be made to uncover a sign. Catholics, like witches, were also feared because of their secret difference. For did not priests, disguised as normal and harmless folk, enter the realm and 'privily minister poison to our souls'?[26] In 1571 a bill against Popish priests disguised in servingmen's apparel was introduced into Parliament. It passed its three readings in the Commons apparently without dispute, and in the minimal time of two days. Put into committee in the Lords, it was then referred to the Privy Council.[27] Issued twenty years later, an anti-Catholic proclamation of 1591 stated that it was common knowledge and common experience that priests arrived in England 'disguised both in their names and persons'. It proceeded to describe the looks and apparel – 'yea, in all colors and rich feathers' – that might be assumed.[28] This sounds like, and may have been, irrational over-reaction, but the circumstances of falsely apparelled Catholics were real enough. Despite persecution, the years between 1580 and 1641 witnessed the growth of the Catholic community, and the numbers of ministering Jesuits also increased 'dramatically'. Correspondingly, so too did the paranoia about these 'Protean disguisers'.[29] Of course, from the persecuted priest's position it was only sensible to assume a disguise. English Jesuit, John Gerard, recorded his reasons for donning the dress of a moderately wealthy gentleman:

> It was thus that I used to go about before I became a Jesuit and I was therefore more at ease in these clothes than I would have been if I had assumed a role that was strange and unfamiliar to me. Besides, I had to move in public and meet many Protestant gentlemen, and I could never have mixed with them and brought them slowly back to love of the faith and a virtuous life had I dressed in any other way.

When arrested he appeared again in his Jesuit cloak and gown. His enemies were, he wrote, 'wild with rage'. '"Why didn't you go about in these clothes before?" they said. "Instead, you had a disguise and assumed a false name. No decent person behaves like that."'[30]

Disguise was, of course, a particularly vexed issue for Catholic priests, already demonized by Protestant opinion for their 'jesuitical' manipulations of the truth. Nevertheless, viewing this incident through Gerard's words alerts us to an inconsistency in the suspicion that altering appearances engendered. It was, in fact, only untrustworthy in *others*. In oneself it was an allowable move in the game of self-presentation, a possible ploy resorted to when circumstances dictated. Indeed, it was not so much cunning as prudent, for we find individuals writing of their disguised experiences in contexts of caution and danger. In these situations it seems as if the responsible course of action was to don a disguise. Also noteworthy is the frequency with which diarists record this happening. Scholars have long remarked the ubiquity of the topos in early modern drama but, more surprisingly, it was mirrored in a minor way by off-stage practice. Disguise was a cultural tool, a way of thinking that offered practicable solutions, that was at the disposal of dramatists and diarists alike. Furthermore, its real life practice outlasted the sixteenth- and early seventeenth-century heyday of stage counterfeit. For example, in the turmoil and uncertainty that preceded the Restoration, as an active member of the Interregnum government Bulstrode Whitelocke found himself liable to imprisonment. He therefore 'thought fitt to absent & conceale himselfe att some friends house'. To make this journey incognito, Whitelocke 'accoutred himselfe with a long grey Coate, & a great Baskethilted sword'. About two miles out of town he 'rode in att a gate to a close & there under the hedge he putt on a great perwicke, which with his unusuall clothes did much disguise him'. Understandably, from what we have seen of the suspicious nature of another's counterfeiting, this caused consternation for the man waiting on Whitelocke. He 'looked strangely att it, fearing (as he S[ai]d afterwards[)] lest his Master might have some design to robbe'.[31]

Also finding herself in danger, Lady Ann Fanshawe (1625–80) disguised her identity. Unlike Bulstrode Whitelocke, this entailed masking her gender. She and her diplomat husband were sailing to Spain when a Turkish galley approached. Fearing they would be attacked, Sir Richard sought to trick the Turks into thinking the ship was a military vessel, and ordered Lady Ann to keep to her cabin. For 'if they saw women, they would take us for merchants and boord us'. Although locked in against her will Lady Ann – who had described herself in youth as 'a hoyting girle' – knocked and called:

> untill at length a cabine boy came and opened the door. I, all in teares, desired him to be so good as to give me his blew throm cap he wore and his tarred coat, which he did, and I gave him half a crown, and putting them on and flinging away my night's clothes, I crept up softly and stood upon the deck by my husband's side.

By this time the two vessels, having taken measure of one another's forces, decided on a discreet and mutual retreat. Sir Richard then turned around and 'looking upon me he blessed himself and snatched me up in his armes, saying, "God God, that love can make this change!"'. Although dangerous and unconventional, both he and Lady Ann appear to have been secretly pleased at the exploit: 'And though he seemingly chid me, he would laugh at it as often as he remembered that voyage.'[32]

Charles II's Boscobel escape after the Battle of Worcester is well documented. He himself narrated to Samuel Pepys his 'resolution of putting myself into a disguise, and endeavouring to get a-foot to London, in a country fellow's habit, with a pair of ordinary gray-cloth breeches, a leathern doublet, and a green jerkin . . . I also cut my hair very short, and flung my clothes into a privy-house, that nobody might see that any body had been stripping themselves'.[33] Less commonly known is the manner of his brother's flight from England three years earlier, clothed as a female. At that point the young Duke of York, then aged fourteen, had been confined under guard to St James's Palace. Lady Halkett recorded how she helped Colonel Bampfield, a Royalist spy who had access to James, 'gett the Duke's cloaths made and to drese him in his disguise'. Rather than buying or borrowing an outfit, Lady Halkett desired the Colonel 'to take a ribban with him and bring mee the bignese of the Duke's wast and his lengh to have cloaths made fitt for him'. But this concern to have authentic props for their real life piece of theatre was very nearly their undoing:

> When I gave the measure to my tailor to inquire how much mohaire would serve to make a petticoate and wastcoate to a young gentlewoman of that bignese and stature, hee considered it a long time and said hee had made many gownes and suites, butt hee had never made any to such a person in his life. I thought hee was in the right; butt his meaning was, hee had never seene any women of so low a stature have so big a wast. However, hee made itt as exactly fitt as if hee had taken the measure himselfe. It was a mixt mohaire of a light haire couler and blacke, and the under petticoate was scarlett.

James, smuggled away from the Palace by river, was taken to a house where Lady Anne was waiting ready. 'His Highese called, "Quickly, quickly, drese mee", and putting off his cloaths I dresed him in the wemen's habitt that was prepared, which fitted His Hignese very well and was very pretty in itt.'[34] In this guise James then escaped successfully to the Continent.

If we include Charles I's assumption of the false beard that started this investigation, we now have contexts in which three Stuart kings took to disguise as a serious and prudent course of action.[35] According to Sir James Melville, Scottish ambassador to England, he offered the same opportunity to Elizabeth. The Queen, Melville said, had again wished she might see Mary, the Scottish monarch. Melville's response was as follows:

'I offered to convey her secretly to Scotland by post, clothed like a page; that under this disguise she might see the Queen, as James V had gone in disguise to France with his own Ambassador.' According to Melville, Elizabeth's reaction was not one of outrage or disbelief, but more like to wistfulness at unattainable freedoms. 'She appeared to like that kind of language, only answered it with a sigh, saying, Alas! if I might do it thus.'[36]

In order to mask identity and put on the characteristics of another sort of person, there needed to exist a shared understanding of how different social groups acted and appeared. There was a tacit agreement, at least, as to dress, posture, demeanour, voice and speech. It was this communal expectation that enabled Charles II to escape looking like a 'country fellow', and made sense of James Melville's suggestion to Elizabeth that she be 'clothed like a page'. Failure to fulfil such expectations appropriately led to the failure of Charles I's anonymous venture to Spain. An accepted typology of characters embeds many instances of early modern disguise, as James Clavell's description of a highwayman playing a country bumpkin illustrates. 'That one amongst them, who can act it right, / Shall be appareld like a Country wight, / Cloathed in russet, or a leatherne slop, / Which roules of rotten hay shall underprop, / Meeting his hobnaild shoes halfe way the legg; / His wastcote buckled with a hathorne pegg; / His steeple felt, with greasie brims, inch broad.'[37]

The prevalence of such social typology within real life assumptions, suggests that early modern identity was perceived as being both fixed, and role based. For the latter, people primarily understood themselves and others as being described by rank and occupation. One was a gentleman, a servant, a housewife, a monarch. The evidence for this inner identity lay in externalities: the king was the king because he looked, dressed and behaved in a kingly way. Thus, as a working proposition – a useful fiction – a transparency was assumed between outer and inner qualities; between appearance and essence. But, as we have seen, it was also an accepted ploy, or play, to mask this identity through disguise, disrupting the correspondence between external and internal truths. Both propositions, however, relied on the belief that internal identity was permanent and essential. Neither Sir James nor Elizabeth felt that his suggestion to dress her as a page would alter her Queenly nature; it would merely mask it. Similarly Charles II clearly felt that his Boscobel adventures dressed first as a labourer and then as a servingman, had not compromised his identity as monarch. On the contrary, the events became an important part of the myth of his kingship, and in subsequent years his escape 'became his favourite topic of reminiscence'.[38] In Charles's retelling of the story to

Pepys he suggests that disguising was his idea, and in a rather disparaging aside about his companion, Lord Wilmot, Charles implicitly foregrounds his own theatrical resourcefulness. 'I could never get my Lord Wilmot to put on any disguise, he saying that he should look frightfully in it, and therefore did never put any on.'[39] Disguising, then, did not change identity, it simply altered its appearance. A successful disguise misled the viewer; a failed disguise was one that was 'seen through'.

Actors and Courtiers

If identity is understood as essential, then disguise is interpreted as a mechanism for changing not the wearer's essence, but the viewer's perceptions. This belief was most frenziedly articulated in anti-theatrical polemic. Although part of an intellectual tradition reaching to classical origins, in England the late sixteenth century saw a resurgence of anti-theatrical debate which, growing in vigour, culminated in the 1642 closure of playhouses. The many polemics produced during this period argued that the whole theatrical experience was one of counterfeit and was therefore untrustworthy, or even Satanic. They also argued that the performance – or the counterfeiting – moved the viewers as if the dramatic enterprise was reality. Through the 'privie entries' of the eyes and ears the dissembling players beguiled the spectators' senses, leading them to believe that what was falsely staged was, in fact, true.[40] John Northbrooke, the writer of one of the earliest of these tracts, warned that watching plays 'you shall learne all things that appertayne to craft, mischiefe, deceytes, and filthinesse'.[41] 'The divel is not ignorant', warned Stephen Gosson, 'how mightely these outward spectacles effeminate, & soften the hearts of men, vice is learnt w[ith] beholding, sense is tickled, desire pricked, & those impressions of mind are secretly counveyed over to the gazers, which the plaiers do counterfeit on the stage.'[42]

The anti-theatrical texts, which repeat, expand, and toss among themselves these and other ideas, culminated in William Prynne's extraordinary polemic of 1633, *Histriomastix*. Within the thousand pages of specious argument, spurious reasoning and exhaustingly repetitive detail, Prynne writes of the manner of acting:

> If we seriously consider the very forme of acting Playes, we must needes acknowledge it to be nought else but grosse hypocrisie. All *things are counterfeited, feined, dissembled; nothing really or sincerely acted. Players are always counterfeiting, representing the persons, habits, offices, callings, parts, conditions, speeches, actions, lives,; the passions, the affections, the*

anger, hatred, cruelty, love, revenge, dissentions; yea, the very vices, sinnes, and lusts; the adulteries, incests, rapes, murthers, tyrannies, thefts, and such like crimes of other men, of other sexes, of other creatures; yea oft-times of the Divell himselfe, and Pagan Divell-gods. They are alwayes *acting others*, not themselves: they vent notorious lying fables, as undoubted truthes: they put false glosses upon Histories, persons, virtues, vices, all things they act, representing them in feined colours: the whole action of Playes is nought else but feining, but counterfeiting, but palpable hypocrisie and dissimulation which God, which men abhore: therefore it must needs be sinfull.[43]

This exhaustive listing of the ways players dissemble is reminiscent of the detailed descriptions in rogue literature that forewarned the reader in what ways the sturdy beggar might be disguised. And this brings us to a further overlap between rogue and anti-theatrical discourse. For those that visited theatres were stigmatized as vagrant and masterless, who instead of pursuing legitimate activity – worship or work – idly congregated 'to be frivolously entertained by counterfeiters'.[44] Labelled as vagrants by polemic the audience nevertheless escaped more lightly than the actors they watched, who were *legally* defined as masterless rogues and beggars. From 1572 the law classified as sturdy poor all players not licensed by either nobles or Justices of the Peace. Anyone taken in this capacity was to be punished as a wandering rogue. In 1597/8 the law squeezed tighter, and only players licensed by nobles were recognized as legitimate. Finally, the Jacobean statute of 1603/4 ordered punitive retribution for all players found on the road, irrespective of their being licensed or not. A nobleman's sanction was no longer adequate to protect them from the whippings and brandings that in theory permanently identified the roguish dissembler.[45]

This legal interpretation of actors as social illegitimates who obtained money by dishonest practice was adopted gleefully by anti-stage writers. From Northbrooke at the start of the movement, to Prynne at the close, most at some point called on the laws of the land to justify their position. Furthermore, they called for the statutes to be enforced and detailed the punishments due. To paraphrase Prynne's lengthily expressed opinion on the matter, all common stage players, by whomsoever licensed, were but vagabonds, rogues, or sturdy beggars who ought to suffer legal pains and punishments in every degree. All magistrates should in this regard enforce the statutes fully, as 'both in law and conscience' they were bound to do.[46]

The anti-theatricalists' response, then, to the counterfeiting practices of stage and players, was to call for the abolition of the one, and the 'fixing' of the other – branding and marking the bodies of idle actors so that they could no longer work their tricks of identity. The bitter irony of this is that Prynne, whose vehement espousal of this position was close to pathology, was made to experience – if not accept – the subjective nature of interpretation. His vast tirade against the theatre, which included comments about actresses and courtly entertainments, was taken by the powerful as criticism of Queen Henrietta Maria, royal theatricals, and the state. In 1634 the Privy Council tried Prynne for sedition and libel, and found him guilty. By the end of his long engagement with the legal process, Prynne had been pilloried, had his ears cropped, and had the letters SL, for seditious libeller, branded on his face. Thus the man who had so desperately wanted to fix the appearance of others, was in turn marked with his 'true' identity.

The reception of Prynne's ill-judged work indicates that, despite its familiar anti-theatrical arguments, it differed in one crucial way from earlier texts: *Histriomastix* attacked the powerful. Jean Howard points out that there was a selectivity about anti-theatrical polemic that aimed only at the margins. It demonized the theatrical practices of subordinate groups, but silently legitimized those of the upper orders.[47] Yet as the Star Chamber proceedings reveal, the Court was most concerned with the book's slurs on the Queen and King, and the mechanisms of government. Sir John Finch voiced the opinions of all his colleagues when he reminded them, they had 'heard this monster of men and nature spitt his venome against the people in generall, the magistrates, and his Ma[ties] howse and household, they shall nowe see him spitt his venome att the throane it selfe'.[48] Of course, the 'people in general' counted for nothing. What mattered was Prynne's daring to castigate the elite.

There were, however, self-dramatizing strategies that not even the outspoken Prynne identified. These strategies were fundamental to the dominant and rising groups, for whom the road to self-advancement lay through favour and patronage, and the entrée to spheres of influence was affected by personal presentation. The gentleman courtier, then, could be said to have consciously adopted models of behaviour in much the same way as the disguised beggar. The rules of comportment for the former, however, were socially acceptable and codified not in rogue literature, but in conduct books.[49] As Stephen Greenblatt has written in his seminal *Renaissance Self-Fashioning*:

> Theatricality, in the sense both of disguise and histrionic self-presentation, arose from conditions common to almost all Renaissance courts: a group of men and women alienated from the customary roles and revolving uneasily around a centre of power, a constant struggle for recognition and attention, and a virtually fetishistic emphasis on manner. The manuals of court behavior which became popular in the sixteenth century are essentially handbooks for actors, practical guides for a society whose members were nearly always on stage.[50]

Nor was this dramatizing confined to court circles, for Anna Bryson has noted that in London at large, and even in rural locations, gentlemen were pressured to 'validate their status with social behaviour informed by the theatricality' laid out within the pages of advice literature.[51]

Conduct books were 'how to' manuals that in varying levels of detail instructed as to appearance, conversation and desirable achievements. All of them recommended the reader to adapt himself to his surroundings and to be, as far as possible, universally popular. The quintessential conduct book, Castiglione's *The Courtier*, suggested that the ideal gentleman should 'frame himselfe according to the inclination of them he accompanieth him selfe withall'. Sir Thomas Elyot's more theoretical text, *The Governor*, advised that 'Affabilitie is of a wonderfull efficacie or power in procurynge love'; and Giovanni Della Casa's extremely practical *Galateo* insisted that 'plesaunt & gentle behaviours, have power to draw their harts & mynds unto us, with whome we live'.[52] Thus one's appearance and outward behaviour could affect viewers and, to a certain extent, manipulate their responses. But presenting a self-conscious model like this – a predetermined mien of affability and politic good nature – could run extremely close to deceit, and disguise. For the cultivated exterior was not a 'true' mirroring of internal reality. Conduct books recommended the reader to *appear* better than he was: more knowledgeable, more skilled, wittier, more urbane. 'Dissimulation and feigning', writes Greenblatt, 'are an important part of the instruction given by almost every court manual'.[53] *The Courtier* made explicit both sides of this argument. Following a disquisition of how a gentleman may enhance the appearance of his personal attributes, the character Lord Gasper Pallavicin speaks out. 'I thinke not this an arte, but a very deceite, and I believe it is not meet for him that will be an honest man to deceive at any time.' Sir Frederick Fregoso replies, somewhat equivocally, that this 'is rather an ornament that accompanieth the thing he doth, than a deceite: and though it be a deceite, yet it is not to be disalowed'. Within the pages of *The Courtier*, 'a certaine warie dissimulation' wins the day.[54]

By placing the discursive treatment of players and wandering poor beside the genre of conduct literature, we see clearly how the early modern vision of disguise splintered along the lines of class. Deceit and counterfeit were inherently suspicious, but only in the marginal and socially inferior. For the elite 'dissimulation' could be an acceptable tool that, wielded skilfully, might help achieve advancement and repute. However, personal narratives suggest that this 'us and them' attitude can be further distilled into a 'me and others' stance. The adoption of disguise might always be suspicious deceit in someone else but, for the individual concerned it was a prudent and clever manipulation of appearances. But however disguise was interpreted, it was always understood as masking, rather than changing, internal truth. The appearances of identity could be altered, but not – unless by God – its essence. For Charles I to dress up and put on a false beard was, in his cultural circumstances therefore, a 'good' idea. Certainly he and his companions were not very skilled in the subtleties of disguise, or their appearance would not have aroused comment and unease. However, he was able to reveal his underlying identity and thus allay, through privilege, all suspicion that deceit engendered.

Wo to Men

The controversy surrounding the nature and place of women has a long history. However, like anti-theatrical sentiment, it burgeoned in the middle of the sixteenth century into a vigorous and energetically waged pamphlet war. Tracts attacking, and also defending, female nature were produced – sometimes by the same author – as rhetorical exercises in this popular debate. While these treatises 'provided a formal framework' for the controversy, interest in the topic was immense and, as with other cultural preoccupations, the argument spilled over into ballads, sermons, conduct books, poetry and drama.[55]

A standard theme in controversial literature linked women with the foolish pursuit of fashionable dress. Vain and greedy they rated fine clothing above reputation, sexual honesty or financial prudence. Inevitably these negative exemplars always finished unhappily. In Stephen Gosson's *Quips for Vpstart, Newfangled Gentlewomen*, a verse tract of 1595, women of all ages are tempted – quite literally – by the devil's work. '(*Don Sathan*) Lord of fained lies, / All these new fangles did devise.' More originally, Gosson provided the reader with a supposed genealogy of the farthingale: originally the frame was used by whores suffering from the pox to keep their skirts from being soiled by dirty undergarments. 'These hoopes that hippes and haunch do hide' also masked the prostitute's other occupational hazard: pregnancy.[56] Eight years later in *The Batchelar's Banquet*, a manual cautioning men to the single life, female lust for apparel was central to the plot and argument of the first five chapters.[57] In Chapter 1, for example, the chief cause of marital strife is a newly wed wife's desire for beautiful clothes. Although they can't afford it she manipulates her husband into giving her a new outfit, as a result of which they end in hardship and misery. In the following chapter a finely dressed woman wishes to go out and show off her clothes. Conflating sartorial greed and sexual appetite, the text soon leads her into adultery.

Around 1620 this theme took a particular turn, however, and crys-
tallized into the motif of women who apparelled themselves as men. It is
this topos that forms the subject of two much quoted pamphlets, *Hic
Mulier* and *Haec-Vir*, licensed within a week of each other in 1620. The
ungrammatical Latin gives a clear indication of their content, as do their
full titles. *Hic Mulier: Or, The Man-Woman: Being a Medicine to cure the
Coltish Disease of the Staggers in the Masculine-Feminines of our Times*,
is an attack on women dressed, and acting, in a masculine mode. *Haec-
Vir: Or The Womanish-Man: Being an Answere to a late Booke intituled
Hic Mulier*, which purports to be a riposte, is structured as a dialogue
between the two eponymous characters. The text begins with both these
figures mistaking the gender of the other. Once the confusion is clarified
Hic Mulier opens her defence, which ranges over the positive nature of
variety and change, the importance of freedom of choice, and the limitations of socially constructed customs. She then turns to her main, and
more conservative argument – a counter attack on the Womanish-Man and
his appropriation of the accoutrements of femininity. Since, Hic Mulier
argues, there must be a distinction between the sexes, women have had no
choice but to take up 'those manly things which you have forsaken'. All
that needs to be done to restore the old and rightful order, is for Haec Vir
to relinquish his effeminate apparel: 'Cast then from you our ornaments,
and put on your owne armours.' The two characters then swap clothing
and titles, and the newly named Haec Mulier and Hic Vir close the text
happily as 'true men, and true women'.[58]

These two short pamphlets have spawned a disproportionate amount
of secondary comment, and have formed the evidential base for numerable
claims about the cross-dressing craze of seventeenth-century London.[59]
But in claiming that men and women wore one another's apparel, what are
these texts actually saying? Firstly, a closer look at the text and title pages
banishes our modern assumption of women in breeches. The main charges
levelled against women involved head wear, and the apparelling of the
torso. Hic Mulier has exchanged:

> the modest attire of the comely Hood, Cawle, Coyfe, handsome Dresse or
> Kerchiefe, to the cloudy Ruffianly broad-brim'd Hatte, and wanton Feather,
> the modest upper parts of a concealing straight gowne, to the loose, lascivious
> civill embracement of a French doublet, being all unbutton'd to entice . . . and
> extreme short wasted to give a most easie way to every luxurious action: the
> glory of a faire large hayre, to the shame of most ruffianly short lockes; the
> side, thicke gather'd, and close guarding savegards, to the short, weake, thinne,
> loose, and every hand-entertaining short basses; for Needles, Swords; for

Prayer bookes, bawdy legs . . . and for womens modestie, all Mimicke and apish incivilitie. [60]

In support of the text, the title page illustration pictures two women in, one assumes, front fastening 'doublets'(Figure 23). One of them shame-lessly wears a hat and feather – her shame indicated by her gazing into a mirror, a common emblem of vanity. The other is hatless, in order that the barber can tend or further cut her short hair. While presumably a potent image to contemporaries, the significations of the pictured hats and shoulder-length hair are generally lost on modern viewers. The charges in *Haec-vir* are almost identical, warning Hic Mulier that:

till you weare hats to defend the Sunne, not to cover shorne locks, Caules to adorne the head, not *Gregorians* to warme braines, till you weare innocent white Ruffes, not jealous yellow jaundis'd bands, well shapt, comely and close Gownes, not light skirts and French doublets, for Poniards, Samplers, for Pistols Prayer-bookes, and for ruffled Bootes and Spurres, neate Shooes and clean-garterd Stockings, you shal never lose the title of *Basenesse, Unnaturalnes, Shamelesnesse,* and *Foolishnesse.*

She counters Haec Vir's accusations, asking him in turn:

why doe you curle, frizell and powder your haiyres . . . why doe you rob us of our Ruffes, of our Earerings, Carkanets, and Mamillions, of our Fannes and Feathers, our Busks and French bodies, nay, of our Maskes, hoods, Shadowes and Shapynas? Not so much as the very Art of Painting, but you have so greedily ingrost it. [61]

Again the title page illustration shows a female figure in a skirt and front fastening 'doublet' (Figure 24). Underneath her large hat and feather her hair is short, and beneath her skirts she is wearing spurs. In one hand she carries a pistol, and with the other she holds the hilt of a sword. From her girdle hangs a dagger. These references to women carrying weapons perhaps allude to the custom of females wearing knives fastened at the girdle, a practice that 'appears to have been pretty general among the European women at the end of the sixteenth century'. It may have been that knives were given to women as wedding gifts, as being valuable domestic utensils. [62] By contrast, the complementary male figure in the illustration is holding a mirror, and what appears to be a feathered fan. His hose are decorated with elaborate knots of ribbon.

So, even in extreme polemic, far from accusing women of appro-priating breeches and men of lacing themselves into dresses, both were

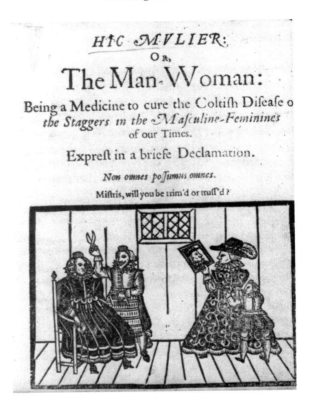

Figure 23 Title page, *Hic Mulier: or, The man-woman* (London, 1620) [Shelfmark: C.40.d.27(1)]. By permission of the British Library.

castigated for the cut of their existing garments and their use of fashionable accessories and techniques. Given that in some cases the same items were censured for both men and women indicates that the context of wear was highly important in generating meaning, and that use was differently gendered. For example, hair was immodest on women when cut 'short' and on men when 'over' tended. Both were accused of misusing ruffs and, similarly, feathers. The female transgression in the matter of the former concerned colour. The starch that was used to set neck and wrist wear into their large elaborate shapes, when died yellow, had significations of immorality. Ruffs in general – entirely non-functional and impractical confections of fashion – had long been a favourite object of reforming zeal and comment. When coloured they became especially

Figure 24 Title page, *Haec-Vir: or, The womanish-man* (London, 1620) [Shelfmark: C.40.d.27(2)]. By permission of the British Library.

potent signs of pride, vanity and abandonment. They were even implicated in the *cause célèbre* of the Overbury murder as Anne Turner, the woman hanged in 1615 for her part in poisoning Sir Thomas, was linked in the public mind with a vision of flaunting yellow ruffs.[63]

This insistence on the fashionable nature of their transgressions should make us question whether the disguise of gender was, in fact, the real target of polemical attack. Certainly in these contexts disguise was used as a literary ploy, but no one was really taken in. The clothing and comportment complained of were not serious attempts to mask gender but essays in chic and avant-garde fashion. Indeed, far from making women look like men, the styles offended because they made the wearer bolder and more flamboyant. Rather than disguising, they drew attention to the female body, making it immodest and sexually available – a charge, incidentally, levelled against different styles of women's dress throughout the ages.[64] So the doublet style is contrasted with the gown, the one being 'modest' and 'concealing', the other 'loose' and 'lascivious', 'all unbutton'd to entice . . . and extreme short wasted to give a most easie way to every luxurious action'. Similarly the safeguard – a garment worn like an apron for protection against the dirt – becomes a protector of chastity; it is 'close guarding'. By contrast the slightly shorter skirts pictured in *Haec-Vir* are 'short, weake, thinne, loose, and every hand-entertaining'.[65] Clearly these were spurious accusations for they imputed characteristics to garments that were not implied by cut or construction. Even the crucial opposition of doublet versus bodice was an imposed one, for the basic principles of design and fastening were identical. However, the point of the attacks was not a realistic analysis of form and function but a condemnation of the most adventurous of styles and wearers.

In keeping with this discursive concern about fashion, we find in the *Hic Mulier* text particularly a huge number of references to deformity and monstrosity. As already noted in the previous chapter, extremes of fashion pushed at the hitherto accepted boundaries of the body, creating new and 'unnatural' configurations. 'Come then, you Masculine-women, for you are my Subject', wrote the *Hic Mulier* author, 'with a deformitie never before dream'd of, that have made your selves stranger things that ever *Noahs* Arke unladed . . . 'Tis of you, I intreat, and of your monstrous deformitie; You that have made your bodies . . . not halfe man, halfe woman; halfe fish, halfe flesh; half beast, halfe Monster; but all Ody ous, all Divell.'[66] Scholars have been misled, then, in imagining a subculture of cross-dressed men, and particularly women, who appropriated the apparel of the other gender in order to make some kind of social or political point. It was fashionable, rather than cross-gendered, apparel that was being vilified.

Furthermore, despite an apparent crescendo of disapprobation, none of this was new. The *Hic Mulier* and *Haec-Vir* tracts appeared in 1620, shortly after an outburst by James against women's attire. Our report of this comes via John Chamberlain who, on 25 January 1620 wrote to Dudley Carleton that:

> Yesterday the bishop of London called together all his clergie about this towne, and told them he had expresse commaundment from the King to will them to inveigh vehemently and bitterly in theyre sermons against the insolencie of our women, and theyre wearing of brode brimd hats, pointed dublets, theyre haire

cut short or shorne, and some of them stillettaes or poinards, and such other trinckets of like moment.

Over a month later Chamberlain reported the rather confused outcome, for it seems one cleric either seized the opportunity, or confused the order, to preach against those inflammatory yellow ruffs. However, as Chamberlain tells it, the elite favourers of this fashion, having the ear of the King, won the day:

> The Deane of Westminster hath ben very strict in his church against Ladies and gentlewomen about yellow ruffes and wold not suffer them to be admitted into any pew, which beeing yll taken and the King moved in yt, he is come to disadvowe him, and sayes his meaning was not for yellow ruffes but for other man-like and unseemly apparell.[67]

Literary historians have coupled the appearance of the *Hic Mulier* texts with James's order, and arrived at 'a short-lived phenomenon, at its height in the early 1620s'.[68] Lawrence Stone, too, sited 'manly' female fashions squarely in Jacobean England, even going so far as to impute a causal relationship between courtly homosexuality and women's attire.[69] Not only is there no evidence for this, but what information we do have indicates the contrary: that these complaints about female dress have a long and continuous history, and are not a phenomenon specific either to James's reign, or the 1620s.[70] For example, almost fifty years previously George Gascoigne's satire *The Steele Glas* in part turned its attention to fashionably apparelled, painted and perfumed ladies. 'What should these be? . . . / They be not men: for why? they have no beards. / They be no boyes, which wear such side long gowns. / They be no Gods, for al their gallant glosse./ They be no divels, (I trow) which seme so saintish. / What be they? women? masking it in mens weedes? / With dutchkin dublets, and with Jerkins jaggde? / With Spanish spangs, and ruffes fet out of France, / With high copt hattes, and fethers flaunt a flaunt? / They be so sure even *Wo* to *Men* in deede.'[71]

Unsurprisingly Philip Stubbes, who covered so much in his resounding *Anatomie of Abuses*, spared time to condemn – repetitively – the by now familiar target of women in doublets. They are:

> buttoned up the brest, and made with wings, welts and pinions on the shoulder points, as mans apparel is, for all the world, & though this be a kinde of attire appropriate onely to man, yet they blush not to wear it, and if they could as wel chaunge their sex, & put on the kinde of man, as they can weare apparel assigned onely to man, I think they would as verely become men indeed as now

Figure 25 Elizabeth I, Unknown artist, *c.* 1575. By courtesy of the National Portrait Gallery, London.

they degenerat from godly sober women, in wearing this wanton lewd kinde of attire proper onely to man.[72]

For Stubbes, then, it was but a small leap from bodices styled after men's doublets, to gender fluidity and transposition of sexual categories. But, as by now should be clear, this is a discursive leap only and not one that was made anywhere but on the page.

Figure 26 Anne of Denmark, Paul van Somer (*c.* 1576–1621/2). The Royal Collection ©
2003, Her Majesty Queen Elizabeth II.

One of the women in Stubbes's time who 'did not blush to wear' a
doublet, was Elizabeth herself (Figure 25). In 1617 her successor's
consort, Anne of Denmark, posed ready for the hunt – in doublet, hat and
feather (Figure 26); and Catherine of Braganza was yet another Queen
given to 'manly' styles. Pepys reported with approval the fashions that she
and her courtly entourage adopted, for 'it was pretty to see the young
pretty ladies dressed like men; in velvet coats, caps with ribbands, and

with laced bands just like men'. The following year, however, this had earned his censure:

> Walking here in the galleries, I find the Ladies of Honour dressed in their riding garbs, with coats and doublets with deep skirts, just for all the world like men, and buttoned their doublets up the breast, with perriwigs and with hats; so that, only for a long petticoat dragging under their men's coat, nobody could take them for women in any point whatever – which was an odde sight, and a sight did not please me.[73]

It is abundantly clear by now that the clothes which caught the polemicists' attention were the styles of high fashion. The elite and aspirant wearers were not donning men's garments, but wearing clothes cut for females with alterations of decoration and form to *resemble* male attire. As the author of *Hic Mulier* acknowledged of the class specific character of the phenomenon, 'the greater the person is, the greater is the rage of this sicknesses, and the more they have to support the eminence of their Fortunes, the more they bestowe in the augmentation of their deformities'.[74] For evidence about the lower orders, we must look to an extremely different source: court cases.

Cross-dressing

Little research has been done on actual recorded instances of early modern gender disguise. The chief contribution, coming from Rudolf Dekker and Lotte van de Pol, deals almost exclusively with Dutch incidents of this type.[75] Michael Shapiro, in a primarily literary study, does discuss a number of cases unearthed in the Repertoires of the Aldermen's Court of London and the Minute Books of Bridewell Hospital.[76] F.G. Emmison's well-known work with Essex records has also thrown up a few instances in the context of presentments to the Church courts.[77] Apart from these few studies, the only other additions to the scholarship have been one-off explorations of chance found incidents.[78] The scarcity of the scholarship reflects, it seems, the paucity of primary material. For despite Dekker and Van de Pol's claim that transvestism was a 'deeply rooted' and 'widespread' tradition, there is very little evidence of it from sixteenth- and seventeenth-century England.[79] In fact, David Cressy has described such archival material that introduces to us actual, non-fictional cross-dressers as 'that rarest of rare birds'.[80]

The first thing to note about the cases that have come to light is that they treat almost exclusively with men and women from the lower orders. Typical subjects are maid servant Magdalen Gawyn, or fruit seller Margaret Bolton.[81] Secondly, the women (and very occasionally men) charged with cross-dressing were not donning fashionable garments that only resembled the clothes of the opposite sex. Rather, they were attiring themselves in the specific, and relatively humble, garments usually worn by the other gender. Thus a Littlebury woman, in 1585, 'did wear man's apparel disorderly in her master's house'. Jacob Cornwall's wife, the court was told in 1592, 'used to wear young men's garters and said she would so to do till they came for them'.[82]

From their evidence, Dekker and Van de Pol have concluded that the strategy of masculine dressing was resorted to by some women as a way of circumventing their sexual vulnerability. Often the women in their study claimed that being apparelled as men enabled them to avoid prostitution brought on by poverty, or follow a way of life unhampered by unwanted sexual overtures. 'By far the greater part of our women were unmarried, and cross-dressing served them as a means to maintain their virginal state, or in any case, to avoid having to marry.'[83] This seems to have grown out of the medieval tradition of chaste, transvestite female saints who took to men's clothes in order to escape persecution and lead lives of sanctity.[84] However in early modern England, discursively at least, the opposite seems to have been true. Rather than cross-dressing having a possible component of chastity, it is almost exclusively linked with sexual incontinence.[85] While the actual motivations of the women involved are lost to us, in the cultural imagination at least, dressing in male attire was almost always a flagrantly provocative sexual act. For example, in 1576 Dorothy Clayton, spinster, was found guilty – 'contrary to all honestye of womanhood' – of going about the city 'apparyled in mans attyre'. She was also found to have 'abbusyed her bodye with sundry persons by reason of her incontynancy of Lyfe'.[86] Not only, as in this case, was cross-dressing was the indicator of immorality. In some instances a woman disguising her gender provided the 'proof' of her dishonesty. In 1601 Elizabeth Griffyn, alias Partridge, was sent to the Bridewell Court only 'upon suspicon of ill and lewd liefe'. Once there 'yt was evidentlie proved to this Courte that she hath used to goe in manes apparrell': case closed.[87]

Punishments for offences involving cross-dressing were frequently of the shaming variety, in which the transgressor's misdemeanours were made humiliatingly public. So Magdalen Gawyn, a maid servant taken in man's clothing, was pilloried having her hair – a powerful sign of femininity – hanging over her shoulders, but 'apparelyd in th'attyre wherewith she ys nowe clothyd'. Likewise Dorothy Clayton was pilloried in Cheapside for the space of two hours, 'apparyled in suche manner and

sorte and in such kynde of mans apparell, as at the tyme of her apprehension did [wear]'. Afterwards, both were committed to Bridewell.[88]

However, the offence, and punishments, of gender disguise were
themselves gender specific. Firstly, it was far less common for a man to
dress as a woman than the other way round. It may be that there was little
to gain for men to assume a role that offered them less freedom of action
and public agency. In a patriarchal society the step from male to female
could only be seen as a retrograde one, moving down rather than up the
evolutionary ladder – or, in more contemporary terms, the great chain of
being. Secondly, when the very few cases of male transvestism did come
to trial, they seem to have been treated more leniently than instances of
female cross-dressing. David Cressy's article explores a case heard before
an Oxfordshire church court in 1633. In it Thomas Salmon, a midwife's
servant, admitted masquerading as a woman in order to participate in the
gossips' merrymaking, which followed a safe delivery. The 'church
accepted Thomas Salmon's confession and assigned him a formal penance.
The incident closed with punishments that were remarkably mild. The
court had done its duty in disciplining youthful folly but found nothing
gravely amiss by the laws of church or state.'[89] A similar attitude can be
seen in a case that came before the Aldermen's Court almost eighty years
earlier, in 1556. In it two men, Robert Chetwyn and Richard Myles, had
been committed to ward for being inappropriately clothed in a public
place. Chetwyn had gone abroad the previous day 'in a womans apparell',
and Myles had gone before him 'with a scarf on his necke'. Instead of
being pilloried, whipped, or sent to Bridewell, Chetwyn and Myles were
merely 'pardonyd of theire folye' and discharged. In addition Chetwyn
was ordered to find himself a master and thus, one assumes, enter a more
sober and responsible life path.[90] Clearly, if these two instances are
anything to go by, male cross-dressing was not transgressive in the same
way as was female transvestism. Even this latter variety was an infringement of a relatively minor sort. Like sexual misdemeanours, female cross-
dressing was a potential challenge to good morals and a well-ordered
community, rather than signalling 'a sex-gender system under pressure'.[91]
It was unseemly and offensive to the establishment (and perhaps intri-
guing and erotic, too), but it did not represent a serious threat. Even less
so did male cross-dressing, which was read as a prank or jest; a possibly
irritating, but ultimately pardonable, folly. Given this leniency towards
male transvestism, an alternative explanation presents itself for the
extreme scarcity of documented cases. It is just possible that, being
unworthy of punishment, incidents never reached the courts at all.

However, even with the tolerance shown towards men, the official attitude displayed to the sartorial transgressions of the lower orders is a far cry from the tone employed around elite manipulations of disguise. We have only to recall Lady Fanshawe's proudly writing of borrowing the cabin boy's clothes, or Lady Halkett's description of the future James II in a gentlewoman's habit, to realize that something very different was going on. For the middling and upper sort gender disguise – as with other maskings of identity – was culturally sanctioned in necessity. When personal safety was threatened, transvestism became a perfectly acceptable, and even praiseworthy, strategy. Sir John Reresby took the trouble to note an incident from the life of his uncle, Sir Tamworth Reresby, which showed such resource and initiative. Sir Tamworth was taken prisoner during the Civil War and sent to Ely House in London. 'He continued ther four months, till by favour of a woeman whos hous joined to the chamber wher he lay he broak a passage into her hous and escaped in woeman's apparell.'[92]

Two more famous escapes concern women. The first occurred in 1605 when Lady Elizabeth Southwell fled the country with her lover, Sir Robert Dudley. Leaving a previous wife and children, Dudley nevertheless took with him a page – the disguised Lady Elizabeth. They settled on the continent, received a papal dispensation to marry, and apparently found their somewhat uncertain history of bigamy and transvestism no impediment to social acceptance.[93] A less happy ending awaited Lady Arbella Stuart, who in 1611 also escaped the country to be with her husband, William Seymour. As James I's cousin and an heir to the English succession, Stuart's marriage was a matter for state management. However, having wed Seymour – another potential claimant for the throne – without James's consent, Lady Arbella and her husband were imprisoned. They both contrived to escape their separate confinements: Stuart by 'drawing a pair of great French-fashioned Hose over her Petticotes, putting on a Man's Doublet, a man-lyke Perruque with long Locks over her Hair, a blacke Hat, black Cloake, russet Bootes with red Tops, and a Rapier by her Syde';[94] Seymour, apparelled in 'wig, beard and a carter's clothing'.[95] They were caught and returned, but although imprisoned, their disguised manner of escape went unrebuked.

This resort to the play of gender disguise *in extremis* was deeply ingrained in contemporary thought. A standard plot in innumerable plays, episodes of cross-dressing were also common in Renaissance prose romances, where 'a male protagonist for reasons of intrigue, love stratagem, or escape from danger puts on female clothes'.[96] These literary examples presumably grow out of classical and medieval antecedents, in which such tactics win the day for the side of the 'right'. Even polemical literature in rabid opposition to transvestite practices had at least to acknowledge, if only to counter, this broadly accepted strand of thought. Anti-theatricalist John Rainoldes, staunchly opposed to the standard practice of using male actors to play female roles, rather testily confessed that he supposed a man might put on woman's apparel, 'For saving of his life or countrie'.[97] The author of *Haec-Vir*, more grudgingly still, decided that: 'It is disputable amongst our Divines, whether upon any occasion a woman may put on mans attyre, or no: all conclude unfit; and the most indifferent will allow it, but only to escape persecution.'[98] Even that most extreme of anti-theatricalists, William Prynne, gave a conditional admission of transvestism's acceptability, but linked it to a renewed refutation. 'Firstly, admit it were lawful for a man to put on womans apparell to save his life, or to avoid some imminent danger . . . yet it followes not hence, that therefore it is lawfull for Men-actors to put on womens aray to act a Play.' During Prynne's trial this very point was raised to illustrate the 'weaknes of his argumentes', for 'yf a man in his howse were beseidged by pagans would hee nott disguise himselfe in his maide's apparell to escape'.[99]

Despite the prevalence of this sanction it was, as we have seen, very selectively applied. Only to the wealthy and already privileged was given the approval to manipulate their appearance and disguise their status, role or gender. To ordinary folk such attempts were met with varying degrees of disapprobation or even, as in the case of the Godmans, brutal punishment. Helped by her husband John, Johan Godman 'disgised and appareled in all thinges like a souldier' went about the city as a lackey. No reason for this subterfuge is given. When found guilty both were set in the pillory, whipped naked to the waist, and then kept at Bridewell.[100]

Just as with the disguise of identity in general, then, the disguise of gender was a tool more freely available to the elite. Ordinary folk might make use of it, but they risked – especially as women – censure or retribution. As Stephen Orgel has written, 'contexts are everything . . . The proprieties of gender have everything to do with the proprieties of social class.'[101] This attitude helps us locate Chamberlain's extraordinarily casual reaction to Henrietta Maria's appearance, with her ladies, in the Shrovetide Masque in 1626. 'On Shrovetuisday the Quene and her women had a maske or pastorall play at Somerset House, wherein herself acted a part, and some of the rest were disguised like men with beards. I have knowne the time when this wold have seemed a straunge sight, to see a Quene act in a play but *tempora mutantur et nos*.'[102] With a shrug, therefore, Chamberlain accepts the sight of the Queen on stage as odd, but a sign of the changing times. The vision of court ladies in false beards, however, seems to him to be not in the least peculiar or worrying. In an appropriately exclusive context, bearded women go unremarked.

Notes

1. According to Chamberlain these were Endymion Porter and James Leviston, both Grooms of the Bedchamber; Kirke, a Scot; and Richard Grimes, a servant of Buckingham's. Buckingham was created Duke later that year, on 18 May.
2. *The Letters of John Chamberlain*, ed. by Norman Egbert McClure, 2 vols (Philadelphia, 1939), II, 480–1. A further version of these events is recounted by Dudley Carleton, see PRO, SP14/138/51.
3. Barry Taylor, *Vagrant Writing: Social and Semiotic Disorders in the English Renaissance* (London, 1991), p. 65.
4. A.L. Beier, *Masterless Men: The Vagrancy Problem in England 1560–1640* (London, 1985), p. xxii. See also John Pound, *Poverty and Vagrancy in Tudor England* (London, 1971); A.L. Beier, 'Vagrants and the Social Order in Elizabethan England', *Past and Present*, 64 (1974), 3–29; and Paul Slack, 'Vagrants and Vagrancy in England 1598–1664 ', in *Migration and Society in Early Modern England*, ed. by Peter Clark and David Souden (London, 1987), pp. 49–76.
5. Beier, *Masterless Men*, pp. 14–28, esp. pp. 19–22.
6. Raphaell Holinshed, William Harrison and others, *The First and Second Volumes of Chronicles* (London, 1587), p. 182.
7. Ibid., p. 183.
8. Paul Slack, *Poverty and Policy in Tudor and Stuart England* (London, 1988), p. 23.
9. *William Lambarde and Local Government: His 'Ephemeris' and Twenty-Nine Charges to Juries and Commissions*, ed. by Conyers Read (Ithaca, 1962), pp. 168–71.
10. William C. Carroll, *Fat King, Lean Beggar: Representations of Poverty in the Age of Shakespeare* (Ithaca, 1996), p. 36.
11. Gilbert Walker's pamphlet, *A Manifest Detection of Dice Play*, may have had up to three editions published about 1552. This was followed in 1561 by John Awdeley's *The Fraternity of Vagabonds*, and in 1566 by Thomas Harman's *A Caveat for Common Cursitors*, both of which went into further editions. While twenty-five rogue

pamphlets are extant, those by Robert Greene and Thomas Dekker dominate. Greene had five works appear over the years 1591–2 (*A Notable Discovery of Cozenage*, 1591; The *Second Part of Cony-Catching*, 1591; *The Third and Last Part of Cony-Catching*, 1592; *A Disputation between a He Cony-Catcher and a She Cony-Catcher*, 1592; *The Black Book's Messenger*, 1592), and in 1608 Dekker published *The Bellman of London* and *Lantern and Candlelight*. Rogue literature was also popular in sixteenth-century Spain, France and Germany. German models in particular influenced the development of the genre in England.

12. Carroll, *Fat King, Lean Beggar*, p. 39.
13. Gilbert Walker, *A Manifest Detection of Dice-Play* (c. 1552), in *Cony-Catchers and Bawdy Baskets: An Anthology of Elizabethan Low Life*, ed. by Gāmini Salgādo, (Harmondsworth, 1972), p. 40.
14. *A Royalist's Notebook: The Commonplace Book of Sir John Oglander of Nunwell*, ed. by Francis Bamford (London, 1936), pp. 137–8.
15. John Clavell, *A Recantation of an Ill Led Life, 1634*, in J.H.P. Pafford, *John Clavell 1601–1643: Highwayman, Author, Lawyer, Doctor* (Oxford, 1993), pp. 6, 8.
16. Robert Greene, *A Notable Discovery of Cozenage* (1591), in *Cony-Catchers and Bawdy Baskets*, ed. by Salgādo, p. 162.
17. Thomas Harman, *A Caveat or Warening for Commen Cursetors* (1567), in *Awdeley's Fraternitye of Vacabondes, Harman's Caveat etc*, ed. by Edward Viles and F.J. Furnivall, Early English Text Society, extra ser., 9 (1869), p. 22.
18. Carroll, *Fat King, Lean Beggar*, p. 42.
19. *SR*, 22 Hen. VIII, c. 12.
20. *SR*, 27 Hen. VIII, c. 25, (1535–6).
21. *SR*, 1 Edw. VI, c. 3, 1547; 14 Eliz. I, c. 5, 1572; 39 Eliz. I, c. 4, 1597/8; 1 Jac. I, c. 7, 1603–4.
22. *SR*, 1 Jac. I, c. 7, 1603–4.
23. Slack, *Poverty and Policy*, pp. 91–100.
24. Beier, *Masterless Men*, p. 160.
25. Harman, *A Caveat*, pp. 20–1.
26. *William Lambarde*, ed. by Read, p. 96.
27. *CJ*, I, 86, 87. *LJ*, I, 677, 678. See also *CSPD* 1547–80, p. 410. After having been referred to the Privy Council, the bill seems to have disappeared.
28. Proclamation 18 October 1591, 33 Elizabeth I (738), see *Tudor Royal Proclamations*, ed. by Paul Hughes and James Larkin, 3 vols (New Haven, 1969).

29. Arthur F. Marotti, 'Alienating Catholics in Early Modern England: Recusant Women, Jesuits and Ideological Fantasies', in *Catholicism and Anti-Catholicism in Early Modern English Texts*, ed. by Arthur F. Marotti (Houndmills, Basingstoke, 1999), pp. 1–34 (pp. 14, 12).

30. John Gerard, *The Autobiography of an Elizabethan*, trans. by Philip Caraman (London, 1951), pp. 17–18, 94.

31. *The Diary of Bulstrode Whitelocke*, ed. by Ruth Spalding, Records of Social and Economic History, new ser., 13 (London, 1990), p. 557. 'Perwicke' seems to be a combination of peruke and periwig.

32. *The Memoirs of Anne, Lady Halkett and Ann, Lady Fanshawe*, ed. by John Loftis (Oxford, 1979), pp. 127–8. Woollen thrummed hats were common among the lower orders.

33. 'An Account of His Majesty's Escape from Worcester: Dictated to Mr Pepys by the King Himself' (1680), in *The Boscobel Tracts*, ed. by J. Hughes, 2nd edn (Edinburgh, 1857), p. 150.

34. *Memoirs of Lady Halkett*, pp. 24–5. Interestingly, in 1644 Sir Samuel Luke, a Parliamentary commander and Governor of Newport Pagnell, ordered his subordinates to apprehend, among others, the Earls of Lindsey and Peterborough. He advised them to search diligently, and to 'be as careful as you can that no men deceive you in women's habits', see *The Letter Books, 1644–45, of Sir Samuel Luke*, ed. by Harry Gordon Tibbutt, HMC, Joint Publication Ser., 4 (London, 1963), p. 119.

35. Charles I was also disguised in his escape from Oxford in the Civil War. It was mentioned by contemporary diarists, among whom figure Lucy Hutchinson and Ralph Josselin, see *Memoirs of the Life of Colonel Hutchinson*, ed. by N.H. Keeble (London, 1995), p. 206; and *The Diary of Ralph Josselin 1616–1683*, ed. by Alan Macfarlane, Records of Social and Economic History, new ser., 3 (London, 1976), p. 59. In 1688 James II again attempted escaping in disguise, but was caught and initially taken for a Jesuit. He wore 'a short black wig [and] a patch on his upper lip on the left side', see John Miller, *James II: A Study in Kingship* (Hove, 1978), p. 206.

36. *Memoirs of Sir James Melville of Halhill 1535–1617*, ed. by A. Francis Steuart (London, 1929), p. 97.

37. Clavell, *A Recantation*, p. 28.

38. Richard Ollard, *The Image of the King: Charles I and Charles II* (London, 1979), p. 85.

39. 'An Account of His Majesty's Escape', in *Boscobel Tracts*, pp. 150, 169.

40. Stephen Gosson, *The Schoole of Abuse* (1579), in *Markets of Bawdrie: The Dramatic Criticism of Stephen Gosson*, ed. by Arthur Kinney (Salzburg, 1974), p. 89.
41. John Northbrooke, *A Treatise against Dicing, Dancing, Plays, and Interludes with Other Idle Pastimes* (1577), ed. by J.P. Collier, The Shakespeare Society, 14 (London, 1843), p. 94.
42. Stephen Gosson, *Playes Confuted in Fiue Actions* (1582), in *Markets of Bawdrie*, ed. by Kinney, pp. 177, 192–3.
43. William Prynne, *Histriomastix* (1633), Garland facsimile edn (New York, 1974), p. 156. Emphasis in the original.
44. Jean Howard, *The Stage and Social Struggle in Early Modern England* (London, 1994), p. 27.
45. *SR*, 14 Eliz. I, c. 5 (1572); 39 Eliz. I, c. 4 (1597–8); 1 Jac. I, c. 7 (1603–4).
46. Prynne, *Histriomastix*, pp. 496–7.
47. Howard, *The Stage and Social Struggle*, p. 16 and Chapter 2, pp. 22–46.
48. *Documents Relating to the Proceedings Against William Prynne, in 1634 and 1637*, ed. by S.R. Gardiner, Camden Society, new ser., 18 (1877), p. 10.
49. Jonas Barish, *The Anti-Theatrical Prejudice* (Berkeley, 1981), pp. 167–85.
50. Stephen Greenblatt, *Renaissance Self-Fashioning: From More to Shakespeare* (Chicago, 1980), p. 162.
51. Anna Bryson, *From Courtesy to Civility: Changing Codes of Conduct in Early Modern England* (Oxford, 1998), p. 207.
52. Baldassare Castiglione, *The Book of the Courtier*, trans. by Sir Thomas Hoby (London, 1928), p. 121. Sir Thomas Elyot, *The Book Named the Governor* (1531, repr. Menston, 1970), fol. 1015^v [irregular pagination]. John della Casa, *A Treatise of the Maners and Behauiours*, trans. by Robert Paterson, The English Experience, 120 (London, 1576; repr. Amsterdam, 1969), p. 3.
53. Greenblatt, *Renaissance Self-Fashioning*, p. 163.
54. Castiglione, *The Courtier*, p. 132. It must be noted that this view was not universally accepted. For example, the French author Philibert de Vienne wrote a satire of such models of courtiership, which was translated by George North and published in England in 1575 under the title *The Philosopher of the Court*. For contemporary objections to civility as codified in conduct books, including the charge of hypocrisy, see Bryson, *From Courtesy to Civility*, pp. 199–223.

55. Katherine Usher Henderson and Barbara McManus, *Half Human-kind: Contexts and Texts of the Controversy about Women in England, 1540–1640* (Urbana, 1985), pp. 11–12.

56. Stephen Gosson's *Quips for Vpstart, Newfangled Gentlewomen* (London, 1595), sigs A4ʳ, Bᵛ.

57. *The Batchelar's Banquet: or A Banquet for Batchelars: Wherein is prepared sundry daintie dishes to furnish their Table, curiously drest, and seriously serued*, in *The Non-Dramatic Works of Thomas Dekker*, ed. by Alexander B. Grosart, 5 vols (New York, 1963), I, 149–275. The text has been mis-attributed to Dekker.

58. *Haec-Vir: or, The womanish-man* (London, 1620), sigs [C2ᵛ, C4ʳ]. A third tract, *Muld Sacke: Or The Apologie of Hic Mulier: To the Late Declamation against her*, was also published in 1620. Although trading on the back of the two earlier pamphlets, it quickly moves from the topic to widely criticize all manner of social types and behaviours.

59. For example: Linda Woodbridge, *Women and the English Renaissance: Literature and the Nature of Womenkind, 1540–1620* (Urbana, 1984); Sandra Clark, 'Hic Mulier, Haec Vir and the Controversy Over Masculine Women', *Studies in Philology*, 82 (1985), 157–83; Susan Shapiro, 'Amazons, Hermaphrodites, and Plain Monsters: The "Masculine" Women in English Satire and Social Criticism from 1580–1640', *Atlantis*, 13 (1987), 66–76; Valerie Lucas, 'Hic Mulier: The Female Transvestite in Early Modern England', *Renaissance and Reformation / Renaissance er Réforme*, 24 (1988), 65–84.

60. *Hic Mulier: or, The man-woman* (London, 1620), sigs [A4ʳ-A4ᵛ].

61. *Haec-Vir*, sigs B4ᵛ, Cʳ.

62. Francis Douce, 'Observations on certain ornaments of Female Dress', *Archaeologia*, 12 (1796), 215–16. C.W. Cunnington and P. Cunnington state that in the first half of the sixteenth century a dagger might be worn from the girdle, but that this was rare, see *Handbook of English Costume in the Sixteenth Century* (London, 1954), p. 85. In a dialogue from 1605 written by Peter Erondell, a lady orders her maid to 'give me my girdle and see that all the furniture be at it: looke if my Cizers, the pincers, the pen-knife, the knife to close Letters, with the bodkin, the ear-picker and my Seale be in the case', see *The Elizabethan Home: Discovered in Two Dialogues by Claudius Hollyband and Peter Erondell*, ed. by M. St.Clare Byrne (London, 1949), p. 40. A slightly earlier reference is found in 'A New Courtly Sonet, of the Lady Greensleves', in which one of the verses runs 'Thy purse, and eke thy gay gilt knives', see *Satirical Songs and*

Poems on Costume, ed. by Frederick Fairholt, Percy Society, Early English Poetry, Ballads, and Popular Literature of the Middle Ages, 27 (London, 1849), pp. 96–100 (p. 97).

63. See Alastair Bellany, 'Mistress Turner's Deadly Sins: Sartorial Transgression, Court Scandal, and Politics in Early Stuart England', *Huntington Library Quarterly*, 58 (1997), 179–210; Peter Stallybrass and Ann Rosalind Jones, *Renaissance Clothing and the Materials of Memory* (Cambridge, 2000), pp. 59–85; Ann Rosalind Jones and Peter Stallybrass, '"Rugges of London and the Diuell's Band": Irish Mantles and Yellow Starch as Hybrid London Fashion', in *Material London, ca. 1600*, ed. by Lena Cowen Orlin (Philadelphia, 2000), pp. 128–49; and David Lindley, *The Trials of Frances Howard: Fact and Fiction at the Court of King James* (London, 1993), pp. 6–10.

64. Laura Gowing interprets this literature in a similar way, noting the androgynous body as being sexually charged, see *Domestic Dangers: Women, Words and Sex in Early Modern London* (Oxford, 1996), p. 83.

65. *Hic Mulier*, sig. [A4^v].

66. Ibid., sigs A3^v-[A4^r].

67. *Letters of John Chamberlain*, II, 286–87; 294, 11 March 1620.

68. Clark, 'Controversy over Masculine Women', p. 157.

69. Lawrence Stone, *The Crisis of the Aristocracy 1558–1641* (Oxford, 1965), p. 666.

70. Susan Shapiro offers a brief survey of 'transvestite' fashions, testifying to the 'persistence of this phenomenon' in 'Sex, Gender, and Fashion in Medieval and Early Modern Britain', *Journal of Popular Culture*, 20 (1987), 113–28 (p. 113).

71. George Gascoigne, *The Steele Glas* (1576), in *George Gascoigne: The Complete Works*, ed. by John W. Cunliffe, Anglistica & Americana Ser., 82, 2 vols (Hildesheim, 1974), II, 173–4.

72. Philip Stubbes, *The Anatomie of Abuses*, The English Experience, 489 (London, 1583; repr. Amsterdam, 1972), sigs [F5^r-F5^v].

73. *Diary*, VI, 172, 27 July 1665; VII, 162, 12 June 1666. On the development of women's riding dress, and its masculine characteristics, see Janet Arnold, 'Dashing Amazons: The Development of Women's Riding Dress, *c.* 1500–1900', in *Defining Dress: Dress and Object, Meaning and Identity*, ed. by Amy de la Haye and Elizabeth Wilson (Manchester, 1999), pp. 10–29.

74. *Hic Mulier*, sig. B2^r.

75. Rudolf Dekker and Lotte van de Pol, *The Tradition of Female Transvestism in Early Modern Europe* (Basingstoke, 1989).

76. Michael Shapiro, *Gender in Play on the Shakespearean Stage: Boy Heroines and Female Pages* (Ann Arbor, 1994), pp. 16–20. A transcription of the thirteen cases, compiled by Mark Benbow and Alasdair Hawkyard, is printed with Shapiro's text in Appendix C, pp. 225–34.
77. F.G. Emmison, *Elizabeth Life II: Morals and Church Courts* (Chelmsford, 1973), p. 8.
78. David Cressy, 'Gender Trouble and Cross-Dressing in Early Modern England', *Journal of British Studies*, 35 (1996), 438–65. Patricia Crawford and Sara Mendelson, 'Sexual Identities in Early Modern England', *Gender and History*, 7 (1995), 363–77. Stephen Greenblatt in 'Fiction and Friction', in *Reconstructing Individualism: Autonomy, Individuality, and the Self in Western Thought*, ed. by Thomas Heller, Morton Sosna and David Wellbery (Stanford, 1986), pp. 30–52 touches on transvestism, and includes in his notes a synopsis of a cross-dressing/gender disguise case in Virginia in 1629.
79. Dekker and Van de Pol, *Female Transvestism*.
80. Cressy, 'Gender Trouble', p. 445.
81. Repertories 18: 372 and Bridewell Court Minutes, 2: 89^v-90^v. Bridewell Court Minutes 2: 163^v, 168^v. Transcribed in Shapiro, *Gender in Play*.
82. Emmison, *Morals and Church Courts*, p. 8.
83. Dekker and Van de Pol, *Female Transvestism*, pp. 39, 45.
84. See, for example, Vern L. Bullough, 'Transvestites in the Middle Ages', *American Journal of Sociology*, 79 (1973–74), 1381–94; John Anson, 'The Female Transvestite in Early Monasticism: The Origin and Development of a Motif', *Viator*, 5 (1974), 1–32; and J.L. Welch, 'Cross-Dressing and Cross-Purposes: Gender Possibilities in the Acts of Thecla', in *Gender Reversal and Gender Cultures*, ed. by Sabrina Petra Ramet (London, 1996), pp. 66–78. Valerie Hotchkiss, *Clothes Makes the Man: Female Cross Dressing in Medieval Europe* (New York, 1996), covers many aspects of medieval transvestism, including that which appears in hagiography.
85. Jean Howard, 'Cross-Dressing, the Theatre, and Gender Struggle in Early Modern England', in *Crossing the Stage: Controversies on Cross-Dressing*, ed. by Lesley Ferris (London, 1993), pp. 20–46 (pp. 25–6).
86. Repertories, 19: 93. Transcribed in Shapiro, *Gender in Play*.
87. Bridewell Court Minutes, 4: 270. Transcribed in Shapiro, *Gender in Play*.
88. Repertories, 18: 372; Repertories, 19: 93. Transcribed in Shapiro, *Gender in Play*.

89. Cressy, 'Gender Trouble', p. 450.
90. Repertories 13: 426^v. Transcribed in Shapiro, *Gender in Play*.
91. Howard, 'Cross-Dressing, the Theatre, and Gender Struggle', p. 20.
92. *Memoirs of John Reresby*, ed. by Andrew Browning (Glasgow, 1936), p. xxxix.
93. Recounted in Stephen Orgel, *Impersonations: The Performance of Gender in Shakespeare's England* (Cambridge, 1996), pp. 113–14.
94. Winwood, *Memorials of Affairs of State in the Reigns of Q. Elizabeth and K. James I collected chiefly from the original papers of the Right Honourable Sir Ralph Winwood, Kt.* 3 vols (London, 1725) III, 279, quoted in G.P.V. Akrigg, *Jacobean Pageant* (London, 1962), p. 121.
95. *The Letters of Lady Arbella Stuart*, ed. by Sara Jayne Steen (Oxford, 1994), pp. 68–9.
96. Winfried Schleiner, 'Male Cross-Dressing and Transvestism in Renaissance Romances', *Sixteenth-Century Journal*, 19 (1988), 606–19 (p. 607).
97. John Rainoldes, *Th'overthrow of Stage-Playes* (1599, repr. New York, 1974), p. 14.
98. *Haec-Vir*, sig. B4^r.
99. Prynne, *Histriomastix*, p. 182. *Proceedings Against William Prynne*, ed. by Gardiner, p. 3.
100. Repertories, 16: 522. Transcribed in Shapiro, *Gender in Play*.
101. Orgel, *Impersonations*, pp. 120–1.
102. *Letters of John Chamberlain*, II, 630. The importance of costumes and cross-dressing in Shrovetide masques is discussed in Barbara Ravelhofer, 'Bureaucrats and Courtly Cross-Dressers in the *Shrovetide Masque* and *The Shepherd's Paradise*', *English Literary Renaissance*, 29 (1999), 75–96.

Conclusion: From Riches to Rags

In 1641 William Calley wrote a letter describing a theft:

> on Saturday the 10th of this instant Aprill betweene twelve and one of the Clocke at night wee lost eight payres of new Canvas sheetes layd in the garden to bee whited but whether over burdened or out of running (like the Lapwing with cryeng to draw further from his nest) they dropped three payres in two severall places openly to bee seene as if they had gone that way which I cannot believe they did, neither doe I thinke they were straungers altogeather; we have used the best diligence wee can by searching but found noething more then what before I sayd was left.[1]

In losing their canvas sheets, William's household were the victims of an extremely common form of crime. So frequently were textiles stolen that rogue pamphlets even alleged a particular type of criminal specialized in pilfering cloth and clothing. It was said these 'hookers', 'anglers' or 'curbers' – named after their long poles fitted with iron hooks – would use this tool of trade to pluck items of apparel through windows and open doors, or from where garments lay drying in the sun.[2] Working from the less debatable evidence of court records, historians agree both on the reality of clothing theft, and its frequency.[3] When soldiers ransacked his daughter's house, Bulstrode Whitelocke wrote that by force they took goods, money and plate. They also took away the couple's 'wering apparell, & even to her childbed linnen'.[4] Similarly, on a trip to Jersey sailors broke open the trunks belonging to Lady Fanshawe. They stole 'a quantity of gold lace, with our best clothes and linnen and all my combs, gloves, ribonds, which amounted to near three hundred pounds'.[5]

Clothing theft is now very rare. A promise to be 'tough on crime and tough on the causes of crime' hardly brings to mind the threat of stolen garments. The practice of taking apparel has diminished, as has the monetary worth of the garments themselves. For early modern clothing crime was a direct reflection of contemporary value. Not only was dress relatively more expensive than today, it had relatively more importance. For in a society in which there were fewer 'things' to own, clothing was more economically visible. For us these experiences, however, open a window on to a world of re-use. It is a world markedly different from our own, in which garments are worn and discarded. Unwanted, clothing is perhaps given to charity, but very rarely is it converted for another wearer, or to another function. Today we even buy our rags new – but call them dish cloths, paper towels and tissues, dusters, and disposable nappies. By contrast, the early modern experience was one that husbanded this valuable resource, tailoring it – figuratively and literally – to a number of needs.

We have seen that the capital garments represented could be realized by the simple expedient of theft. Sartorial investment could also be turned into ready cash by its sale. For example Pepys, on the rise in his professional life but still financially cautious, bought a second-hand velvet cloak. Interestingly, he spent two pounds more for it than had the seller, but Pepys still considered it 'worth my money'. Some years later, when better off himself, he noted the 'sad condition' of a Mrs Williams who 'hath been fain of late to sell her best clothes and Jewells to get a little money upon'.[6] More commonly recorded by personal narratives was a visit to the pawn shop. In 1629 Sir Francis Harris wrote a letter of appeal to his aunt, Lady Barrington. He hoped that 'some freind reedemes me a doblett and hose of black which lyeth for 21s'.[7] This method of converting worn assets to hard cash could be employed apparently regardless of income, social standing, or political and religious persuasion. The staunchly pious Alice Thornton pawned her husband's sword, and the staunchly royalist Duchess of Newcastle was told by her husband 'that I must of necessity pawn my cloaths to make so much Money as would procure a Dinner'. For Henry Newcome, a poor parishioner with a shiftless husband who pawned her coat was a moral exemplar.[8] At the other end of the social scale Queen Henrietta Maria, with a husband in a different plight, pawned the crown jewels. For sixteenth- and seventeenth-century men and women, the pawnbrokers was a universal place of transformation, turning apparel from capital into cash, and then back again.

Garments might be circulated through many other mechanisms. They were passed on to dependants, left as testamentary bequests, given to local churches for making into vestments, and re-used within the household. Lady Clifford's diary illustrates some of these multiple uses. In November 1617 she gave to the Queen, by my Lady Ruthven, the gift of 'the skirts of a White Satin Gown all pearl and embroidered with colours'. Clearly these skirts were new and not second-hand, and cost Lady Anne 'fourscore pounds without the Satin'. Earlier that year, however, in February, she mentioned she had passed on her daughter's old clothes to her steward, so that Legge could give them to his wife.[9] Also in 1617 Lady Anne noted her then husband's plans to refurbish their country house, Knole, in part re-using his own apparel for the furnishings. Along with the Earl of Dorset's orders to the steward to dress up the rooms 'as fine as he could', he 'determined to make all his old clothes in purple stuff for the gallery & Drawing Chamber'.[10] Two years later Lady Anne noted that she gave away her sable muff to Sir Robert Taxley. Perhaps most interestingly of all, despite being one of the wealthiest women in the country, that month Lady Anne also wrote that 'My Lord gave me 3 Shirts to make Clouts of'.[11]

So clothes in early modern England were an asset, costly to begin with, but if carefully managed imbued with the potential of bringing in more money. They were material items in which utility, investment and social possibility combined to create unique value. Garments could pass through many different hands by re-circulating through theft, and also re-sale, pawning, bequest and gift. At each stage of their ownership they were wrung of still more value, until finally there was nothing left to exploit. As illustrated by Lady Anne's re-use of her husband's shirts, the sixteenth- and seventeenth-century story of clothes was literally a tale of riches to rags.

It is hardly surprising that something as materially significant as dress should also be charged with values over and above its financial and utilitarian worth. In exploring the ways that clothing participated in the lives of the upper and middling sort, this study has sought to uncover some of this cultural significance. Firstly, it required wearers to have an expertise in the 'making' of garments. Although they were sewn by a tailor, the consumer had an active role, commonly first selecting and buying the right quantity and type of fabric, deciding on cut and style, and exercising choice over the finishing and trimming of a garment in order to achieve their desired appearance. Once made up, elite wearers demonstrated a prowess in the manipulation of their dress, styles to the 1620s in particular demanding that they negotiate their world through the medium of padded, stiffened and multi-layered forms. Clothing had many other implications for the body. From swaddling at birth to death's shroud, clothes were a positive presence that people felt managed, protected and sustained their physical progress through life. Outer garments were a decorative barrier against disease and cold. Inner linen garments resided somewhere between flesh and fabric. A publicly glimpsed suggestion of intimacy, linen was skin-like and sexually evocative. Its white abundance also spoke of the luxury of wealth and the gentility of a disciplined physicality.

The social body, too, was profoundly affected by costume, as individuals used it to signal and perform aspects of personality. However, this was by no means always a consensual activity, as the imposed persona of the socially marginalized was frequently achieved through the medium of dress. The powerful nature of the appearential text also emerges through scrutiny of the acts and proclamations of apparel, measures that sought to control access to the dress styles of the elite. The transformation of appearances was policed less overtly through the attitude of authority towards disguise. For the privileged, the manipulation of outward personae was an allowable, and sometimes praiseworthy, strategy. For the humble, it was deceitful, subversive and punishable. While tracing these stories of use through legal discourse, written public debate, and individual claims and reminiscences, I have tried to draw attention to the agency of dress. Certainly garments were put on and manipulated by their wearers but, to a certain extent, they also exercised a reverse influence. Clothes shaped the configurations of the body, affected the spaces and interactions between people, and altered the perceptions of the wearer and viewers. As William Shakespeare had Perdita say, 'sure this robe of mine does change my disposition'.[12]

There is, however, a coda to this riches to rags story which was so profoundly entwined in people's lives. It opens with Endymion Porter, who has so far made only a peripheral appearance (Figure 16). A Stuart courtier, Porter accompanied Charles in his disguised Spanish venture. He was also connected, through the favours of patronage, to the Calley household. In 1640 Porter and three others petitioned the king for a monopoly on the making of white writing paper. As fundamental to the success of the venture, they also requested a prohibition on the export of linen rags, instead desiring that the rags be sold to them.[13] For the making of paper was dependent on the tattered remains of textiles, and represents an after-life to the long cycle of cloth re-use. As John Taylor, the Water Poet, observed of these rags:

> And some of these poore things perhaps hath beene
> The linnen of some Countesse or some Queene,
> Yet lyes now on the dunghill, bare and poore
> Mix'd with the rags of some baud, theefe, or whore.
> And these things have beene in better states
> Adorning bodies of great Potentates [...]
> May not the torne shirt of a Lords or Kings
> Be pasht and beaten in the Paper mill
> And made Pot-paper by the workemans skill?[14]

In order to approach the meanings of dress, this investigation has assumed that textiles, then as now, operated in a way analogous to text.

That is, bringing interpretative strategies to bear on the dressed figure, viewers produced a range of complex and multiple readings. We end, however, by confronting the literal truth of the fabrication of meaning. Worn too thin and tattered to sustain further re-use, garments yet began a second life. Transformed from rags to writing paper, textiles, in the early modern world, again became text.

Notes

1. PRO, SP16/479/78.
2. Thomas Harman, *A Caveat or Warening for Commen Cursetors* (1567), in *Awdeley's Fraternitye of Vacabondes, Harman's Caveat etc*, ed. by Edward Viles and F.J. Furnivall, Early English Text Society, extra ser., 9 (1869), pp. 21, 35–6.
3. For example, in sampled evidence from Cheshire in the 1590s to the 1660s, Garthine Walker has demonstrated that clothing and household linens were the most popular goods stolen by both men and women, see 'Women, Theft and the World of Stolen Goods', in *Women, Crime and the Courts in Early Modern England*, ed. by J. Kermode and G. Walker (London, 1994), pp. 81–105 (esp. pp. 87–8).
4. *The Diary of Bulstrode Whitelocke*, ed. by Ruth Spalding, Records of Social and Economic History, new ser., 13 (London, 1990), p. 621.
5. *The Memoirs of Anne, Lady Halkett and Ann, Lady Fanshawe*, ed. by John Loftis (Oxford, 1979), p. 118.
6. *Diary*, III, 84, 17 May 1662; VIII, 314, 1 July 1667. On the second-hand trade, including its links with the theft and pawning of garments, see the work by Beverly Lemire esp. 'Consumerism in Preindustrial and Early Industrial England: The Trade in Secondhand Clothes', *Journal of British Studies*, 27 (1998), 1–24; 'Peddling Fashion: Sales-men, Pawnbrokers, Taylors, Thieves and the Second-hand Clothes Trade in England, *c*. 1700–1800', *Textile History*, 22 (1991), 67–82; and *Dress, Culture and Commerce: The English Clothing Trade before the Factory, 1660–1800* (Basingstoke, 1997). On the second-hand market in early modern Italy, see Patricia Allerston, 'Reconstructing the Second-hand Clothes Trade in Sixteenth- and Seventeenth-Century Venice', *Costume*, 33 (1999), 46–56.

7. *Barrington Family Letters 1628–1632*, ed. by Arthur Searle, Camden 4th ser., 28 (London, 1983), p. 114.

8. *The Autobiography of Mrs. Alice Thornton*, Surtees Society, 62 (1875), p. 163. *The Lives of William Cavendishe, Duke of Newcastle, and of his wife, Margaret Duchess of Newcastle*, ed. by Mark Antony Lower (London, 1872), p. 71. *The Autobiography of Henry Newcome, M.A.,* ed. by Richard Parkinson, 2 vols, Chetham Society, 26, 27 (1852), I, 85.

9. *The Diaries of Lady Anne Clifford*, ed. by D.J.H. Clifford (Stroud, 1990), pp. 64, 49.

10. Ibid., p. 55. While the Earl of Dorset's wardrobe inventory does include a purple suit, it does not record the re-use of its fabrics as furnishings. However, this same inventory does note that caparisons were re-made into such items as chairs, stools, cushions and canopies for Knole. It also provides evidence that the Earl gave some of his garments away to dependants, see Peter Mactaggart and Ann Mactaggart, 'The Rich Wearing Apparel of Richard, 3rd Earl of Dorset', *Costume*, 14 (1980), 41–55.

11. *Diaries of Lady Clifford*, p. 81.

12. William Shakespeare, *The Winter's Tale*, IV, 4, 134.

13. *CSPD* 1640, p. 226. Porter and his colleagues were not the first to request this. In 1585 a London stationer, Richard Tottyl, had petitioned for the right to make white paper, and for the prohibition of rag export. While Tottyl failed, in 1589 jeweller and papermaker John Spilman was granted the monopoly for rags. Although most paper used in England was imported, between 1601 and 1650 there were forty-one paper mills; see Richard L. Hills, *Papermaking in Britain 1488–1988* (London, 1988), pp. 50–2.

14. John Taylor, 'The Praise of Hemp-Seed', in *All the Workes of John Taylor the Water Poet* (London, 1630; repr. 1977), III, 68–70 (irregular pagination).

Select Bibliography

Manuscript

BIHR, York, Cons. AB. 33 (1570–2).
BIHR, York, Prob. Ex. 1607–46.
BL, London, Harley MS 6064.
BL, London, Harley MS 6079.
Bod. Lib., Oxford, Ashmole MS 836.
Bod. Lib., Oxford, Ashmole MS 840.
Bod. Lib., Oxford, Ashmole MS 857.
CA, London, Vincent MS 151.
PRO, London, SP16/392/15.
PRO, London, SP16/392/16.
PRO, London, SP16/400/62.
PRO, London, SP16/400/76.
PRO, London, SP16/410/46.
PRO, London, SP16/413/11.
PRO, London, SP16/414/66.
PRO, London, SP16/414/67.
PRO, London, SP16/454/100.
PRO, London, SP16/458/10.
PRO, London, SP16/471/67.
PRO, London, SP16/471/68.
PRO, London, SP16/473/56.
PRO, London, SP16/473/81.
PRO, London, SP16/473/91.
PRO, London, SP16/478/77.
PRO, London, SP16/479/21.
PRO, London, SP16/479/78.
PRO, London, SP16/480/30.

Printed Primary

Æ., I. H., 'The Mirrour of Worldly Fame' (1603), in *Harleian Miscellany*,
  8 vols (London, 1744–6) VIII, 31–46.

Allestree, Richard, *The Whole Duty of Man* (London, 1671).

*Articles Agreed upon by the Lordes . . . for a Reformation of their seru-
  auntes in certayne Abuses of Apparell*, (20 October 1559) STC 7903.

Ascham, Roger, *The Scholemaster* (1570), English Linguistics 1500–1800
  Facsimile Reprints, 20 (Menston, 1967).

Assheton, Nicholas, *The Journal of Nicholas Assheton*, ed. by F.R. Raines,
  Chetham Society, 14 (Manchester, 1848).

Bacon, Francis, *The Essays*, ed. by John Pitcher (Harmondsworth, 1985).

Barbon, Nicholas, *A Discourse of Trade*, (1690; repr. Baltimore, 1905).

Barrington Family Letters 1628–1632, ed. by Arthur Searle, Camden 4th
  ser., 28 (London, 1983).

Barrow, Henry, *The Writings of Henry Barrow 1587–1590*, ed. by Leland
  H. Carlson (London, 1962).

Becon, Thomas, *Prayers and Other Pieces of Thomas Becon*, ed. by John
  Ayre, Parker Society, 12 (Cambridge, 1844).

Bonham, Thomas, *The Chyrurgeons Closet*, The English Experience, 31
  (London, 1630; repr. Amsterdam, 1968).

Bright, Timothy, *The Sufficiencie of English Medicines*, The English
  Experience, 854 (London, 1580; repr. Amsterdam, 1977).

B[ulwer], J[ohn], *Anthropometamorphosis: Man Transfrom'd: Or, the
  Artificall Changling* (London, 1653).

Burton, Robert, *The Anatomy of Melancholy*, 6 vols (Oxford, 1989–2000).

Byrne, M. St.Clare (ed.), *The Elizabethan Home: Discovered in Two
  Dialogues by Claudius Hollyband and Peter Erondell* (London, 1949).

Camden, William, *Remains Concerning Britain* (London, 1870).

Carey, Robert, *The Memoirs of Robert Carey*, ed. by F.H. Mares (Oxford,
  1972).

Carleton, Dudley, *Dudley Carleton to John Chamberlain 1603–1624
  Jacobean Letters*, ed. by Maurice Lee, Jr. (New Brunswick, 1972).

Carpenter, Richard, *Experience, Historie, and Divinitie* (London, 1642).

Castiglione, Baldassare, *The Book of the Courtier*, trans. by Sir Thomas
  Hoby (London, 1928).

Cavendish, Margaret, *The Lives of William Cavendishe, Duke of Newcastle, and of his Wife, Margaret Duchess of Newcastle*, ed. by Mark
  Antony Lower (London, 1872).

Chamberlain, John, *The Letters of John Chamberlain*, ed. by Norman
  Egbert McClure, 2 vols (Philadelphia, 1939).

Clavell, John, *A Recantation of an Ill Led Life, 1634*, in J.H.P. Pafford, *John Clavell 1601–1643: Highwayman, Author, Lawyer, Doctor* (Oxford, 1993).

Cleland, James, *The Institution of a Young Nobleman* (1607; repr. Bristol, 1994).

Clifford, Lady Anne, *The Diaries of Lady Anne Clifford*, ed. by D.J.H. Clifford (Stroud, 1990).

Commons Debates 1621, ed. by Wallace Notestein, Frances Relf and Hartley Simpson, 7 vols (New Haven, 1935).

Courthop, George, 'The Memoirs of George Courthop', in *The Camden Miscellany 11*, Camden Society, 3rd ser., 13 (London, 1907).

Dekker, Thomas, *The Non-Dramatic Works of Thomas Dekker*, ed. by Alexander B. Grosart, 5 vols (New York, 1963).

della Casa, John, *A Treatise of the Maners and Behauiours*, trans. by Robert Paterson, The English Experience, 120 (London, 1576; repr. Amsterdam, 1969).

de Maisse, *De Maisse: A Journal of All that was Accomplished by Monsieur de Maisse Ambassador in England*, trans. and ed. by G.B. Harrison (London, 1931).

de Vienne, Philibert, *The Philosopher of the Court*, trans. by George North (1575).

Digby, Sir Kenelm, *Private Memoirs of Sir Kenelm Digby, Gentleman of the Bedchamber to King Charles the First* (London, 1827).

Donne, John, *The Complete English Poems*, ed. by A.J. Smith (Harmondsworth, 1986).

Drayton, Michael, *The Works of Michael Drayton*, ed. by J. William Hebel, 5 vols (Oxford, 1961).

Earle, John, *Microcosmography or a Piece of the World Discovered in Essays and Characters*, ed. by Harold Osborne (London, n.d.).

Edward VI, *Literary Remains of King Edward VI*, ed. by J.G. Nichols (London, 1857; repr. New York, 1964).

Elyot, Sir Thomas, *The Book Named the Governor* (1531; repr. Menston, 1970).

Erasmus, Desiderius, *Collected Works of Erasmus* (Toronto, 1974–97).

Evelyn, John, *The Diary of John Evelyn*, ed. by E.S. de Beer, 6 vols (Oxford, 1955).

Fairholt, Frederick (ed.), *Satirical Songs and Poems on Costume*, Percy Society, Early English Poetry, Ballads, and Popular Literature of the Middle Ages, 27 (London, 1849).

Fanshawe, Lady Ann, *The Memoirs of Anne, Lady Halkett and Ann, Lady Fanshawe*, ed. by John Loftis (Oxford, 1979).

Finet, John, *Ceremonies of Charles I: The Note Books of John Finet 1628–1641*, ed. by Albert J. Loomie (New York, 1987).

Fox, George, *The Journal of George Fox*, ed. by John L. Nickalls (Cambridge, 1952).

Frere, W.H. and Douglas C.E. (eds), *Puritan Manifestoes* (London, 1907).

Fuller, Thomas Fuller, *The Holy State and the Profane State* (1642), ed. by James Nichols (London, 1841).

Gardiner, S.R. (ed.), *Documents Relating to the Proceedings Against William Prynne, in 1634 and 1637*, Camden Society, new ser., 18 (London, 1877).

Gascoigne, George, *George Gascoigne: The Complete Works*, ed. by John W. Cunliffe, Anglistica & Americana Ser., 82, 2 vols (Hildesheim, 1974).

Gawdy, Philip, *Letters of Philip Gawdy*, ed. by Isaac Herbert Jeayes, The Roxburghe Club, 148 (London, 1906).

Gerard, John, *The Autobiography of an Elizabethan*, trans. by Philip Caraman (London, 1951).

Gosson, Stephen, *Quips for Vpstart, Newfangled Gentlewomen* (London, 1595).

Haec-Vir: or, The womanish-man (London, 1620).

Halkett, Lady Anne, *The Memoirs of Anne, Lady Halkett and Ann, Lady Fanshawe*, ed. by John Loftis (Oxford, 1979).

Hall, Joseph, *The Works of Joseph Hall*, ed. by Joseph Pratt and Peter Hall, 12 vols (Oxford, 1837–9).

Hammond, Walter, 'A Paradox: Proving the Inhabitants of the Island, called Madagascar, or St. Lawrence (in things temporal) to be the happiest People in the World' (1640), in *Harleian Miscellany*, 8 vols (London, 1744–6), I, 256–7.

Hane, Joachim, *The Journal of Joachim Hane*, ed. by C.H. Firth (Oxford, 1896).

Harington, John, *The Letters and Epigrams of Sir John Harington*, ed. by Norman Egbert McClure (New York, 1977).

Harington, John, *Nugae Antiquae: Being a Miscellaneous Collection of Original Papers*, ed. by Thomas Park, 2 vols (London, 1804).

Harley, Lady Brilliana, *Letters of The Lady Brilliana Harley*, ed. by Thomas Taylor Lewis, Camden Society, 58 (London, 1854).

Harrison, G.B., *The Elizabethan Journals*, 3 vols, rev. edn (London, 1938).

Hawes, Richard, *The Poore-Mans Plaster-Box*, The English Experience, 664 (London, 1634; repr. Amsterdam, 1974).

Hazlitt, W.C. (ed.), *Inedited Tracts: Illustrating the Manners, Opinions, and Occuptions of Englishment During the Sixteenth and Seventeenth Centuries*, Burt Franklin Research and Source Works Series, 49 (New York, 1963).

Herbert, Lord Edward, *The Life of Edward, First Lord Herbert of Cherbury, Written by Himself*, ed. by J.M. Shuttleworth (London, 1976).

Hic Mulier: or, The man-woman (London, 1620).

Hilliard, Nicholas, *A Treatise Concerning the Arte of Limning*, ed. by R.K.R. Thornton and T.G.S. Cain (Ashington, 1981).

Hindley, Charles (ed.), *The Old Book Collector's Miscellany*, (London, 1872).

Hoby, Lady Margaret, *The Private Life of an Elizabethan Lady: The Diary of Lady Margaret Hoby, 1599–1605*, ed. by Joanna Moody (Stroud, 1998).

Hodgson, John, *Autobiography of Captain John Hodgson, of Coley Hall, near Halifax; His Conduct in the Civil Wars, and his Troubles after the Restoration*, ed. by J. Horsfall Turner (Brighouse, 1882).

Holinshed, Raphaell; Harrison, William and others, *The First and Second Volumes of Chronicles* (London, 1587).

Hoppit, Julian (ed.), *Failed Legislation, 1660–1800: Extracted from the Commons and Lords Journals* (London, 1997).

Hughes, J. (ed.), *The Boscobel Tracts*, 2nd edn (Edinburgh, 1857).

Hughes, P.L. and Larkin, J.F. (eds), *Tudor Royal Proclamations*, 3 vols (New Haven, 1964–9).

Hughes, P.L. and Larkin, J.F. (eds), *Stuart Royal Proclamations, Volume I* (Oxford, 1973).

Hutchinson, Lucy, *Memoirs of the Life of Colonel Hutchinson*, ed. by N.H. Keeble (London, 1995).

Josselin, Ralph, *The Diary of Ralph Josselin 1616–1683*, ed. by Alan Macfarlane, Records of Social and Economic History, new ser., 3 (London, 1976).

Judges, A.V., *The Elizabethan Underworld* (London, 1930).

Kinney, Arthur F. (ed.), *Markets of Bawdrie: The Dramatic Criticism of Stephen Gosson*, (Salzburg, 1974).

Kinney, Arthur F. (ed.), *Rogues, Vagabonds and Sturdy Beggars: A New Gallery of Tudor and Early Stuart Rogue Literature* (Amherst MA, 1990).

Lambarde, William, *William Lambarde and Local Government: His 'Ephemeris' and Twenty-Nine Charges to Juries and Commissions*, ed. by Conyers Read (Ithaca, 1962).

Larkin, J.F. (ed.), *Stuart Royal Proclamations, Volume II* (Oxford, 1983).

Lower, Richard, *De Catarrhis* (1672), trans. by Richard Hunter and Ida Macalpine (London, 1963).

Luke, Sir Samuel, *The Letter Books, 1644–45, of Sir Samuel Luke*, ed. by Harry Gordon Tibbutt, HMC, Joint Publication Ser., 4 (London, 1963).

M., I., *A Health to the Gentlemanly Profession of Serving-Men 1598*, ed. by A.V. Judges, Shakespeare Association Facsimiles, 3 (1931).

Machyn, Henry, *The Diary of Henry Machyn, Citizen of London, 1550–1563*, ed. by John Gough Nichols, Camden Society, 42 (London, 1847).

Mactaggart, Peter and Mactaggart, Ann, 'The Rich Wearing Apparel of Richard, 3rd Earl of Dorset', *Costume*, 14 (1980), 41–55.

Manningham, John, *The Diary of John Manningham of the Middle Temple 1602–1603*, ed. by Robert Parker Sorlien (Hanover NH, 1976).

Markham, Gervase, *The English Housewife* (1615), ed. by Michael R. Best (Montreal, 1994).

Melville, Sir James, *Memoirs of Sir James Melville of Halhill 1535–1617*, ed. by A. Francis Steuart (London, 1929).

Mildmay, Lady Grace, *With Faith and Physic: The Life of a Tudor Gentlewoman Lady Grace Mildmay 1552–1620*, ed. by Linda Pollock (London, 1993).

Montaigne, Michel Eyquem de, *Montaigne's Essays: John Florio's Translation*, ed. by J.I M. Stewart, 2 vols (London, 1931).

Moore, Giles, *The Journal of Giles Moore*, ed. by Ruth Bird, The Sussex Record Society, 68 (Lewes, 1971).

More, George, *A True Discourse Concerning the Certaine Possession and Dispossessi of 7 Persons in one Familie in Lancashire* (London?, 1600).

Mortimer, Ian (ed.), *Berkshire Probate Accounts 1583–1712*, Berkshire Record Society, 4 (Reading, 1999).

Moryson, Fynes, *An Itinerary*, 4 vols (Glasgow, 1907).

Mun, Thomas, *England's Treasure by Forraign Trade* (Oxford, 1959).

Nashe, Thomas, *Christs Teares Over Jerusalem* (London, 1593; repr. Menston, 1970).

Nashe, Thomas, *The Works of Thomas Nashe*, ed. by R.B. McKerrow, 5 vols (repr. Oxford, 1958).

Newcome, Henry, *The Autobiography of Henry Newcome, M.A.*, ed. by Richard Parkinson, 2 vols, Chetham Society, 26, 27 (Manchester, 1852).

Norgate, Edward, *Miniatura or the Art of Limning*, ed. by Martin Hardie (Oxford, 1919).

North, Sir Dudley, *Discourses upon Trade* (1691), in Richard Grassby, *The English Gentleman in Trade: The Life and Works of Sir Dudley North, 1641–1691* (Oxford, 1994).

North, Roger, *The Autobiography of the Hon. Roger North*, ed. by Augustus Jessop (London, 1887).

Northbrooke, John, *A Treatise against Dicing, Dancing, Plays, and Interludes with Other Idle Pastimes* (1577), ed. by J.P. Collier, The Shakespeare Society, 14 (London, 1843).

Oglander, Sir John, *A Royalist's Notebook: The Commonplace Book of Sir John Oglander of Nunwell*, ed. by Francis Bamford (London, 1936).

Overbury, Thomas, *The Miscellaneous Works in Prose and Verse of Sir Thomas Overbury*, ed. by Edward Rimbault (London, 1890).

Peacham, Henry, *The Truth of our Times* (1638), in Henry Peacham, *The Complete Gentleman and Other Works*, ed. by Virgil Heltzel (Ithaca, 1962).

Peele, George, *Polyhmnia*, in *The Life and Minor Works of George Peele*, ed. by David Horne (New Haven, 1952).

Penn, William, *No Cross, No Crown:, Or Several Sober Reasons against Hat-Honour* (London, 1669).

Pepys, Samuel, *The Diary of Samuel Pepys*, ed. by Robert Latham and William Matthews, 11 vols (London, 1970–83).

Pett, Phineas, *The Autobiography of Phineas Pett*, ed. by E.G. Perrin, Navy Records Society, 51 (London, 1918).

Proceedings in Parliament 1614, ed. by Maija Jansson (Philadelphia, 1988).

Proceedings in Parliament 1628, ed. by Mary Frear Keeler, Maija Jansson Cole and William B. Bidwell, 6 vols (New Haven, 1978).

Proceedings in the Parliaments of Elizabeth I, ed. by T.E. Hartley, 3 vols (Leicester, 1981–95).

Prynne, William, *The Vnlouelinesse of Love-Lockes* (London, 1628).

Prynne, William, *Histriomastix* (1633), Garland facsimile edn (New York, 1974).

Prynne, William, *A Gagge for Long-Hair'd Rattle-Heads who Revile all Civill Round-heads* (London, 1646).

Rabelais, François, *The Works of Rabelais*, trans. by Sir Thomas Urquhart, intro. by J. Lewis May, 2 vols (London, 1933).

Rainoldes, John, *Th'overthrow of Stage-Plays* (1599, repr. New York, 1974).

Reresby, John, *Memoirs of John Reresby*, ed. by Andrew Browning (Glasgow, 1936).

Rye, William Brenchley (ed.), *England as Seen by Foreigners* (London, 1865).

Salgādo, Gāmini (ed.), *Cony-Catchers and Bawdy Baskets: An Anthology of Elizabethan Low Life* (Harmondsworth, 1972).

Segar, William, *Honor Military, and Ciuill, Contained in Foure Books* (London, 1602).

Shakespeare, William, *Much Ado About Nothing*, ed. by Sheldon P. Zitner (Oxford, 1993).

Shakespeare, William, *The Winter's Tale*, ed. by Stephen Orgel (Oxford, 1996).

Simotta, George, *A Theater of the Planetary Houres For All Dayes of the Yeare*, The English Experience, 414 (London, 1631; repr. Amsterdam, 1971).

Smith, Sir Thomas, *A Discourse of the Commonweal of This Realm of England*, ed. by Mary Dewar, The Folger Shakespeare Library (Charlottesville, 1969).

Spenser, Edmund, *Two Cantos of Mutabilitie*, Stanzas 1, 6 (1609), in Edmund Spenser, *The Faerie Queene*, 2 vols, facsimile edn (London, 1976).

Stern, Elizabeth, 'Peckover and Gallyard, Two Sixteenth-Century Norfolk Tailors', *Costume*, 15 (1981), 13–23.

Stowe, John, *Three Fifteenth-Century Chronicles with Historical Memoranda by John Stowe*, ed. by James Gairdner, Camden Society, new ser., 28 (London, 1880).

Stuart, Lady Arbella, *The Letters of Lady Arbella Stuart*, ed. by Sara Jayne Steen (Oxford, 1994).

Stubbes, Philip, *The Anatomie of Abuses*, The English Experience, 489 (London, 1583; repr. Amsterdam, 1972).

Sutcliffe, Matthew, *An Answere to a Certaine Libel Svpplicatorie* (London, 1592).

Taylor, John, *All the Workes of John Taylor the Water Poet* (London, 1630; repr. 1977).

Thornton, Alice, *The Autobiography of Mrs. Alice Thornton*, Surtees Society, 62 (Durham, 1875).

Townshend, Dorothea, *The Life and Letters of Endymion Porter* (London, 1897).

Verney, Frances Parthenope Lady, *Memoirs of the Verney Family*, 4 vols (London, 1892–1899).

Viles, Edward and Furnivall, F.J. (eds), *Awdeley's Fraternitye of Vacabondes, Harman's Caveat etc.*, Early English Text Society, extra ser., 9 (London, 1869).

Warwick, Mary Countess of, *Autobiography of Mary Countess of Warwick*, ed. by T. Clifton Croker, Percy Society, 22 (London, 1848).

Weever, John, *Ancient Funerall Monuments* (London, 1631).

Select Bibliography

Whitelocke, Bulstrode, *The Diary of Bulstrode Whitelocke*, ed. by Ruth Spalding, Records of Social and Economic History, new ser., 13 (London, 1990).
Whitelocke, Sir James, *Liber Famelicus of Sir James Whitelocke*, ed. by John Bruce, Camden Society, 70 (London, 1858).
Whitgift, John, *The Works of John Whitgift*, ed. by John Ayre, 3 vols, Parker Society, 40 (Cambridge, 1851–3).
Winthrop Papers Volume I 1498–1628 (Massachusetts, 1929).
Winthrop Papers Volume II 1623–1630 (Massachusetts, 1931).
Woolton, John, *The Christian Manual*, Parker Society, 41 (Cambridge, 1851), p. 90.
Wright, Louis B. (ed.), *Advice to a Son: Precepts of Lord Burghley, Sir Walter Raleigh, and Francis Osborne* (Ithaca, 1962).

Secondary

Adams, Simon, 'Eliza Enthroned? The Court and its Politics', in *The Reign of Elizabeth I*, ed. by Christopher Haigh (Basingstoke, 1984), pp. 55–77.
Akrigg, G.P.V., *Jacobean Pageant* (London, 1962).
Allerston, Patricia, 'Clothing and Early Modern Venetian Society', *Continuity and Change*, 15 (2000), 367–90.
Allerston, Patricia, 'Reconstructing the Second-hand Clothes Trade in Sixteenth- and Seventeenth-Century Venice', *Costume*, 33 (1999), 46–56.
Anson, John, 'The Female Transvestite in Early Monasticism: The Origin and Development of a Motif', *Viator*, 5 (1974), 1–32.
Appleby, Joyce Oldham, *Economic Thought and Ideology in Seventeenth-Century England* (Princeton, 1978).
Arnold, Janet, 'Dashing Amazons: The Development of Women's Riding Dress, c. 1500–1900', in *Defining Dress*, ed. by de la Haye and Wilson, pp. 10–29.
Arnold, Janet, *Patterns of Fashion: The Cut and Construction of Clothes for Men and Women c. 1560–1620* (London, 1985).
Arnold, Janet, *Queen Elizabeth's Wardrobe Unlock'd* (Leeds, 1988).
Ashelford, Jane, *Dress in the Age of Elizabeth I* (London, 1988).
Ashelford, Jane, *The Art of Dress: Clothes and Society 1500–1914* (London, 1996).
Aydelotte, Frank, *Elizabethan Rogues and Vagabonds* (Oxford, 1913).
Baclawski, Karen, *The Guide to Historic Costume* (London, 1995).

Baldwin, Frances, *Sumptuary Legislation and Personal Regulation in England* (Baltimore, 1926).

Banner, Lois, 'The Fashionable Sex, 1100–1600', *History Today*, 42 (1992), 37–44.

Barish, Jonas, *The Anti-Theatrical Prejudice* (Berkeley, 1981).

Beier, A.L., 'Vagrants and the Social Order in Elizabethan England', *Past and Present*, 64 (1974), 3–29.

Beier, A.L., *Masterless Men: The Vagrancy Problem in England 1560–1640* (London, 1985).

Beier, Lucinda McCray, *Sufferers and Healers: The Experience of Illness in Seventeenth-Century England* (London, 1987).

Bell, Clifford and Ruse, Evelyn, 'Sumptuary Legislation and English Costume, An Attempt to Assess the Effect of an Act of 1337', *Costume*, 6 (1972), 22–31.

Bell, Quentin, *On Human Finery: The Classic Study of Fashion Through the Ages*, rev. edn (London, 1976).

Bellany, Alastair, 'Mistress Turner's Deadly Sins: Sartorial Transgression, Court Scandal, and Politics in Early Stuart England', *Huntingdon Library Quarterly*, 58 (1996), 179–210.

Belsey, Andrew and Belsey, Catherine, 'Icons of Divinity: Portraits of Elizabeth I', in *Renaissance Bodies: The Human Figure in English Culture c.1540–1660*, ed. by Lucy Gent and Nigel Llewellyn (London, 1990), pp. 11–35.

Berger, Arthur Asa, *Reading Matter: Multidisciplinary Perspectives on Material Culture* (New Brunswick, 1992).

Bourdieu, Pierre, *Distinction: A Social Critique of the Judgement of Taste*, trans. by Richard Nice (London, 1984).

Bradfield, Nancy, *Historical Costumes of England 1066–1968*, rev. edn (London, 1970).

Braudel, Fernand, *The Structures of Everyday Life: The Limits of the Possible*, trans. by Siân Reynolds (London, 1981).

Breward, Christopher, *The Culture of Fashion: A New History of Fashionable Dress* (Manchester, 1995).

Broadbent, John, 'The Image of God, or Two Yards of Skin', in *The Body as a Medium of Expression*, ed. by Jonathan Benthall and Ted Polhemus (London, 1975), pp. 303–26.

Bryson, Anna, *From Courtesy to Civility: Changing Codes of Conduct in Early Modern England* (Oxford, 1998).

Buck, Anne, 'Clothing and Textiles in Bedfordshire Inventories, 1617–1620', *Costume*, 34 (2000), 25–38.

Bullough, Vern L., 'Transvestites in the Middle Ages', *American Journal of Sociology*, 79 (1973–4), 1381–94.

Butler, Judith, *Gender Trouble: Feminism and the Subversion of Identity* (New York, 1990).

Byrde, Penelope, *The Male Image: Men's Fashion in England 1300–1970* (London, 1971).

Carrier, J.G., *Gifts and Commodities: Exchange and Western Capitalism Since 1700* (London, 1995).

Carroll, William C., *Fat King, Lean Beggar: Representations of Poverty in the Age of Shakespeare* (Ithaca, 1996).

Chirelstein, Ellen, 'Emblem and Reckless Presence: The Drury Portrait at Yale', in *Albion's Classicism: The Visual Arts in Britain, 1550–1650* (New Haven, 1995), ed. by Lucy Gent, pp. 287–312.

Chirelstein, Ellen, 'Lady Elizabeth Pope: The Heraldic Body', in *Renaissance Bodies: The Human Figure in English Culture c.1540–1660*, ed. by Lucy Gent and Nigel Llewellyn (London, 1990), pp. 36–59.

Clark, Sandra, '*Hic Mulier, Haec Vir* and the Controversy Over Masculine Women', *Studies in Philology*, 82 (1985), 157–83.

Cliffe, J.T., *The Puritan Gentry* (London, 1984).

Collinson, Patrick, *The Puritan Character: Polemics and Polarities in Early Seventeenth-Century English Culture* (Los Angeles, 1989).

Constructing Race: Differentiating Peoples in the Early Modern World, a special edition of *The William and Mary Quarterly*, 3rd ser., 54, no. 1 (1997).

Corfield, Penelope, 'Dress for Deference and Dissent: Hats and the Decline of Hat Honour', *Costume*, 23 (1989), 64–79.

Craik, Jennifer, *The Face of Fashion: Cultural Studies in Fashion* (London, 1994).

Crawford, Patricia, and Mendelson, Sara, 'Sexual Identities in Early Modern England', *Gender and History*, 7 (1995), 363–77.

Cressy, David, 'Death and the Social Order: the Funerary Preferences of Elizabethan Gentleman', *Continuity and Change*, 5 (1989), 99–119.

Cressy, David, 'Gender Trouble and Cross-Dressing in Early Modern England', *Journal of British Studies*, 35 (1996), 438–65.

Cressy, David, *Birth, Marriage and Death: Ritual, Religion and the Life-Cycle in Tudor and Stuart England* (Oxford, 1997).

Cressy, David, *Travesties and Transgressions in Tudor and Stuart England: Tales of Discord and Dissension* (Oxford, 2000).

Cunnington, C.W. and Cunnington, P., *Handbook of English Costume in the Sixteenth Century* (London, 1954; repr. 1962).

Cunnington, C.W. and Cunnington, P., *Handbook of English Costume in the Seventeenth Century*, 2nd edn (London, 1966).

Cunnington, C.W. and Cunnington, P., *The History of Underclothes*, rev. edn (London, 1981).

Cunnington, Phillis and Lucas, Catherine, *Costume for Births, Marriages and Deaths* (London, 1972).

Davis, Fred, *Fashion, Culture and Identity* (Chicago, 1992).

Dawson, Mark S., 'Histories and Texts: Refiguring the Diary of Samuel Pepys', *Historical Journal*, 43 (2000), 407–31.

Day, J.F.R., 'Death be very proud: Sidney, Subversion, and Elizabethan heraldic funerals', in *Tudor Political Culture*, ed. by Dale Hoak (Cambridge, 1995), pp. 179–203.

de Beer, Esmond S., 'King Charles II's own Fashion; an Episode in Anglo-French Relations', *Journal of the Warburg and Courtauld Institutes*, 2 (1938–9), 105–15.

de la Haye, Amy and Wilson, Elizabeth (eds), *Defining Dress: Dress as Object, Meaning and Identity* (Manchester, 1999).

de Marly, Diana, 'King Charles II's Own Fashion: The Theatrical Origins of the English Vest', *Journal of the Warburg and Courtauld Institutes*, 37–38 (1974–5), 378–82.

de Marly, Diana, 'Pepys and the Fashion for Collecting', *Costume*, 21 (1987), 34–43.

Dean, David, *Law-making and Society in Late Elizabethan England: The Parliament of England, 1584–1601* (Cambridge, 1996).

Dekker, Rudolf and Van de Pol, Lotte, *The Tradition of Female Transvestism in Early Modern Europe* (Basingstoke, 1989).

Douce, Francis, 'Observations on certain ornaments of Female Dress', *Archaeologia*, 12 (1796), 215–16.

Durston, Christopher and Eales, Jacqueline (eds), *The Culture of English Puritanism 1560–1700* (Houndmills, Basingstoke, 1996).

Eales, Jacqueline, *Puritans and Roundheads: The Harleys of Brampton Bryan and the Outbreak of the English Civil War* (Cambridge, 1990).

Edwards, Lesley, '"Dres't Like a May-Pole": A Study of Two Suits c.1600–1662', *Costume*, 19 (1980), 75–93.

Elton, G.R., *The Parliament of England 1559–1581* (Cambridge, 1986).

Elton, G.R., *England Under the Tudors*, 3rd edn (London, 1991).

Emmison, F.G., *Elizabethan Life I: Disorder* (Chelmsford, 1970).

Emmison, F.G., *Elizabethan Life II: Morals and the Church Courts* (Chelmsford, 1973).

Epstein, Julia and Straub, Kristina (eds), *Body Guards: The Cultural Politics of Gender* Ambiguity (London, 1991).

Evenden, Doreen, *The Midwives of Seventeenth-Century London* (Cambridge, 2000).

Feher, Michel; Naddaff, Ramona and Tazi, Nadia (eds), *Fragments for a History of the Human Body*, 3 vols (New York, 1989).

Finkelstein, Joanne, *The Fashioned Self* (Cambridge, 1991).

French, H.R., 'The Search for the "Middle Sort of People" in England, 1600–1800', *Historical Journal*, 43 (2000), 277–93.

Freudenberger, Herman, 'Fashion, Sumptuary Laws, and Business', *Business History Review*, 37 (1963), 37–48.

Fritz, Paul, '"From Public to Private": the Royal Funerals in England, 1500–1830', in *Mirrors of Mortality: Studies in the Social History of Death*, ed. by Joachim Whaley (London, 1981), pp. 61–79.

Frye, Susan, *Elizabeth I: The Competition for Representation* (Oxford, 1993).

Fumerton, Patricia, '"Secret" Arts: Elizabethan Miniatures and Sonnets', *Representations*, 15 (1986), 57–97.

Fumerton, Patricia and Hunt, Simon (eds), *Renaissance Culture and the Everyday* (Philadelphia, 1999).

Gent, Lucy (ed.), *Albion's Classicism: The Visual Arts in Britain, 1550–1650* (New Haven, 1995).

Gent, Lucy and Llewellyn, Nigel (eds), *Renaissance Bodies: The Human Figure in English Culture c. 1540–1660* (London, 1990).

Gittings, Clare, *Funerals in England 1580–1640: The Evidence of Probate Accounts* (unpublished B. Litt. thesis, University of Oxford, 1978).

Gittings, Clare, *Death, Burial and the Individual in Early Modern England* (London, 1984).

Gowing, Laura, *Domestic Dangers: Women, Words and Sex in Early Modern London* (Oxford, 1996).

Greaves, Richard, *Society and Religion in Elizabethan England* (Minneapolis, 1981).

Greenblatt, Stephen, *Renaissance Self-Fashioning: From More to Shakespeare* (Chicago, 1980).

Greenblatt, Stephen, 'Fiction and Friction', in *Reconstructing Individualism: Autonomy, Individuality, and the Self in Western Thought*, ed. by Thomas Heller, Morton Sosna and David Wellbery (Stanford, 1986), pp. 30–52.

Greenfield, Kent Robert, *Sumptuary Law in Nürnberg: A Study in Paternal Government* (Baltimore, 1918).

Griffiths, Paul, *Youth and Authority: Formative Experiences in England 1560–1640* (Oxford, 1996).

Guy, Ali; Green, Eileen and Banim, Maura (eds), *Through the Wardrobe: Women's Relationships with Their Clothes* (Oxford, 2001).

Guy, John, 'The 1590s: the second reign of Elizabeth I?', in *The Reign of Elizabeth I: Court and Culture in the Last Decade*, ed. by John Guy (Cambridge, 1995).

Haigh, Christopher (ed.), *The Reign of Elizabeth I* (Basingstoke, 1984).

Hale, J.R., *Artists and Warfare in the Renaissance* (New Haven, 1990).

Hart, Avril, 'The Mantua: its Evolution and Fashionable Significance in the Seventeenth and Eighteenth Centuries', in *Defining Dress: Dress as Object, Meaning and Identity*, ed. by Amy de la Haye and Elizabeth Wilson (Manchester, 1999), pp. 93–103.

Harte, N.B., 'State Control of Dress and Social Change in Pre-Industrial England', in *Trade, Government and Economy in Pre-Industrial England*, ed. by D.C. Coleman and A.H. John (London, 1976), pp. 132–65.

Heal, Felicity, 'The Idea of Hospitality in Early Modern England', *Past and Present*, 102 (1984), 66–93.

Heal, Felicity, *Hospitality in Early Modern England* (Oxford, 1990).

Heinze, Rudolph, *The Proclamations of the Tudor Kings* (Cambridge, 1976).

Henderson, Katherine Usher and McManus, Barbara, *Half Humankind: Contexts and Texts of the Controversy about Women in England, 1540–1640* (Urbana, 1985).

Hillman, David and Mazzio, Carla (eds), *The Body in Parts: Fantasies of Corporeality in Early Modern Europe* (London, 1997).

Hills, Richard L., *Papermaking in Britain 1488–1988* (London, 1988).

Hodgen, Margaret, *Early Anthropology in the Sixteenth and Seventeenth Centuries* (Philadelphia, 1964).

Hollander, Anne, *Seeing Through Clothes*, (Berkeley, 1993).

Hooper, Wilfred, 'The Tudor Sumptuary Laws', *English Historical Review*, 30 (1915), 433–49 .

Hotchkiss, Valerie, *Clothes Makes the Man: Female Cross Dressing in Medieval Europe* (New York, 1996).

Houlbrooke, Ralph, *Church Courts and the People During the English Reformation 1520–1570* (Oxford, 1979).

Houlbrooke, Ralph, *English Family Life, 1576–1716: An Anthology from Diaries* (Oxford, 1988).

Houlbrooke, Ralph, 'Death, Church and the Family in England Between the Late Fifteenth and the Early Eighteenth Centuries', in *Death, Ritual and Bereavement*, ed. by Ralph Houlbrooke (London, 1989).

Houlbrooke, Ralph, ' "Public" and "Private" in the Funerals of the later Stuart Gentry: Some Somerset Examples', *Mortality*, 1, (1996), 163–76.

Houlbrooke, Ralph, *Death, Religion, and the Family in England, 1480–1750* (Oxford, 1998).

Howard, Jean, 'Cross-Dressing, the Theatre, and Gender Struggle in Early Modern England', in *Crossing the Stage: Controversies on Cross-Dressing*, ed. by Lesley Ferris (London, 1993), pp. 20–46.

Howard, Jean, *The Stage and Social Struggle in Early Modern England* (London, 1994).

Hughes, Diane, 'Distinguishing Signs: Ear-Rings, Jews and Franciscan Rhetoric in the Italian Renaissance City', *Past and Present*, 112 (1986), 3–59.

Hughes, Diane, 'Sumptuary Laws and Social Relations in Renaissance Italy', in *Disputes and Settlements: Law and Human Relations in the West*, ed. by John Bossy (Cambridge, 1983), pp. 69–99.

Hunt, Alan, *Governance of the Consuming Passions: A History of Sumptuary Law* (London, 1996).

Ingram, Martin, 'Ridings, Rough Music and the "Reform of Popular Culture" in Early Modern England', *Past and Present*, 105 (1984), 79–113.

Ingram, Martin, *Church Courts, Sex and Marriage in England, 1570–1640* (Cambridge, 1987).

Jardine, Lisa, *Still Harping on Daughters: Women and Drama in the Age of Shakespeare*, 2nd edn (London, 1989).

Jenner, Mark, 'Body, Image, Text in Early Modern Europe', *Social History of Medicine*, 12 (1999), 143–54.

Johnston, Flora, 'Jonet Gothskirk and the "Gown of Repentance"', *Costume*, 33 (1999), 89–94.

Jones, Ann Rosalind, and Stallybrass, Peter, '"Rugges of London and the Diuell's Band": Irish Mantles and Yellow Starch as Hybrid London Fashion', in *Material London, ca.1600*, ed. by Lena Cowen Orlin (Philadelphia, 2000), pp. 128–49.

Jordan, W.K., *Edward VI: the Threshold of Power* (London, 1970).

Jütte, Robert, *Poverty and Deviance in Early Modern Europe* (Cambridge, 1994).

Kasson, John F., *Rudeness and Civility: Manners in Nineteenth-Century America* (New York, 1990).

Kelso, Ruth, *The Doctrine of the English Gentleman in the Sixteenth Century* (Gloucester, MA, 1964).

Kelso, Ruth, *Doctrine for the Lady of the Renaissance* (Urbana, 1978).

Kent, Joan, *Social Attitudes of Members of Parliament with Special Reference to the Problem of Poverty, circa 1590–1624* (unpublished Ph.D. thesis, University of London, 1970).

Kent, Joan, 'Attitudes of Members of the House of Commons to the Regulation of "Personal Conduct" in Late Elizabethan and Early Stuart England', *Bulletin of the Institute of Historical Research*, 46 (1973), 41–65 .

Killerby, Catherine Kovesi, 'Practical Problems in the Enforcement of Italian Sumptuary Law, 1200–1500', in *Crime, Society and the Law in Renaissance Italy*, ed. by Trevor Dean and K.J.P. Lowe (Cambridge, 1994), pp. 99–120.

Knoppers, Laura Lunger, *Constructing Cromwell: Ceremony, Portrait, and Print 1645–1661* (Cambridge, 2000).

Koch, Mark, 'The Desanctification of the Beggar in Rogue Pamphlets of the English Renaissance, in *The Work of Dissimilitude*, ed. by D. Allen and R. White (Newark, 1992), pp. 91–104.

Kuchta, David, 'The Making of the Self-Made Man: Class, Clothing, and English Masculinity, 1688–1832', in *The Sex of Things: Gender and Consumption in Historical Perspective*, ed. by Victoria de Grazia with Ellen Furlough (Berkeley, 1996), pp. 54–78.

Kupperman, Karen Ordahl , 'Presentment of Civility: English Reading of American Self-Presentation in the Early Years of Colonization', *The William and Mary Quarterly*, 3rd ser., 54, no. 1 (1997), 193–228.

LaMar, Virginia A., 'English Dress in the Age of Shakespeare', in *Life and Letters in Tudor and Stuart England*, ed. by Louis B.Wright and Virginia A. LaMar (Ithaca, 1962), pp. 383–426 .

Laqueur, Thomas, *Making Sex: Body and Gender from the Greeks to Freud* (Cambridge MA, 1990).

Laslett, Peter, *The World We Have Lost* (London, 1965).

Laslett, Peter, *The World We Have Lost Further Explored* (Cambridge, 1983).

Laver, James, *Dress* (London, 1950).

Laver, James, *Modesty in Dress: An Enquiry into the Fundamentals of Fashion* (London, 1969).

Lehmberg, Stanford E., *The Reformation of Parliament 1529–1536* (Cambridge, 1970).

Lemire, Beverly, 'The Theft of Clothes and Popular Consumerism in Early Modern England', *Journal of Social History*, 24 (1990), 255–76.

Lemire, Beverly, *Fashion's Favourite: The Cotton Trade and the Consumer in Britain, 1660–1800* (Oxford, 1991).

Lemire, Beverly, 'Peddling Fashion: Salesmen, Pawnbrokers, Taylors, Thieves and the Second-hand Clothes Trade in England, c. 1700–1800', *Textile History*, 22 (1991), 67–82.

Lemire, Beverly, *Dress, Culture and Commerce: The English Clothing Trade before the Factory, 1660–1800* (Basingstoke, 1997).

Lemire, Beverly, 'Consumerism in Preindustrial and Early Industrial England: The Trade in Secondhand Clothes', *Journal of British Studies*, 27 (1998), 1–24.

Lemire, Beverly, '"In the hands of work women": English Markets, Cheap Clothing and Female Labour,1650–1800', *Costume*, 33 (1999), 23–35.

Lemire, Beverly, 'Second-hand Beaux and "Red-armed Belles": Conflict and the Creation of Fashions in England, *c.* 1660–1800', *Continuity and Change*, 15 (2000), 391–417.

Levine, Laura, *Men in Women's Clothing: Anti-theatricality and Effeminization, 1579–1642* (Cambridge, 1994).

Lindemann, Mary, *Medicine and Society in Early Modern Europe* (Cambridge, 1999).

Lindley, David, *The Trials of Frances Howard: Fact and Fiction at the Court of King James* (London, 1993).

Linthicum, M. Channing, *Costume in the Drama of Shakespeare and his Contemporaries* (Oxford, 1936).

Litten, Julian, *The English Way of Death: The Common Funeral Since 1450* (London, 1991).

Llewellyn, Nigel, *The Art of Death: Visual Culture in English Death Ritual c.1500–c.1800* (London, 1991).

Loach, Jennifer, *Edward VI*, ed. by George Bernard and Penry Williams (New Haven, 1999).

London Bodies: The Changing Shape of Londoners from Prehistoric times to the Present Day, complied by Alex Werner (London, 1998).

Lucas, Valerie, '*Hic Mulier*: The Female Transvestite in Early Modern England', *Renaissance and Reformation / Renaissance et Réforme*, 24 (1988), 65–84.

Lyons, Bridget Gellert, *Voices of Melancholy: Studies in the Literary Treatments of Melancholy in Renaissance England* (London, 1971).

Mabey, Richard, *Flora Britannica* (London, 1996).

MacDonald, Michael, *Mystical Bedlam: Madness, Anxiety and Healing in Seventeenth-Century England* (Cambridge, 1981).

Marotti, Arthur F., 'Alienating Catholics in Early Modern England: Recusant Women, Jesuits and Ideological Fantasies', in *Catholicism and Anti-Catholicism in Early Modern English Texts*, ed. by Arthur F. Marotti (Houndmills, Basingstoke, 1999), pp. 1–34.

Marshall-Ward, Jackie, 'Mode and Movement', *Costume*, 34 (2000), 123–8.

Mauss, Marcel, *The Gift: Forms and Functions of Exchange in Archaic Societies*, trans. by Ian Cunnison (New York, 1967).

McMullan, John L., *The Canting Crew: London's Criminal Underworld 1550–1700* (New Brunswick, 1984).

Miller, John, *James II: A Study in Kingship* (Hove, 1978).

Miller, Sylvia, 'Old English Laws Regulating Dress', *Journal of Home Economics*, 20 (1928), 89–94.

Mukerji, Chandra, *From Graven Images: Patterns of Modern Materialism* (New York, 1983).

Neale, J.E., *Elizabeth I and her Parliaments 1559–1581* (London, 1953).

North, Gary, 'The Puritan Experiment with Sumptuary Legislation', *Freeman*, 24 (1974), 341–55.

Ollard, Richard, *The Image of the King: Charles I and Charles II* (London, 1979).

Orgel, Stephen, *Impersonations: The Performance of Gender in Shakespeare's England* (Cambridge, 1996).

Orlin, Lena Cowen (ed.), *Material London, ca.1600* (Philadelphia, 2000).

Pagden, Anthony, *The Fall of Natural Man: The American Indian and the Origins of Comparative Ethnology* (Cambridge, 1982).

Parker, Rozsika, *The Subversive Stitch: Embroidery and the Making of the Feminine*, rev. edn (London, 1996).

Peacock, John, 'The Politics of Portraiture', in *Culture and Politics in Early Stuart England*, ed. by Kevin Sharpe and Peter Lake (Houndmills, Basingstoke, 1994), pp. 199–228.

Pelling, Margaret, 'Appearance and Reality: Barber-Surgeons, the Body and Disease', in *London 1500–1700:The Making of a Metropolis*, ed. by A.L. Beier and Roger Finlay (London, 1986), pp. 82–112.

Perrot, Philippe, 'Suggestions for a Different Approach to the History of Dress', *Diogenes*, 114 (1981), 157–76.

Perrot, Phillipe, *Fashioning the Bourgeoisie: A History of Clothing in the Nineteenth Century*, trans. by Richard Bienvenu (Princeton NJ, 1994).

Piper, David, *The English Face* (London, 1957).

Piponnier, Françoise and Mane, Perrine, *Dress in the Middle Ages*, trans. by Caroline Beamish (New Haven, 1997).

Pound, John, *Poverty and Vagrancy in Tudor England* (London, 1971).

Prest, Wilfred, *The Inns of Court under Elizabeth I and the Early Stuarts 1590–1640* (London, 1972).

Purkiss, Diane, 'Material Girls: The Seventeenth-Century Woman Debate', in *Women, Texts and Histories 1575–1760*, ed. by Clare Brant and Diane Purkiss (London, 1992), pp. 69–101.

The Pursuit of Beauty: Five Centuries of Body Adornment in Britain, text by Clare Gittings (London, 1997).

Quaife, G.R., *Wanton Wenches and Wayward Wives: Peasants and Illicit Sex in Early Seventeenth Century England* (London, 1979).

Rainey, Ronald, 'Dressing Down the Dressed-Up: Reproving Feminine Attire in Renaissance Florence', in *Renaissance Society and Culture*, ed. by John Monfasani and Ronald G. Musto (New York, 1991), pp. 217–37.

Ramet, Sabrian Petra, *Gender Reversal and Gender Cultures* (London, 1996).

Ravelhofer, Barbara, 'Bureaucrats and Courtly Cross-Dressers in the *Shrovetide Masque* and *The Shepherd's Paradise*', *English Literary Renaissance*, 29 (1999), 75–96.

Ribeiro, Aileen, *The Gallery of Fashion* (London, 2000).

Ribeiro, Aileen and Cumming, Valerie, *The Visual History of Costume* (London, 1989).

Roche, Daniel, *The Culture of Clothing: Dress and Fashion in the Ancien Régime*, trans. by Jean Birrell (Cambridge, 1996).

Rose, Mary Beth, *The Expense of Spirit: Love and Sexuality in English Renaissance Drama* (Ithaca, 1988).

Rose, Mary Beth, 'Women in Men's Clothing: Apparel and Social Stability in *The Roaring Girl*', *English Literary Renaissance*, 14 (1984), 367–91.

Salgādo, Gāmini, *The Elizabethan Underworld* (London, 1977).

Sawday, Jonathan, *The Body Emblazoned: Dissection and the Human Body in Renaissance Culture* (London, 1995).

Schleiner, Winfried, 'Male Cross-Dressing and Transvestism in Renaissance Romances', *Sixteenth-Century Journal*, 19 (1988), 606–19.

Sekora, John, *Luxury: The Concept in Western Thought, Eden to Smollet* (Baltimore, 1977).

Shaaber, M.A., *Some Forerunners of the Newspaper in England 1476–1622* (Philadelphia, 1929).

Shapiro, Michael, *Gender in Play on the Shakespearean Stage: Boy Heroines and Female Pages* (Ann Arbor, 1994).

Shapiro, Susan, 'Amazons, Hermaphrodites, and Plain Monsters: The "Masculine" Women in English Satire and Social Criticism from 1580–1640', *Atlantis*, 13, (1987), 66–76.

Shapiro, Susan, 'Sex, Gender, and Fashion in Medieval and Early Modern Britain', *Journal of Popular Culture*, 20 (1987), 113–28.

Sharpe, J.A., *Judicial Punishment in England* (London, 1990).

Sharpe, J.A., '"Last Dying Speeches": Religion, Ideology and Public Execution in Seventeenth-Century England', *Past and Present*, 107 (1985), 144–67.

Slack, Paul, 'Vagrants and Vagrancy in England 1598–1664', in *Migration and Society in Early Modern England*, ed. by Peter Clark and David Souden (London, 1987), pp. 49–76.

Slack, Paul, *Poverty and Policy in Tudor and Stuart England* (London, 1988).

Spicer, Joaneath, 'The Renaissance Elbow', in *A Cultural History of Gesture*, ed. by Jan Bremmer and Herman Roodenburg (Oxford, 1991), pp. 84–128.

Spufford, Margaret, *The Great Reclothing of Rural England: Petty Chapmen and their Wares in the Seventeenth Century* (London, 1984).

Squire, Geoffrey, *Dress, Art and Society* (New York, 1984).

Stallybrass, Peter, 'Worn worlds: clothes and identity on the Renaissance stage', in *Subject and Object in Renaissance Culture*, ed. by Margreta de Grazia, Maureen Quilligan and Peter Stallybrass (Cambridge, 1996), pp. 289–320.

Stallybrass, Peter and Jones, Ann Rosalind, *Renaissance Clothing and the Materials of Memory* (Cambridge, 2000).

Stannard, David, *The Puritan Way of Death: A Study in Religion, Culture and Social Change* (New York, 1977).

Steele, Valerie, 'Letter from the Editor', *Fashion Theory: The Journal of Dress and Body Culture*, 1 (1997), 1–2.

Stone, Lawrence, *The Crisis of the Aristocracy 1558–1641* (Oxford, 1965).

Stone, Lawrence, 'Social Mobility in England, 1500–1700', *Past and Present*, 33 (1966), 16–55.

Strong, Roy, *The English Icon: Elizabethan and Jacobean Portraiture* (London, 1969).

Strong, Roy, *Gloriana: The Portraiture of Queen Elizabeth I* (London, 1987).

Styles, John, 'Clothing the North: The Supply of Non-élite Clothing in the Eighteenth-Century North of England', *Textile History*, 25 (1994), 139–66.

Tarrant, Naomi, *The Development of Costume* (Edinburgh, 1994).

Taylor, Barry, *Vagrant Writing: Social and Semiotic Disorders in the English Renaissance* (London, 1991).

Taylor, Lou, *Mourning Dress: A Costume and Social History* (London, 1983).

Thirsk, Joan, *Economic Policy and Projects: The Development of a Consumer Society in Early Modern England* (Oxford, 1978).

Tiramani, Jenny, 'Janet Arnold and the Globe Wardrobe: Handmade Clothes of Shakespeare's Actors', *Costume*, 34 (2000), 118–22.

Tiramani, Jenny, Information panel for 'Patterns of Fashion' exhibition, Victoria & Albert Museum, Gallery 40, 1 February 1999 – 22 August 1999.

Tseëlon, Efrat, 'Ontological, Epistemological and Methodological Clarifications in Fashion Research: From Critique to Empirical Suggestions', in *Through the Wardrobe: Women's Relationships with Their*

Clothes, ed. by Ali Guy, Eileen Green and Maura Banim (Oxford, 2001), pp. 237–54.

Veblen, Thorstein, *The Theory of the Leisure Class* (New York, 1899).

Vicary, Grace Q., 'Visual Art as Social Data: The Renaissance Codpiece', *Cultural Anthropology*, 4 (1989), 3–25.

Vigarello, Georges, *Concepts of Cleanliness: Changing Attitudes in France since the Middle Ages*, trans. by Jean Birrell (Cambridge, 1988).

Vigarello, Georges, 'The Upward Training of the Body', in *Fragments for a History of the Human Body*, ed. by Michel Feher, Ramona Naddaff and Nadia Tazi, 3 vols (New York), II, 148–99.

Vincent, John M., *Costume and Conduct in the Laws of Basel, Bern, and Zurich 1370–1800* (1935; repr. New York, 1969).

Walker, Garthine, 'Women, Theft and the World of Stolen Goods', in *Women, Crime and the Courts in Early Modern England*, ed. by J. Kermode and G. Walker (London, 1994), pp. 81–105.

Wardle, Patricia, '"Divers necessaries for his Majesty's use and service": seamstresses to the Stuart Kings', *Costume*, 31 (1997), 16–27.

Warwick, Alexandra and Cavallaro, Dani, *Fashioning the Frame: Boundaries, Dress and the Body* (Oxford, 1998).

Weatherill, Lorna, 'Consumer Behaviour, Textiles and Dress in the Late Seventeenth and Early Eighteenth Centuries', *Textile History*, 22 (1991), 297–310.

Weatherill, Lorna, *Consumer Behaviour and Material Culture in Britain 1660–1760*, 2nd edn (London, 1996).

Welch, J.L., 'Cross-Dressing and Cross-Purposes: Gender Possibilities in the Acts of Thecla', in *Gender Reversal and Gender Cultures*, ed. by Sabrina Petra Ramet (London, 1996), pp. 66–78.

Whigham, Frank, *Ambition and Privilege: The Social Tropes of Elizabethan Courtesy Theory* (Berkeley, 1984).

Williams, Tamsyn, '"Magnetic Figures": Polemical Prints of the English Revolution', in *Renaissance Bodies: The Human Figure in English Culture c.1540–1660*, ed. by Lucy Gent and Nigel Llewellyn (London, 1990), pp. 86–110.

Wilson, Adrian, 'The Ceremony of Childbirth and its Interpretation', in *Women as Mothers in Pre-Industrial England*, ed. by Valerie Fildes (London, 1990), pp. 68–107.

Woodbridge, Linda, *Women and the English Renaissance: Literature and the Nature of Womenkind, 1540–1620* (Urbana, 1984).

Woodward, Jennifer, *The Theatre of Death: The Ritual Management of Royal Funerals in Renaissance England 1570–1625* (Woodbridge, 1997).

Wright, Pam, 'A Change in Direction: The Ramifications of a Female Household, 1558–1603', David Starkey and others, *The English Court: from the Wars of the Roses to the Civil War* (London, 1987), pp. 147–72.

Wrightson, Keith, *English Society 1580–1680* (London, 1982).

Yates, Frances, *Astraea: The Imperial Theme in the Sixteenth Century* (London, 1975).

Youngs, Frederic, *The Proclamations of the Tudor Queens* (Cambridge, 1976).

Index

Index

Lightning Source UK Ltd.
Milton Keynes UK
UKOW022359291111

182842UK00007B/30/P

9 781859 737514